DEC 1 4 2009

D0742131

DEFINING MOMENTS
THE ATTACK ON
PEARL HARBOR

DEFINING MOMENTS
THE ATTACK ON
PEARL HARBOR

Laurie Collier Hillstrom

Omnigraphics

P.O. Box 31-1640
Detroit, MI 48231

Omnigraphics, Inc.

Kevin Hillstrom, *Series Editor*
Cherie D. Abbey, *Managing Editor*

Peter E. Ruffner, *Publisher*
Matthew P. Barbour, *Senior Vice President*

Elizabeth Collins, *Research and Permissions Coordinator*
Kevin M. Hayes, *Operations Manager*

Allison A. Beckett and Mary Butler, *Research Staff*
Cherry Stockdale, *Permissions Assistant*
Shirley Amore, Martha Johns, and Kirk Kauffman, *Administrative Staff*

Copyright © 2009 Omnigraphics, Inc.
ISBN 978-0-7808-1069-3

Library of Congress Cataloging-in-Publication Data

Hillstrom, Laurie Collier, 1965-
    The attack on Pearl Harbor / by Laurie Collier Hillstrom.
        p. cm. -- (Defining moments)
    Summary: "Provides a detailed account of the Pearl Harbor attack and the war in the Pacific. Covers the dramatic events of December 7, 1941; chronicles America's victory over Japan; and explores the legacy of Pearl Harbor. Features include a narrative overview, biographies, primary source documents, chronology, glossary, bibliography, and index"--Provided by publisher.
    Includes bibliographical references and index.
    ISBN 978-0-7808-1069-3 (hardcover : alk. paper) 1. Pearl Harbor (Hawaii), Attack on, 1941. I. Title.
    D767.92.H536 2009
    940.54'26693--dc22
                                                                2009004236

The information in this publication was compiled from the sources cited and from other sources considered reliable. Additional copyright information can be found on the photograph credits page of this book and accompanying every reprinted source. While every possible effort has been made to ensure reliability, the publisher will not assume liability for damages caused by inaccuracies in the data, and makes no warranty, express or implied, on the accuracy of the information contained herein.

This book is printed on acid-free paper meeting the ANSI Z39.48 Standard. The infinity symbol that appears above indicates that the paper in this book meets that standard.

Printed in the United States of America

TABLE OF CONTENTS

PRIMARY SOURCES

PREFACE

Throughout the course of America's existence, its people, culture, and institutions have been periodically challenged—and in many cases transformed—by profound historical events. Some of these momentous events, such as women's suffrage, the civil rights movement, and U.S. involvement in World War II, invigorated the nation and strengthened American confidence and capabilities. Others, such as the McCarthy era, the Vietnam War, and Watergate, have prompted troubled assessments and heated debates about the country's core beliefs and character.

Some of these defining moments in American history were years or even decades in the making. The Harlem Renaissance and the New Deal, for example, unfurled over the span of several years, while the American labor movement and the Cold War evolved over the course of decades. Other defining moments, such as the Cuban missile crisis and the terrorist attacks of September 11, 2001, transpired over a matter of days or weeks.

But although significant differences exist among these events in terms of their duration and their place in the timeline of American history, all share the same basic characteristic: they transformed the United States' political, cultural, and social landscape for future generations of Americans.

Taking heed of this fundamental reality, American citizens, schools, and other institutions are increasingly emphasizing the importance of understanding our nation's history. Omnigraphics' *Defining Moments* series was created for the express purpose of meeting this growing appetite for authoritative, useful historical resources. This series will be of enduring value to anyone interested in learning more about America's past—and in understanding how those historical events continue to reverberate in the twenty-first century.

Each individual volume of *Defining Moments* provides a valuable one-stop resource for readers interested in learning about the most profound events in our nation's history. Each volume is organized into three distinct sections—Narrative Overview, Biographies, and Primary Sources.

- The **Narrative Overview** provides readers with a detailed, factual account of the origins and progression of the "defining moment" being examined. It also explores the event's lasting impact on America's political and cultural landscape.

- The **Biographies** section provides valuable biographical background on leading figures associated with the event in question. Each biography concludes with a list of sources for further information on the profiled individual.

- The **Primary Sources** section collects a wide variety of pertinent primary source materials from the era under discussion, including official documents, papers and resolutions, letters, oral histories, memoirs, editorials, and other important works.

Individually, each of these sections is a rich resource for users. Together, they comprise an authoritative, balanced, and absorbing examination of some of the most significant events in U.S. history.

Other notable features contained within each volume in the series include a glossary of important individuals, places, and terms; a detailed chronology featuring page references to relevant sections of the narrative; an annotated bibliography of sources for further study; an extensive general bibliography that reflects the wide range of historical sources consulted by the author; and a subject index.

Acknowledgements

This series was developed in consultation with a distinguished Advisory Board composed of public librarians, school librarians, and educators. They evaluated the series as it developed, and their comments and suggestions were invaluable throughout the production process. Any errors in this and other volumes in the series are ours alone. Following is a list of board members who contributed to the *Defining Moments* series:

Gail Beaver, M.A., M.A.L.S.
Adjunct Lecturer, University of Michigan
Ann Arbor, MI

Melissa C. Bergin, L.M.S., N.B.C.T.
Library Media Specialist
Niskayuna High School
Niskayuna, NY

Rose Davenport, M.S.L.S., Ed. Specialist
Library Media Specialist
Pershing High School Library
Detroit, MI

Karen Imarisio, A.M.L.S.
Assistant Head of Adult Services
Bloomfield Twp. Public Library
Bloomfield Hills, MI

Nancy Larsen, M.L.S., M.S. Ed.
Library Media Specialist
Clarkston High School
Clarkston, MI

Marilyn Mast, M.I.L.S.
Kingswood Campus Librarian
Cranbrook Kingswood Upper School
Bloomfield Hills, MI

Rosemary Orlando, M.L.I.S.
Library Director
St. Clair Shores Public Library
St. Clair Shores, MI

Comments and Suggestions

We welcome your comments on *Defining Moments: The Attack on Pearl Harbor* and suggestions for other events in U.S. history that warrant treatment in the *Defining Moments* series. Correspondence should be addressed to:

Editor, *Defining Moments*
Omnigraphics, Inc.
P.O. Box 31-1640
Detroit, MI 48231
E-mail: editorial@omnigraphics.com

HOW TO USE THIS BOOK

Defining Moments: The Attack on Pearl Harbor provides users with a detailed and authoritative overview of the events of December 7, 1941, as well as background on the principal figures involved in this pivotal episode in U.S. history. The preparation and arrangement of this volume—and all other books in the *Defining Moments* series—reflect an emphasis on providing a thorough and objective account of events that shaped our nation, presented in an easy-to-use reference work.

Defining Moments: The Attack on Pearl Harbor is divided into three primary sections. The first of these sections, the **Narrative Overview**, provides a detailed, factual account of the Pearl Harbor attack and the war in the Pacific. It explains the political and economic forces behind Japan's decision to attack the United States, as well as the factors that contributed to America's failure to prepare for such an attack. This section also covers the dramatic events of December 7, 1941, from the shocking appearance of enemy aircraft in the skies over Hawaii to the scenes of chaos, destruction, and heroism that occurred at Pearl Harbor and surrounding military facilities. Finally, this section chronicles America's hard-fought victory over Japan in the Pacific during World War II and explores the legacy of Pearl Harbor in the postwar development of both nations.

The second section, **Biographies**, provides valuable biographical background on leading figures involved in the events of December 7, 1941, including Mitsuo Fuchida, the lead pilot in the Japanese attack force; Husband E. Kimmel, the U.S. Navy admiral in charge of the Pacific Fleet at the time of the attack; Doris Miller, a cook on the battleship *West Virginia* whose heroism at Pearl Harbor made him the first African-American sailor to earn the Navy Cross; and Isoroku Yamamoto, the Japanese admiral who developed the attack plan. Each biography concludes with a list of sources for further information on the profiled individual.

The third section, **Primary Sources**, collects essential and illuminating documents related to the attack on Pearl Harbor. This diverse collection includes the detailed Japanese attack plan; dramatic firsthand accounts of the attack from a Japanese pilot, an American sailor, and a high-school student caught in the crossfire; President Franklin D. Roosevelt's famous "Day of Infamy" speech; and the instrument of Japanese surrender that marked the end of World War II.

Other valuable features in *Defining Moments: The Attack on Pearl Harbor* include the following:

- Attribution and referencing of primary sources and other quoted material to help guide users to other valuable historical research resources.
- A glossary of Important People, Places, and Terms.
- Detailed Chronology of events with a *see reference* feature. Under this arrangement, events listed in the chronology include a reference to page numbers within the Narrative Overview wherein users can find additional information on the event in question.
- Photographs of the leading figures and major events associated with the attack on Pearl Harbor and the war in the Pacific.
- Sources for Further Study, an annotated list of noteworthy works about the event.
- Extensive bibliography of works consulted in the creation of this book, including books, periodicals, and Internet sites.
- A Subject Index.

NARRATIVE OVERVIEW

PROLOGUE

President Franklin D. Roosevelt famously described December 7, 1941, as "a date which will live in infamy." On that fateful Sunday morning—as unsuspecting American soldiers, sailors, and civilians on the U.S. Navy base at Pearl Harbor, Hawaii, followed their regular routines—hundreds of Japanese planes suddenly appeared in the sky overhead. Before people on the ground could grasp what was happening, the planes began dropping bombs and torpedoes on the ships in Pearl Harbor and strafing nearby airfields with machine-gun fire. The attack lasted less than two hours, but the Japanese succeeded in destroying 188 U.S. warplanes, sinking or severely damaging 21 warships, and killing 2,388 Americans.

The greatest loss of life took place on the battleship USS *Arizona,* which was struck by an armor-piercing bomb during the first few minutes of the Japanese attack. This bomb struck the ship's forward magazine, a large compartment in the bow that held fifty tons of gunpowder and ammunition. The strike triggered a massive explosion that tore apart the front part of the *Arizona* and sent flaming debris, metal fragments, and human body parts raining down on nearby ships. The *Arizona* disaster took the lives of 1,177 sailors, or about half of the total number of Americans who died in the attack on Pearl Harbor. Only 337 crew members survived.

One of the lucky few was Aviation Machinist's Mate First Class George D. Phraner. Just minutes before the explosion, he left the bow of the *Arizona* to go below deck and help bring up ammunition for the battleship's big guns. "I had begun lifting shells into the hoist when a deafening roar filled the room and the entire ship shuddered," he recalled. "It was the forward magazine. One and a half million pounds of gunpowder exploding in a massive fireball disintegrating the whole forward part of the ship."[1] Phraner managed

3

to find his way back up to the deck in smoke and darkness, then jumped overboard and swam through flaming oil and debris to reach shore.

Another survivor, Gunner's Mate Third Class Leland H. Burk, was at his battle station inside a gun turret when the explosion rocked the *Arizona*. When he came out to help fight the resulting fire, he was confronted with a grisly scene on the deck. "There were guys lying all around moaning and groaning for help," he remembered. "Most of their clothes were either blown or burnt off. I helped move some of the injured and their flesh would stick to your hands when you handled them."[2] After loading some of the casualties into small boats, Burk left the sinking ship and swam to Ford Island. He narrowly escaped death again a few minutes later, when a Japanese bomb landed fifteen feet away from him but did not explode.

As the last of the Japanese planes finally retreated from the skies over Pearl Harbor, the stunned survivors of the *Arizona* could only watch helplessly as the battered remains of their proud ship sank beneath the waves. Everywhere they looked were scenes of devastation, from roaring flames and pillars of black smoke to capsized ships and floating bodies of dead sailors.

Out of the tragedy at Pearl Harbor, though, a nation was roused to action. The surprise attack shocked, outraged, and united the American people like few other events in U.S. history. Immediately afterward, the United States declared war on Japan and officially entered World War II. "In American mythology, Pearl Harbor still represents, even after a half-century, a classic moment of treachery and betrayal," noted a *Time* magazine article commemorating the fiftieth anniversary of the attack. "Certainly it was a moment of historic surprise, a moment when the impossible happened, when warfare suddenly spread, for the first and only time in history, to virtually the whole world."[3]

Notes

[1] Phraner, George D. "George Phraner's Brush with Death aboard the USS *Arizona*." USSArizona.org. Available online at http://www.ussarizona.org/survivors/phraner/index.html.

[2] Burk, Leland Howard. "USS Arizona Survivor Stories." USSArizona.org. Available online at http://www.ussarizona.org/survivors/burk/index.html.

[3] Friedrich, Otto. "Day of Infamy." *Time*, December 2, 1991, p. 30.

Chapter One

EVENTS LEADING UP TO WORLD WAR II

It seems inevitable that a collision should occur between Japan, determined to establish a sphere of interest in East Asia ... and the United States, which is determined to meddle in affairs on the other side of a vast ocean.

—1940 editorial in the Japanese newspaper *Asahi Shimbun*

T he Japanese attack on the U.S. military base at Pearl Harbor, Hawaii, on December 7, 1941, is one of the most infamous events in modern warfare. In the annals of history, it is often presented as a devious sneak attack that came without warning or provocation. It is true that many Americans were shocked and outraged by the sudden and ferocious nature of the attack, as well as by its devastating outcome. But in retrospect, the attack on Pearl Harbor can be viewed as a predictable result of decades of increasing tension and conflict between the United States and Japan. It also followed logically from a series of events in Europe that drew nations around the globe into World War II.

The Aftermath of World War I

Many historians note that one of the main causes of World War II was the outcome of World War I. This conflict, which lasted from August 1914 until November 1918, was called "the war to end all wars." At the time it started, France and Germany were the most dominant military and economic powers in Europe. To protect their borders and interests against each other, both nations had entered into a series of complex alliances with other countries. As political rivalries and tensions increased, it took only a minor incident to ignite all of Europe into war.

If not for timely intervention by the United States, the Central Powers (Germany and its allies Austria-Hungary and the Ottoman Empire) might have won the war. The United States started out by sending money, supplies, and weapons to aid the Allies (France, England, Italy, and Russia) in the fight against Germany. When the U.S. government sent combat troops into the conflict in 1917, it helped turn the tide in the Allies' favor. By the end of the following year, the Allies were victorious. Although 110,000 American soldiers were killed in action or died of disease during the war—and another 230,000 were wounded—the U.S. mainland did not sustain any damage. The United States maintained its military and industrial power after the war and grew into a respected world leader.

Since the United States held the strongest position among the victors, President Woodrow Wilson proposed a settlement that would be fair to all parties involved. His famous "Fourteen Points" were intended to provide a long-term resolution of the issues that had divided Europe. Wilson also led in the creation of the League of Nations, an international body that was designed to help member countries resolve their differences in a peaceful manner.

But the nations that had borne the brunt of German aggression, including France and England, felt a great deal of anger and bitterness in the aftermath of the war. They were determined to punish Germany and ensure that it never again posed a threat to their security or interests. The Treaty of Versailles, which officially ended World War I in 1919, took away German territory, forbade the Germans from raising an army, and forced the German people to pay for damages caused by the war. Naturally, many Germans resented the terms of the treaty, especially as Germany suffered from economic problems over the next few years.

During the postwar period, there were some hopeful signs that the nations involved had learned important lessons from World War I. In 1922, for instance, England, Germany, Japan, and the United States were among the parties that signed an agreement to limit the size of their navies. Four years later, Germany joined the League of Nations. But hopes that Europe might recover from the war grew dim when the Great Depression hit first the United States and then the world.

The Rise of Fascism in Europe

The U.S. economy plunged into the worst depression in its history in October 1929. A crash in the value of the stock market and a series of bank failures cost millions of Americans their life savings. Companies went out of business, people lost their jobs, prices increased rapidly, and American families struggled to pay for food and other basic necessities.

The trouble in the U.S. economy soon spread to Europe, where many nations were still trying to recover financially from World War I. The Great Depression compounded these problems, creating high unemployment and inflation rates. In Germany, for instance, the depression put six million people out of work. Combined with political instability and widespread government corruption, the economic downturn left many European nations reeling. Some European citizens felt so desperate that they became willing to embrace any form of government or leadership that promised to restore order and stability to their lives.

Such feelings contributed to the rise of fascist regimes in Germany and

Residents of New York City wait in line for food during the Great Depression of the 1930s. The economic hardships of this period also contributed to the rise of fascism in Europe.

Italy. The political and social system known as fascism features a strong central government that controls most aspects of citizens' lives. Under fascism, people are pressured to sacrifice their individual rights and freedoms for the "good of the country." Nevertheless, fascism held a great deal of appeal to the people of Germany and Italy at this point in history. The fascists promised to solve their countries' economic problems quickly and restore national pride and international prestige.

Italy's fascist regime was led by Benito Mussolini. After taking control of the government in 1922, Mussolini outlawed rival political parties and threw anyone who disagreed with his policies into prison. Despite the fact that he behaved like a dictator, though, Mussolini remained popular among some Italians. He oversaw a period of economic recovery, industrial expansion, and job creation. His government imposed discipline and order on

Italian society and, as Mussolini liked to boast, ensured that "the trains run on time."

The most infamous fascist to rise to power during this time was Adolf Hitler in Germany. Hitler joined the National Socialist German Workers' Party, or Nazi Party, in the early 1920s. In 1923 the Nazis made an unsuccessful attempt to overthrow the government of a section of Germany called Bavaria. While serving time in prison for his involvement in the plot, Hitler wrote a famous manifesto called *Mein Kampf (My Struggle)*. This book outlined his plan to restore Germany's status as a major world power. It also detailed his hatred of Jews, Asians, Africans, and other races he claimed were inferior to white Anglo-Saxons or Aryans.

When the Great Depression hit Europe, Hitler and the Nazis turned the situation to their advantage. They blamed the nation's economic woes on the high reparations costs that Germany was forced to pay following World War I. They also falsely claimed that Jewish bankers and business owners contributed to the problem by cheating their customers. At a time when many struggling Germans were looking for an outlet for their anger and frustration, the Nazi message held some appeal. Support for Hitler increased steadily until he became the leader of the German government in 1933. He soon signaled his hostile intentions by launching a buildup of the German military—in direct violation of the terms of the Treaty of Versailles—and withdrawing from the League of Nations.

Hitler Goes on the Offensive

Another link was added to the chain of events that led to World War II in March 1936, when Hitler sent German troops into the Rhineland. This neutral territory on the border of France had been taken away from Germany following World War I. Although leaders of France, England, and other European nations were alarmed by Germany's aggression, they did not take action. The horrors of World War I were still fresh in the minds of many Europeans, and they were reluctant to enter into a new conflict with Germany.

As soon as Hitler confirmed that the other European powers would do nothing to stop him, however, he set his sights on conquering even more territory. Claiming that Germany was overcrowded, Hitler systematically began expanding the nation's borders to give his people more "living space." In 1938 the German army took over Austria, a neighboring country where many citizens spoke German and supported the Nazi Party. Next Hitler's army

Under Adolf Hitler (left) and the Nazi Party, Germany conquered much of Europe in the late 1930s and early 1940s.

marched into Sudetenland, a region of Czechoslovakia with a significant number of residents of German descent.

At this point, British Prime Minister Neville Chamberlain negotiated a deal with Hitler. Instead of demanding that Hitler return the occupied territories, the deal allowed Germany to keep all of the land it had already conquered, as long as Hitler agreed not to expand his nation's borders any further. Chamberlain claimed that the arrangement would prevent another war and promote "peace in our time." But many other European leaders criticized the deal and expressed concerns about Hitler's real goals. One of England's rising political stars, Winston Churchill, dismissed the treaty as "appeasement." He predicted that Chamberlain's stance signaled to Hitler that he could do whatever he wanted without fear of British intervention.

This prediction came true in 1939, when the German army took over the rest of Czechoslovakia and then turned its attention toward Poland. Hitler shocked the world by making an arrangement with one of his biggest rivals, Russian dictator Joseph Stalin. The two leaders agreed not to attack each other and to divide Poland between them. On September 1, the German army marched into western Poland. The Soviet Union claimed eastern Poland and also annexed the Baltic states of Latvia, Lithuania, and Estonia.

By making a non-aggression pact with the Soviet Union, Hitler ensured that Germany did not need to worry about defending its eastern border. He was then able to turn the full force of the German army toward western Europe. The leaders of France and England realized that Hitler had no intention of stopping until Germany had conquered all of Europe. On September 3, 1939, France and England declared war on Germany to mark the official start of World War II.

In the spring of 1940 the German army advanced through Norway, Denmark, and Belgium. It then launched a massive attack on France. On June 22, France was forced to surrender. German troops occupied northern France and established a puppet government in Vichy to rule the southern portion of the country. France's defeat meant that England was the only nation that stood between Hitler and German control of all of western Europe. Following the surrender of France, British troops retreated from the mainland and took up defensive positions on their own side of the English Channel.

Japan Dreams of Empire in Asia

While Hitler was rising to power in Germany and conquering large parts of Europe, Japan was embarking on a similar mission to dominate Asia. Like Germany, Japan had been upset about the Treaty of Versailles that ended World War I. Although Japan had fought on the side of the victorious Allies, it had not been invited to participate in the peace negotiations. Instead, Japan was grouped with lesser nations that were consulted as needed. The agreement that was signed in 1919 left Japan feeling frustrated and unappreciated. Japanese leaders believed that they should have received greater respect and more territory in exchange for their contributions to the Allied cause.

Immediately after World War I ended, Japan moved toward establishing a democratic form of government. During this period, however, Japan experienced some disappointing diplomatic setbacks. The United States placed severe restrictions on Japanese immigration, for example, and Great Britain built a naval base in Singapore. Many Japanese citizens criticized the government, complaining that it was too weak to defend the nation's interests against the demands of western powers.

These complaints grew louder in the early 1930s, when the Great Depression rocked Japan's economy. As the Japanese people struggled with high rates of inflation and unemployment, nationalists with ties to the military gained influence in Japan's government. These leaders promised to restore national pride and international prestige by conquering new territory. This stance appealed to the warrior tradition in Japanese culture, which said that men could bring honor to their families by fighting and dying for their country. The government also gained the support of many Japanese citizens by launching an aggressive military buildup that created jobs and improved the nation's economy.

Emperor Hirohito reviews Japanese troops in China at the beginning of Japan's quest to build an empire in Asia.

Before long, the growing Japanese military began expanding Japan's sphere of influence in Asia. Their first target was China, which was going through a period of political upheaval at that time. Chinese Communists, led by Mao Zedong, were fighting for control of the country against Chinese Nationalists, led by Chiang Kai-shek. In September 1931, Japan took advantage of this unstable political situation to take over Manchuria. Control of this region of northeastern China had long been disputed between China, Japan, and Russia. Manchuria contained large deposits of iron and coal, which Japan desperately needed to support its military production.

The United States and the Soviet Union protested against Japan's invasion of Manchuria, as did the League of Nations. Japan's military leaders responded by withdrawing from the League and refusing to honor international arms treaties. On July 7, 1937—following an incident in which Chinese forces supposedly fired upon Japanese troops near Peking (now Bei-

Colonialism in Asia

By the time Japan became the most powerful nation in Asia in the early twentieth century, the United States and a number of European countries had colonized most of the region. European traders and missionaries began visiting South Asia and the Pacific Islands in the 1500s. For the next 200 years, they acquired silk, tea, spices, and other exotic goods that could be sold at a large profit back home.

During the 1800s, the United States and various European nations used their superior military and economic strength to take control of large parts of Asia. The Netherlands controlled the Dutch East Indies (now Indonesia), France held French Indochina (consisting of Vietnam, Laos, and Cambodia), the United States took over Hawaii and Guam, and Great Britain controlled Singapore, Malaya, Hong Kong, and Burma. These colonial powers installed governments that served the interests of the mother country, often at the expense of local people. They used their Asian colonies as sources of raw materials—such as rice, rubber, and timber—and as markets for cloth, machines, and other manufactured goods.

Throughout the colonial era, Japan was controlled by warlords called shogun who followed a policy of isolation. They managed to keep out for-

jing)—Japan launched a full-scale invasion of China. Some historians consider this event to be the true start of World War II.

Following a destructive bombing campaign, Japanese forces captured the Nationalist capital of Nanking in December 1937. Then the army went on a murderous rampage, killing an estimated 300,000 Chinese civilians and raping thousands of Chinese women. By 1938 the Japanese controlled most of China's ports. Although Japan never managed to conquer all of China, its leaders felt confident that they had eliminated their biggest rival for power in Asia.

At this point, Japanese leaders began planning to build an empire in southeast Asia and the Pacific islands. They wanted to create what they called the Greater East Asian Co-Prosperity Sphere. The main idea was to take control of valuable sources of raw materials to fuel Japanese industry. But they eign traders and resist colonization by European powers for two centuries. Japan was finally forced to open its ports to shipping in 1853, when a U.S. naval squadron led by Commodore Matthew Perry sailed into Edo Bay (now Tokyo Bay). Within a few years, Japan's ports were full of merchant vessels bringing goods from foreign lands.

Once Japan was exposed to western goods and ideas, its leaders set out on an ambitious program of modernization. They studied recent innovations in science, technology, and commerce. They also established a formidable military presence by building warships, guns, and planes. In 1905 the well-armed Japanese army defeated Russia in the Russo-Japanese War.

By this time, the biggest challenge facing Japan in its quest to become the dominant power in Asia was its lack of raw materials. The island nation lacked the natural resources needed to fuel modern industry, such as oil, coal, and iron. Although these materials were available in other parts of Asia, most sources were under the control of European or American colonial powers. Japan did not want to depend on other countries to supply it with vital resources. Instead, it wanted to expand its territory in order to control supplies of its own.

also felt that conquering new territory would make Japan the dominant regional power and increase its international standing.

The advance of Hitler's army across Europe in 1940 gave Japan a perfect opportunity to take over the Asian colonies that belonged to England, France, and Holland (see "Colonialism in Asia," p. 12). While they were busy fighting against Germany, these nations did not have military resources available to defend their colonies from a Japanese invasion. After France surrendered to Germany, Japan moved southward to take over French Indochina (modern-day Cambodia, Laos, and Vietnam). By occupying this area, Japanese leaders gained control of naval bases that they could use to attack Thailand, Burma, the oil-rich Dutch East Indies, and the British military base in Singapore.

Germany, Japan, and Italy Form the Axis Powers

Japan became more firmly set on its aggressive course in July 1940, when hard-line militarists took control of the government. Two months later—on September 27, 1940—Japan entered into a formal military alliance with Germany and Italy. Representatives of the three countries signed a document called the Tripartite Pact (see "The Tripartite Pact of 1940," p. 165). They agreed to cooperate with each other in hopes of establishing a new world order. Each nation recognized the others' spheres of interest and promised not to interfere in activities there. They also agreed to come to each others' defense in case of attack. The Italian dictator, Mussolini, described the three-way alliance as the "Axis," because he felt the parties shared many common or intersecting goals.

Many world leaders believed that Nazi Germany, Fascist Italy, and Imperialist Japan formed the Axis Powers in order to send a message to the United States. By the time the three nations signed the Tripartite Pact, America was the lone remaining power with enough military and industrial strength to halt their expansionist plans. Japan was well aware that the U.S. had military bases in the Philippines, for instance, and had recently relocated its Pacific Fleet from California to Hawaii. This put the United States in a strong position to interfere with Japanese plans for expansion in the Pacific.

Japanese leaders also knew, however, that the United States was reluctant to get involved in World War II. They felt that America would be even less likely to enter the conflict if U.S. leaders knew they would face enemies on both the Atlantic and Pacific sides of the continent. They hoped that the Tripartite Pact, and the potential for a two-front war, would convince the Americans to stay out of the conflict. Instead, though, it convinced President Franklin D. Roosevelt and many other U.S. leaders that war was inevitable.

Chapter Two

AMERICA STAYS
ON THE SIDELINES

Japan must deal the U.S. Navy a fatal blow at the outset of the war. It is the only way she can fight with any reasonable prospect of success.

—Isoroku Yamamoto, commander in chief of the Imperial Japanese Combined Fleet, January 1941

U.S. leaders and ordinary citizens alike watched with growing alarm as Nazi Germany conquered most of Europe and Japan threatened to overtake large parts of Asia and the Pacific. They were particularly concerned when Germany, Italy, and Japan formed an alliance in September 1940—one that seemed specifically designed to intimidate the United States and prevent it from entering World War II.

Despite their widespread dismay at German and Japanese aggression, however, the American people still felt a deep reluctance to go to war for a second time in less than twenty-five years. Many citizens argued that the country should mind its own business and stay out of world affairs. Nevertheless, President Franklin D. Roosevelt gradually increased U.S. support for the Allies fighting against Germany in the late 1930s and early 1940s. He also held intensive diplomatic negotiations with Japan—and employed economic sanctions and other nonmilitary weapons—in hopes of avoiding conflict in the Pacific until the Nazis could be defeated. As it turned out, though, Japan had other plans.

War-weariness, Pacifism, and Isolationism
Even though the fighting had taken place overseas, World War I still took a toll on the United States. By the time it ended, the American people

15

felt tired of war and determined to stay out of future overseas conflicts. Many citizens questioned whether the cost—both in terms of human lives and financial support—had been worth it. After all, it became clear fairly quickly that the "war to end all wars" had neither settled the longstanding differences between countries nor secured the future of democracy in Europe. It also became apparent that the League of Nations was too weak to halt the rise of fascism or preserve peace.

The aftermath of World War I had a tremendous impact on national attitudes in the United States. Many war-weary Americans believed that the best way for their country to maintain its power and security was to remain isolated from the rest of the world. They found confidence in the fact that vast oceans separated the U.S. mainland from the problems in Europe and Asia. They argued that the United States should only use its military strength to defend its borders—not to intervene in conflicts elsewhere.

Such isolationist attitudes helped convince the U.S. Congress to pass a series of Neutrality Acts in the 1930s (see "The Neutrality Act of 1937," p. 159). These laws forbade American government agencies, businesses, or citizens from providing money, weapons, or any other type of aid to a nation at war. The acts also prohibited Americans from traveling to war zones or sailing on vessels owned by a nation at war.

Another factor influencing the passage of the Neutrality Acts was a Congressional investigation led by Gerald Nye. The Nye Commission had found that some American banks, corporations, and citizens had profited from U.S. involvement in World War I. Articles in magazines and newspapers claimed that these war profiteers had earned money from the blood of American soldiers and criticized them as "merchants of death." Congress intended for the Neutrality Acts to prevent American financial and industrial institutions from influencing any future U.S. government decisions on going to war.

Increasing Support for the Allies in Europe

Although isolationist feelings were strong among both the American people and members of the U.S. Congress, some citizens argued against this view. They felt that the United States, as one of the most powerful countries in the world, had a responsibility to take a leadership role in world affairs. They wanted the U.S. government to promote democracy, protect human rights, and defend victims of fascist or imperialist aggression around the

German attack submarines, like the U-47 in the foreground of this photograph, disrupted transatlantic shipping and prompted the U.S. government to increase its support for the Allies.

globe. Other people argued that isolationism hurt the U.S. economy. They claimed that the nation could only emerge from the Great Depression by extending American business interests to international markets.

President Franklin D. Roosevelt (see Roosevelt biography, p. 144) was among those who believed that the United States should use its position to influence world affairs. He felt that it was only a matter of time before the nation would be drawn into another conflict. But Roosevelt recognized that the isolationist sentiments of the American people limited what he could do without alienating voters. When Nazi Germany launched its march across Europe in 1937, for instance, the president suggested that the United States and other nations use economic sanctions to punish the fascists for their aggression. The idea met with such a negative public reaction, however, that he was forced to drop it. Instead, Roosevelt quietly provided nonmilitary support to the Allies and worked to sway public opinion in favor of intervention.

As Germany and Japan began waging war on their neighbors, though, isolationist feelings started to erode among the American people. Polls showed that the percentage of Americans who described themselves as "deeply isolationist" declined from 64 percent in 1937 to 39 percent in 1940.[1] Roosevelt took advantage of the shifting attitudes to convince Congress to revise and eventually repeal the Neutrality Acts. When France and England declared war on Germany in 1939, for example, the president arranged to sell weapons and munitions to the Allies on a "cash-and-carry" basis. This revision to the Neutrality Acts allowed the United States to sell materials to nations at war as long as those nations paid immediately in cash and handled the transportation.

> *"We must be the great arsenal of democracy," Roosevelt declared. "We must apply ourselves to our task with the same resolution, the same sense of urgency, the same spirit of patriotism and sacrifice as we would show were we at war."*

In the meantime, Roosevelt also took steps to prepare the nation for possible involvement in the war. He encouraged Congress to pass the Burke-Wadsworth Selective Service Training and Service bill, which instituted a peacetime military draft for the first time in U.S. history. As a concession to the isolationists, however, Congress included provisions that limited the term of required military service to one year and prohibited draftees from being sent overseas. At a campaign stop in Boston in October 1940—one month after the bill passed—Roosevelt famously assured voters that "your boys are not going to be sent into any foreign wars."

After winning reelection that November, however, Roosevelt began speaking out more forcefully about how he viewed the nation's role in stopping fascist aggression. On December 29, 1940, he delivered a famous address designed to rally the American people in support of the Allies. In this "Arsenal of Democracy" speech, the president outlined the growing threat posed by Germany and Japan, which had recently signed the Tripartite Pact. He argued that giving in to the demands of the Axis Powers had only made them stronger. "No nation can appease the Nazis," he explained. "No man can tame a tiger into a kitten by stroking it." Instead, Roosevelt insisted that the United States had a responsibility to supply the arms and equipment needed for the Allies to defeat the Axis. "We must be the great arsenal of democracy," he declared. "We must apply ourselves to our task with the same resolution, the same sense of urgency, the same spirit of patriotism and sacrifice as we would show were we at war."[2]

U.S. support for the Allies increased steadily throughout 1941. Although the nation had clearly abandoned its neutral stance by this time, the American people were not yet ready to commit to direct military intervention. Still, the United States shipped arms and other supplies across the Atlantic Ocean to help Great Britain hold out against the German Army. The Germans used submarine attacks to disrupt these transatlantic shipments and prevent vital materials from reaching England. The German subs, known as U-boats, were terribly effective in destroying British naval and merchant vessels. In fact, the Nazis sunk British ships five times faster than they could be replaced.

In response to this crisis, Roosevelt convinced the U.S. Congress to pass the Lend-Lease Act in March 1941. This legislation gave the United States a way to supply the Allies with warships without officially entering the war. Under this arrangement, the U.S. Navy lent 50 retired destroyers to Great Britain in exchange for a lease on British naval bases in the Caribbean. Roosevelt also prepared for the day when the United States might need to provide direct aid to the Allies. He got Congress to set aside $7 billion to build new ships, planes, tanks, and other military equipment.

During the fall of 1941, the U.S. Navy became involved in several direct confrontations with German submarines. The U.S.S. *Greer* was attacked by a German U-boat in September, for instance, and the U.S.S. *Reuben James* was sunk in October—a tragedy that took the lives of more than 100 American sailors. These events pushed the United States ever closer to joining the fight against Germany. The escalating violence led Roosevelt to arm American merchant vessels and order the navy to shoot German warships on sight.

Embargoes and Sanctions against Japan

In the meantime, tensions increased between the United States and Japan as well. U.S. leaders were highly critical of Japan's decision to invade China in 1937. They provided aid to the Chinese Nationalists to help them fight both the Chinese Communists and the Japanese. In December 1937, an incident occurred that threatened to pull the United States into the conflict. Japanese planes bombed a U.S. Navy gunboat that was escorting American oil tankers on China's Yangtze River. Several American sailors were killed in the attack.

Japanese leaders claimed that it was an accident and issued an official apology. In the face of strong isolationist sentiments among the American people, Roosevelt felt compelled to accept the apology. Many Japanese officials were surprised that the United States did not retaliate. They viewed the lack of

American response to the incident as a sign of weakness and indecision. This perspective made them less hesitant to behave aggressively in the future.

American leaders grew even more alarmed in 1938, when Japan took control of most of China's ports. Certain that Japanese aggression would eventually threaten U.S. interests in the Pacific, Roosevelt worked to improve American defenses in the region. As part of this initiative, he convinced Congress to approve funding to build up the U.S. Navy to more than twice its previous size.

Even so, Roosevelt and most other U.S. officials still believed that Germany posed a much greater threat to world security than Japan. Although they recognized that the United States might someday need to use military action to stop Japanese aggression, they wanted to avoid fighting a war on two fronts—in Europe and the Pacific—at the same time. The top priority for Roosevelt and his advisors was to help the Allies stop Hitler from taking over Europe. They hoped to delay entering into an armed conflict with Japan until after Germany was defeated.

With this goal in mind, Roosevelt decided to use diplomacy and economic sanctions to try to slow down Japanese expansion in Asia and the Pacific. In 1940, when Japan formed an alliance with Germany and Italy with the Tripartite Pact, Roosevelt responded by placing an embargo on aviation gasoline. This measure prohibited the United States and its allies from selling fuel to Japan that could be used in its warplanes. The president also placed restrictions on the sale of scrap iron and steel that could be used to further Japanese military plans.

At the same time, though, Roosevelt continued building up American defenses in the Pacific. He moved American warplanes, including long-range bombers capable of reaching Japan, to military bases in the Philippines. He also sent troops and equipment to the island of Guam. Finally, in February 1940, Roosevelt moved the home base of the U.S. Navy's Pacific Fleet from California to the island of Oahu in Hawaii—about 2,000 miles closer to Japan (see "The History of Pearl Harbor," p. 21).

Some Japanese officials viewed these changes as evidence that the United States was planning to attack Japan. In fact, a few of Roosevelt's advisors favored this plan. They urged the president to destroy Japan's naval forces with one swift attack. They argued that this strategy, if successful, would allow the United States to devote its full attention and military strength to the

The History of Pearl Harbor

The Hawaiian Islands—located 2,400 miles southwest of California in the Pacific Ocean—were first colonized by Polynesians in canoes around 600 A.D. Pearl Harbor, on the island of Oahu, was precious to the native people. Ancient Hawaiians called the shallow, protected bay "Wai Momi," or "Waters of Pearl," because of the abundance of pearl-producing oysters found there. It was also known as an excellent fishing ground, especially in the tidal pools along the shoreline.

The famous British explorer Captain James Cook became the first westerner to land in Hawaii in 1778. In 1810, the eight main islands of Hawaii were united under a single leader, King Kamehameha I. The U.S. Navy arrived in 1826, during a period of American exploration and colonization of the Pacific. A routine Navy survey showed that a coral reef blocked the entrance to Pearl Harbor.

It was not until 1898, when the United States captured the Philippines in the Spanish-American War, that the Navy decided to establish a base in Hawaii to help maintain control of this new acquisition in the western Pacific. The United States annexed Hawaii as a U.S. territory that year. After removing the coral reef to create a navigable waterway, the U.S. Navy established the Pearl Harbor Naval Shipyard in 1908.

Pearl Harbor became the home of the U.S. Pacific Fleet in February 1940. The aircraft carrier USS *Enterprise* was sent there from San Diego, along with 200 airplanes, 17 destroyers, and 7 cruisers. Unfortunately, Japan viewed the increased U.S. military presence in Hawaii as a hostile act. On December 7, 1941, Japan attacked Pearl Harbor in hopes of immobilizing the Pacific Fleet. As the National Park Service noted on the USS *Arizona* Memorial Web site, "the very action taken to protect America from this potential threat would be the thing that made her vulnerable to it."

Source: National Park Service. "Places: The History of Pearl Harbor." USS *Arizona* Memorial site. Available online at http://www.nps.gov/usar/historyculture/places.htm.

fight against Germany. But Roosevelt never seriously considered attacking Japan. Still facing pressure from isolationists, he was committed to using diplomatic methods to discourage Japan from trying to dominate Asia.

Roosevelt used all the nonmilitary weapons at his disposal in July 1941, when Japan took control of French Indochina. The president responded by freezing all Japanese assets in the United States and prohibiting the sale of all raw materials and manufactured goods to Japan. Since Japan did not possess many natural resources of its own, it depended on foreign trade to gain access to oil, coal, iron, steel, and other vital materials. The American embargo thus had the potential to devastate Japan's economy and derail its expansion plans.

Diplomatic Efforts to Avoid War with Japan

The American embargo shocked and angered Japanese leaders. All of their plans for military production and territorial expansion depended on their having continued access to oil and other raw materials from foreign sources. They knew that their nation would be unable to continue on its present course if these supplies were cut off. Once the embargo took effect, Japan was left with only about a year's supply of oil. This became the timetable for Japanese leaders to decide whether they would give in to American demands and halt their expansion efforts, or attempt to take what they needed by force. "Oil was the lifeblood of Japan's military capacity, and the American embargo became the most crucial event in the entire sequence of events leading to war," one writer explained. "Japan was faced with a critical choice: abandon its decade-long effort to control China and return to its home islands, or go to war with the most industrially productive, technologically advanced nation on earth."[3]

Some historians claim that Japan made its choice in October 1941, when leaders with close ties to the military took over the reins of the government. Prince Fumimaro Konoye, who had expressed an interest in maintaining peace with the United States, was forced to resign as prime minister. He was replaced by the war minister, General Hideki Tojo, who believed that Japan's future depended on expanding its reach in Asia, even if that meant war with the United States. "The men who were charting Japan's course," noted Dr. Stanley Hornbeck, an advisor to the U.S. State Department, "had decided that their country had a date with Destiny, that it needed to expand, that it was their function to make secure its actual domain and enlarge the area of its jurisdiction, and that this they would do—by diplomatic processes if possible but if those did not suffice by use of whatever weapons, strategies, and tactics they might be able to bring to bear."[4]

Although war became a distinct possibility as soon as Tojo came to power, Japan continued negotiating with the United States for the next few months. Japan's highest-ranking diplomat in the United States was Ambassador Kichisaburo Nomura, a retired admiral and former foreign minister. He held a series of meetings with the U.S. Secretary of State, Cordell Hull. Nomura recognized three major obstacles in the negotiations: Japan's occupation of China; the Tripartite Pact between Japan, Germany, and Italy; and Japan's expansion into French Indochina. The United States wanted Japan to withdraw its troops from China and French Indochina and back out of its alliance with the Axis Powers. Japan, on the other hand, wanted the United States to stop providing aid to China, quit building up its military forces in the Pacific, and resume supplying Japan with oil.

Japanese ambassador Kichisaburo Nomura and U.S. Secretary of State Cordell Hull, pictured in February 1941, tried to avoid war in the Pacific through diplomacy.

Some historians argue that Japan did not believe a peaceful settlement was possible and only participated in the diplomatic meetings in order to gain time to prepare for an attack. For evidence to support this view, they point to November 20, 1941, when Nomura presented Hull with a proposal that he described as the Japanese government's "last word." The Japanese ambassador suggested that the United States must agree to the proposal if it wanted to avoid war. The proposal demanded that the United States unfreeze Japanese assets, supply Japan with oil, stop giving aid to China, and accept Japan's occupation of French Indochina. In other words, it did not contain any concessions to the American side. Hornbeck noted that Japan's proposal convinced the U.S. government "that the chances of reaching an agreement and of dissuading Japan from her program of conquest were small indeed if existent at all." In fact, he suggested that November 20 might well be considered "the date when, in effect, war between Japan and the United States began."[5]

Despite the lack of concessions offered by the Japanese, Hull did not reject the proposal. Instead, he responded on November 26 with a counterproposal. The United States offered to lift the economic sanctions against Japan and enter into a non-aggression pact, if Japan agreed to reduce its military presence in Indochina and negotiate an end to hostilities with China. Hull and his advisors did not realistically expect Japanese leaders to accept the proposal. They mainly hoped that it would serve as the basis for continued discussions and thus buy time for the United States to deal with the greater threat posed by Germany. Nevertheless, Hull's proposal generated a great deal of criticism within the United States. Newspapers described it as an "ultimatum" that offered no compromises and made war with Japan inevitable.

Japanese Goals and Strategy

Throughout the period when these diplomatic negotiations were going on, Japanese military leaders were also preparing for war. Given Japan's limited access to oil and other materials, they knew that a long, drawn-out conflict would favor the United States. Therefore, they concentrated on developing strategies that involved quick, devastating attacks that might catch American forces off guard. They reasoned that if they could destroy a significant part of the U.S. military presence in the Pacific, then the Americans might be forced to negotiate a settlement on Japanese terms. This plan would allow Japan to continue its expansion in Asia without the threat of U.S. intervention.

The specific strategy that was eventually adopted came from Admiral Isoroku Yamamoto (see Yamamoto biography, p. 152), who had been promoted to commander in chief of the Japanese Combined Fleet on August 30, 1940. Recognizing the strength of the U.S. military and the extent of the nation's resources, Yamamoto felt that Japan should do everything in its power to avoid war with the United States. But when he eventually became convinced that war was inevitable, he advanced a plan for the Japanese navy to launch an attack on the U.S. Pacific Fleet stationed at Pearl Harbor, Hawaii. Yamamoto argued that attacking the U.S. fleet at anchor gave Japan its best chance to gain a significant advantage over the Americans. He anticipated, however, that this advantage would only be temporary. "If I am told to fight regardless of the consequences, I shall run wild for the first six months or a year," Yamamoto told Japanese leaders, "but I have utterly no confidence for the second or third year."[6]

On January 7, 1941, Yamamoto sent a passionate letter to Japan's minister of the navy. He threatened to resign if the government did not adopt his plan to attack the U.S. fleet at Pearl Harbor as its main strategic option in case of war. The Japanese government responded by ordering the navy to begin gathering information and performing training exercises so that they would be prepared to execute Yamamoto's plan. At this point, rumors began circulating in Tokyo about a possible Japanese attack on Pearl Harbor. By January 27, the rumors reached the ears of Joseph C. Grew, the American ambassador to Japan. Grew dutifully informed U.S. officials back in Washington, D.C., but no one took the report seriously because the scenario seemed so unlikely.

Yamamoto's Plan

Yamamoto's plan called for the Japanese navy to send a group of aircraft carriers across the Pacific to Hawaii. When the ships got within range of Pearl Harbor, they would launch entire squadrons of planes from their decks. These planes would carry out the attack—dropping bombs and torpedoes to destroy the U.S. fleet and land-based military bases—and then return to the carriers.

"If I am told to fight regardless of the consequences, I shall run wild for the first six months or a year," Yamamoto told Japanese leaders, *"but I have utterly no confidence for the second or third year."*

At the time, this type of carrier-based air attack represented a new direction in naval warfare. Most earlier naval battles took place between battleships at sea, or between ships and submarines. But two recent events had convinced the Japanese that a carrier-based attack on Pearl Harbor might be effective. In 1938, the U.S. Pacific Fleet itself had conducted training exercises for this type of attack. And on November 11, 1940, the British carrier *Illustrious* had launched a surprise raid using twenty-one obsolete planes that crippled Mussolini's main fleet in Taranto, Italy.

Using these successful carrier-based air raids as inspiration, the Japanese navy prepared its ships and planes for an attack on Pearl Harbor. Since the harbor was relatively shallow, they had to come up with a way to make torpedoes dropped from planes hit their targets rather than get stuck in the bottom. Their solution involved adding wooden fins to make the torpedoes more buoyant. Japanese pilots also did lots of training exercises to practice flying in tight formation and dropping bombs with precision.

Admiral Isoroku Yamamoto, commander in chief of the Imperial Japanese Combined Fleet, came up with the plan to attack Pearl Harbor.

In the meantime, the Japanese tried to improve their chances for success by collecting detailed information about Pearl Harbor and the U.S. Pacific Fleet. They sent a highly trained spy, Takeo Yoshikawa, to Hawaii in March 1941. While pretending to work at the Japanese consulate in Honolulu, he drew maps of the army and navy bases on Oahu, tracked the movements of ships and planes, and took note of the general activities and habits of U.S. military personnel. Yoshikawa gained a great deal of information by chatting with ethnic Japanese civilians (at that time, about one-third of the population of Hawaii was of Japanese origin) who worked on the military bases at Pearl Harbor as drivers, cooks, and gardeners. He relayed all of this data to military planners back in Tokyo, who incorporated it into their attack strategy.

Japanese military planners also sent several merchant ships to Honolulu in the months before the attack. On board one of these ships was a professional spy for the Japanese navy named Suguru Suzuki. Aware of what information was needed to finalize the Pearl Harbor plan, his vessel followed the route across the northern Pacific that had been chosen for the attack force. During the journey, Suzuki took note of the weather conditions and the appearance of any ships or planes. As his boat approached Hawaii, Suzuki saw a U.S. reconnaissance aircraft turn back 200 miles north of Oahu. Figuring that this was the outer perimeter of routine air patrols, he recommended that the Japanese attack be launched from a greater distance. While his ship sat in port within a few miles of Pearl Harbor, Suzuki observed through binoculars that the U.S. military maintained particularly low levels of security and activity on Sunday. This information helped Japanese planners choose a Sunday as the day to launch the attack.

General Tojo formally approved the attack plan on October 20, 1941— just four days after taking power (see "The Japanese Attack Plan," p. 167). Although diplomatic negotiations continued throughout November and early

December, Japan had already decided on war. The main question remaining was whether they would be able to preserve the element of surprise.

Warnings of Imminent Attack

U.S. political and military leaders realized that diplomatic relations between the United States and Japan were deteriorating in the fall of 1941. They understood that Japan resented what it viewed as American interference with its expansion strategy—especially the embargo that Roosevelt placed on oil, steel, and other materials that Japan desperately needed to support its military goals. Even so, many U.S. strategists thought that Japan would never launch a direct attack on the United States.

Some argued that Japan was too weak to pose a threat. As late as December 5, 1941, the War Department issued a report stating that Germany would "remain the only power capable of launching large-scale strategic offensives"[7] through at least the spring of 1942. Other U.S. strategists found it difficult to believe that Japan would choose to provoke a war with the United States. Although American leaders tried to discourage Japanese expansion by strengthening military defenses in the Pacific and placing the embargo on necessary materials, they had no plans to attack Japan. "Had the Japanese confined their aggression to nations they could actually defeat, the United States—given its strong isolationist streak and the Roosevelt administration's preoccupation with Germany—might well have hesitated to declare war on Japan,"[8] noted one writer.

In fact, Roosevelt remained determined to put off armed conflict with Japan until Germany could be defeated. He was committed to pursuing diplomatic solutions as long as possible in order to gain time to end the war in Europe (see "President Franklin D. Roosevelt Appeals for Peace," p. 173). Furthermore, antiwar feelings among the American people and in Congress meant that the president could not be too aggressive in dealing with Japan. If the two countries went to war, he felt, then Japan would be the one that started it. "The administration's known policy of leaving the first shot to Japan appeased the isolationists," one historian explained, "but handed the choice on whether, when, and how war would begin to Japan, with its well-established tradition of starting wars with surprise attacks."[9]

These widely held views led U.S. government officials to consistently underestimate Japan's military strength and its determination to build an

U.S. military code breakers intercepted a number of Japanese messages that provided clues about the coming attack on Pearl Harbor.

empire at any cost. As a result, American leaders misinterpreted several warning signs. Some of the most direct warnings came in the form of intercepted messages between the Japanese government in Tokyo and Japanese consulates in Washington, D.C., and Honolulu, Hawaii. U.S. military code breakers had succeeded in breaking the sophisticated secret code—known as Purple—that Japanese officials used to transmit diplomatic messages. At listening stations around the Pacific Rim, they intercepted and deciphered the instructions that Japan gave to its diplomatic offices. Some of these messages contained important clues about Japan's intention to go to war.

After Japanese Ambassador Kichisaburo Nomura presented his government's "last word" proposal on November 20, for example, code breakers intercepted a message saying that things were "automatically going to happen"[10] if the United States rejected it. On November 26, U.S. Secretary of State Cordell Hull gave the Japanese diplomats the American government's counterproposal. It was unacceptable to Japan, and official negotiations broke down. A few days later, code breakers intercepted a message from Tokyo telling all Japanese consulates and embassies in the United States to destroy their code machines and all sensitive documents. Japanese officials were apparently concerned about these materials falling into American hands in wartime. In another intercepted message, Tokyo asked the Japanese consulate in Hawaii to provide the exact locations of all U.S. Navy ships in Pearl Harbor.

Although these and other messages held important clues about the Japanese attack plan, U.S. officials did not put the pieces together. Part of the problem was that the clues were hidden within the huge amount of raw information collected by the code breakers. In addition, the U.S. government did not have a single agency (the modern Central Intelligence Agency, or CIA, had not been formed yet) assigned to oversee the gathering and evaluation of foreign intelligence. As a result, important information was often missed or misinterpreted. While American leaders suspected that Japan had hostile intentions, they did not expect an attack on the United States. "What now stands out as obvious evidence of an impending attack," one scholar noted, "was at the time buried among a multitude of signs which, taken as a whole, certainly did not single out Hawaii as a target."[11]

U.S. Fails to Prepare

Since political and military leaders in Washington, D.C., did not expect a Japanese attack on Hawaii, they did not do a good job preparing the officers in charge of Pearl Harbor for that possibility. Admiral Husband E. Kimmel (see Kimmel biography, p. 127) was the commander of the U.S. Navy's Pacific Fleet at the time. General Walter C. Short (see Short biography, p. 148) was in charge of the 45,000 U.S. Army soldiers stationed on Oahu to protect the fleet at anchor and the various airfields and other military installations scattered around the island. Although Kimmel and Short got along well and played golf together every week, they did not always share information or coordinate efforts effectively. There was no overall command for the U.S. forces in Hawaii—or for the different branches of the U.S. armed services—because the office of the Joint Chiefs of Staff did not exist at that time.

When diplomatic negotiations between the United States and Japan broke down on November 27, Kimmel received an alert message from Admiral Harold R. Stark, the Chief of Naval Operations, in Washington, D.C. "This dispatch is to be considered a war warning," it read. "Negotiations with Japan have ceased and an aggressive move by Japan is expected within the next few days. Japanese troops and naval task forces indicate an amphibious expedition against either the Philippines, Thai, or Kra Peninsula or possibly Borneo. Execute an appropriate defensive deployment."[12] This message went out to all navy commanders in the Pacific, but it seemed to be directed primarily at those stationed in the locations that were specifically mentioned. Although military leaders in Washington made it clear that war with Japan was imminent, they did not express concern about an attack on Hawaii. Kimmel later described the vague message as "no more than saying that Japan was going to attack someplace."[13]

Admiral Husband E. Kimmel, pictured in the Pacific Fleet headquarters at Pearl Harbor, failed to prepare for a possible Japanese attack.

Short received a similar alert message from the Army Chief of Staff, General George C. Marshall. "Negotiations with Japan appear to be terminated," the warning said. "Japanese future action unpredictable but hostile action possible at any moment. If hostilities cannot, repeat cannot, be avoided, the United States desires that Japan commit the first overt act.... Prior to hostile Japanese action, you are directed to undertake such reconnaissance and other measures as you deem necessary but these measures should be carried out so as not, repeat not, to alarm civil population or disclose intent."[14] Short interpreted the message to mean that he should increase defensive measures in a limited way that would not be noticeable to local residents.

Around the same time, the two commanders received word that military strategists in Washington planned to send fifty of the most advanced warplanes then in Hawaii to Midway and Wake Islands. This decision added to Kimmel and Short's sense of security. They figured that if the top brass was willing to reduce Pearl Harbor's defenses, they must be expecting the Japanese attack to occur further west.

One thing that did make Kimmel and Short nervous was the fact that U.S. tracking systems lost radio contact with a significant part of the Japanese Combined Fleet in early December. The call signs of a major carrier group—nearly two dozen warships, including several aircraft carriers—simply disappeared from the airwaves on December 2. Military intelligence officers hoped that these ships were sitting quietly in Japanese waters, on guard against a possible U.S. attack. But Kimmel knew that they could be anywhere in the Pacific—even approaching Pearl Harbor—and he demanded that the Navy locate them as soon as possible.

Still, the two commanders felt confident in their forces' ability to defend Pearl Harbor against a Japanese land invasion. The coast of Oahu was lined with guns and soldiers on patrol, and the island also had a harbor full of warships and several airfields full of sophisticated fighter planes. As a Honolulu newspaper noted on September 6, "A Japanese attack on Hawaii is regarded as the most unlikely thing in the world, with one chance in a million of being successful. Besides having more powerful defenses than any other post under the American flag, it is protected by distance."[15]

As a result of all these factors, Kimmel and Short took only a few extra precautions against a possible Japanese attack on Pearl Harbor. They ordered increased patrols and reconnaissance flights, and they agreed to operate a new Army radar station between 4:00 and 7:00 A.M. each day to scan for enemy ships and planes. They also took steps to protect military equipment and facilities from possible sabotage by local people of Japanese origin. Instead of being tucked away in hangars, for instance, military planes were parked close together out in the open so they would be easier to guard. In addition, guns and ammunition were locked safely away so they would not be stolen. But aside from these modest measures, everyday operations at Pearl Harbor remained unchanged. Virtually no one believed that a Japanese attack on Hawaii was even a remote possibility.

Notes

[1] "World War II: Background to Involvement, 1939-45." *Discovering U.S. History.* Gale Research, 1997. Reproduced in History Resource Center. Farmington Hills, MI: Gale.

[2] Roosevelt, Franklin D. "Arsenal of Democracy" speech, December 29, 1940. Available online at Wooley, John T., and Gerhard Peters, *The American Presidency Project,* http://www.presidency. ucsb.edu/ws/pid=15917.

[3] "World War II: Background to Involvement, 1939-45."

[4] Hornbeck, Stanley. "Hornbeck Autobiography," Hornbeck Papers, Box 497. Quoted in Prange, Gordon W. *Pearl Harbor: The Verdict of History.* New York: McGraw-Hill, 1986, p. 153.

[5] Hornbeck, Stanley. "Genesis and Character of the American Government Communication to Japan's Spokesmen of November 26, 1941," December 4, 1942. Hornbeck Papers, Box 335. Quoted in Prange, *Pearl Harbor: The Verdict of History,* p. 181.

[6] Quoted in Friedrich, Otto. "Day of Infamy." *Time,* December 2, 1991, p. 30.

[7] Quoted in Conn, Stetson, Rose C. Engelman, and Byron Fairchild. *Guarding the United States and Its Outposts.* Washington, D.C.: U.S. Army Center of Military History, 2000, p. 176. Available online at http://www.history.army.mil/books/wwii/guard-us/ch7.htm.

[8] Posner, Richard A. "Surprise Attack: The Lessons of History." *Commentary,* April 2005, p. 50.

[9] Van der Vat, Dan. *Pearl Harbor: The Day of Infamy—An Illustrated History.* Toronto: Madison Press, 2001, p. 27.

[10] Quoted in Prange, Gordon W. *At Dawn We Slept: The Untold Story of Pearl Harbor.* New York: McGraw-Hill, 1981, p. 369.

[11] Warren, Spencer. "Why America Slept." *National Review,* December 16, 1991, p. 34.

[12] Quoted in Conn, Engelman, and Fairchild, p. 179.

[13] Quoted in Friedrich, p. 30.

[14] Quoted in Conn, Engelman, and Fairchild, p. 178.

[15] Quoted in Harris, Nathaniel. *A Day That Made History: Pearl Harbor.* North Pomfret, VT: David and Charles, 1986, p. 50.

Chapter Three

THE ATTACK
ON PEARL HARBOR

━━◄░◊░►━━

Do you mean to say they [Japanese aircraft carriers] could be
rounding Diamond Head [a volcanic mountain on the island
of Oahu, Hawaii] and you wouldn't know it?

—Admiral Husband E. Kimmel, upon learning that U.S. Navy
intelligence had lost radio contact with the Japanese fleet,
December 2, 1941

As Japan put together its strategy for a surprise attack on the U.S. military base in Hawaii, President Franklin D. Roosevelt and other American leaders knew that the two countries were veering dangerously close to a confrontation. Throughout the fall of 1941—and even in the hours before the attack began—there were a number of ominous warnings that war could break out at any time. But the United States largely misinterpreted or disregarded these signs and failed to prepare for the coming attack.

On the morning of December 7, 1941, therefore, American sailors and soldiers were shocked when Japanese planes suddenly appeared overhead and began dropping bombs and torpedoes on the U.S. Pacific Fleet anchored in Pearl Harbor. The attack was a tremendous victory for the Japanese. They achieved complete surprise and severely crippled American military capabilities in the Pacific.

The Japanese Attack Force Approaches

The ships of the Japanese Combined Fleet assigned to participate in the attack on Pearl Harbor gathered in Hitokappu Bay, a remote outpost in the

33

Kurile Islands north of Japan, in late November. The attack force consisted of 23 warships, including 6 aircraft carriers with nearly 400 planes, 9 destroyers, 3 submarines, 2 battleships, 2 heavy cruisers, and 1 light cruiser. They were accompanied by 8 oil tankers so they could refuel at sea and avoid stopping at any ports where their movements might be observed. The commander of the attack force was Vice Admiral Chuichi Nagumo, a career officer with vast experience at sea. To preserve secrecy, he did not inform the crews of the various ships about their mission until after they had reached Hitokappu Bay.

On November 23, when the last of the ships arrived, Nagumo outlined the attack plan Admiral Isoroku Yamamoto had developed. The attack force would travel east across the northern Pacific and then turn south toward Hawaii. When they reached a point about 230 miles north of Oahu, they would stop and launch two waves of warplanes from the aircraft carriers. The first wave would consist of 189 planes: 50 Nakajima B5N2 "Kate" high-level bombers; 40 Kate torpedo bombers; 54 Aichi D3A1 "Val" low-level dive bombers; and 45 Mitsubishi A6M2 "Zero" fighters. Each Kate carried a three-man crew consisting of a pilot, a navigator-bomber, and a radioman-gunner. Each Val had a two-man crew consisting of a pilot and a gunner. Each speedy Zero carried a solo pilot.

If the Japanese planes managed to arrive without alerting the American defenses, the plan was for the torpedo bombers to strike first. They would fly low over Pearl Harbor and concentrate on destroying the largest U.S. warships—especially aircraft carriers and battleships. Then the high-level bombers would attack the ships at anchor. Meanwhile, the dive bombers would try to destroy as many American warplanes as possible at the various air bases scattered around the island. The Japanese hoped to hit the U.S. planes before they could take off and fight back against the air attack.

After the first wave of Japanese planes used up their bombs, torpedoes, and bullets, then the plan called for a second wave to take over. The second wave would consist of 171 aircraft, including 54 Kates, 81 Vals, and 36 Zeros. All of the Kates in the second wave would be equipped as high-level bombers, because it would be too dangerous to send in more low-flying torpedo bombers once American forces began firing antiaircraft guns. The second wave was supposed to target any ships, airfields, or other facilities that had not been completely destroyed in the first wave of the attack. The overall commander of the planes in the Japanese strike force was Mitsuo Fuchida

34

This photo, captured from the Japanese, shows planes preparing to take off from the aircraft carrier *Shokaku* for the attack on Pearl Harbor.

(see Fuchida biography, p. 123), who would lead the first wave in a high-level Kate bomber.

Finally, the Japanese attack plan also included a separate force of twenty-seven submarines. Five of the full-size subs carried tiny, two-man midget submarines attached to their backs. The full-size submarines were assigned to lurk outside the entrance to Pearl Harbor and destroy any ships that managed to escape the air raid. The midget subs were designed to sneak into the harbor during the attack and cause further damage to the American warships. The submarine portion of the plan was added at the last minute over the objections of Nagumo and other Japanese military leaders. They worried that the subs would be detected in the waters near Hawaii and ruin their chances for achieving surprise.

The Japanese ships set sail from Hitokappu Bay on November 26. As they headed east across the northern Pacific, they stayed well outside of the normal shipping lanes to avoid detection. They also maintained strict radio silence during the ten-day journey. Instead of using their radios, the ships in the attack force communicated with each other by flashing lights or displaying signal flags. This was why the U.S. tracking systems lost radio contact with the ships. The Japanese also tried to confuse American intelligence by leaving the carrier group's normal radio operators behind in home waters, where they sent out routine signals.

On December 2—the same day that Tokyo ordered all Japanese consulates in the United States to destroy their secret code machines and sensitive documents—Nagumo received final confirmation of his mission. Yamamoto sent him a message that said "Climb Mount Niitaka 1208." Mount Niitaka was the highest peak in the Japanese empire. This signal meant that all diplomatic options had been exhausted and the attack was scheduled for December 8 Tokyo time, which was December 7 in Hawaii.

U.S. Forces Discount Suspicious Activity

As dawn approached on that sleepy Sunday morning, about half of the U.S. Navy's Pacific Fleet was moored in Pearl Harbor. There were a total of 185 vessels, including more than 90 warships and an assortment of tugboats, repair ships, tankers, seaplane tenders, and other support vessels. The most impressive section of the anchorage was Battleship Row, located on the southeastern shore of Ford Island in the middle of the harbor. Seven heavily armored battleships with massive guns lining their decks were anchored there, alone or in pairs. Beginning closest to the harbor entrance, there was the USS *California* by itself, the *Oklahoma* anchored outside of the *Maryland*, the *West Virginia* moored outside of the *Tennessee*, the *Arizona* on the inside of the *Vestal* (a repair ship), and the *Nevada* by itself. An eighth battleship, the USS *Pennsylvania*, sat in dry dock nearby.

By sheer coincidence, none of the Pacific Fleet's three aircraft carriers were in Pearl Harbor that morning. The USS *Enterprise* was on its way back from delivering some Marine Corps fighter planes to Wake Island, and the *Lexington* had left two days earlier to deliver some scout bombers to Midway Island. The third carrier, the USS *Saratoga*, was in California undergoing repairs. In addition, 36 destroyers, 18 submarines, and 12 cruisers that were

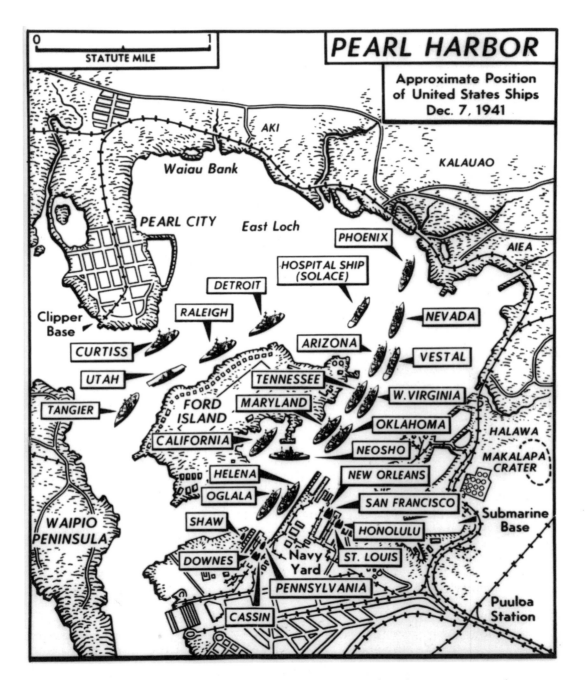

This U.S. Navy map shows the location of ships immediately before the Japanese attack on Pearl Harbor.

normally stationed at Pearl Harbor were out of port on patrol or on various missions that day.

As the Japanese forces crept into position for the coming assault, some of the American ships patrolling outside of the harbor nearly discovered the Japanese attack plan. As Yamamoto and other military planners had feared, it was the separate submarine force that almost gave away the element of surprise. At 3:42 A.M. on December 7—about four hours before the air raid began—the minesweeper *Condor* saw a periscope while on routine patrol. The commanding officer reported it to the destroyer *Ward*, which was under orders to attack any submarines found near the entrance to Pearl Harbor. The *Ward* was unable to find anything by sonar, however, so the commander decided that the *Condor* must have been wrong and did not report the incident to headquarters.

At 6:33 A.M., however, the *Ward* received a second report of a submarine sighting from the stores ship *Antares*. This time, the *Ward* found the sub, attacked, and sank it. This attack—which was reported to Pacific Fleet headquarters at 6:53 A.M.—was technically the first hostile action in the war between the United States and Japan. A few minutes later, a U.S. Navy plane on routine patrol spotted another submarine about a mile from the entrance to Pearl Harbor. The plane dropped depth charges on the sub and reported the incident to headquarters around 7:00 A.M.

Upon learning that his forces had engaged two enemy submarines near the harbor, Kimmel could have informed Short and put the entire base on high alert. The two commanders could have ordered their forces to increase patrols or even man their battle stations. But Kimmel did not tell his Army counterpart about the submarines or take any other action to prepare for a possible attack.

The American forces at Pearl Harbor received one more clue that they were in imminent danger, but once again they did not recognize its importance. At 7:02 A.M., as Privates Joseph Lockard and George Elliott were preparing to end their three-hour shift at the U.S. Army radar station on the northern shore of Oahu, the scanner showed something very strange. It looked as if at least fifty planes were flying toward the island from the north. When the soldiers first noticed the unusual reading, the planes were about 132 miles away.

After making sure that their equipment was working correctly, Lockard and Elliott reported the sighting to Lieutenant Kermit Tyler, the officer on

A view of Pearl Harbor from a Japanese plane as the attack began: torpedo tracks and shock waves are visible in the water near Battleship Row, and white smoke can be seen rising in the distance from Hickam Field.

duty at the Army's main information center. Tyler knew that eleven American B-17 Flying Fortress bombers were expected to arrive from California that morning, on their way to the Philippines. Tyler decided that if the radar operators really did see planes on the relatively new equipment, they must actually be tracking the B-17s. Since information about the planes' arrival was classified, however, Tyler was not allowed to inform the two privates. Instead, he simply told Lockard and Elliott not to worry about the radar images.

Japan Achieves Complete Surprise

Of course, what the American radar operators really saw was the first wave of Japanese warplanes, which had taken off from the aircraft carriers north of Oahu a short time earlier. Fuchida and the other pilots had struggled to launch their planes safely in high winds and rough seas. "We could hear the waves splashing against the ship with a thunderous noise," the commander recalled. "Under normal circumstances, no plane would be permitted to take off in such weather."[1] The poor conditions and mechanical problems combined to prevent ten Japanese planes from taking off. This setback reduced the attack force to 350 aircraft (183 in the first wave and 167 in the second).

Once the planes of the first wave got into the air, Fuchida led them south toward Oahu (see "Japanese Pilot Mitsuo Fuchida Leads the Attack," p. 176). They planned to begin their attack at 8:00 A.M. local time. As they neared the coast of the island at 7:40 A.M., Fuchida fired a flare to indicate his belief that they had achieved complete surprise and should proceed according to plan. Nine minutes later, with all the planes in attack formation, the commander told his pilots, "To, to, to!" (short for *totsugekiseyo,* which means "charge"). Fuchida also sent a famous message to be relayed back to Tokyo: "Tora, tora, tora!" This code word, meaning "tiger," informed Japanese military planners that their strategy had succeeded in catching the Americans off guard.

As the Japanese planes approached Pearl Harbor, Japanese officials sent a message to the United States formally severing all diplomatic ties between the two countries. The message outlined fourteen points of contention between the United States and Japan. It concluded with the following statement: "The Japanese government regrets that it is impossible to reach an agreement through further negotiations."

Ambassador Nomura was supposed to deliver this message to Secretary of State Hull at exactly 1:00 P.M. Washington time (7:30 A.M. in Hawaii) on December 7—just before the attack began. Japanese leaders felt that this timing would allow them to say that they had broken off diplomatic relations before going to war. They did not realize that U.S. military code breakers had intercepted the message and provided the text to President Roosevelt the night before the attack. Even though the Japanese did not declare war in so many words, Roosevelt understood the underlying meaning. "This means war," he told his aide Harry Hopkins.

Hopkins called Admiral Stark and General Marshall to make sure that all U.S. Navy and Army forces were fully prepared for a Japanese attack. The two chiefs agreed that it seemed suspicious that Tokyo had ordered Nomura to deliver the message at a specific time. They felt that the time might indicate when they should expect an attack to occur. But since they had already warned all U.S. military forces in the Pacific to be prepared for a Japanese attack at any time, they decided that no further action was needed.

As it turned out, the message was delayed at the Japanese embassy in Washington. Nomura did not bring the official version to Hull's office until 2:05 P.M. (8:35 A.M. Hawaii time)—about forty-five minutes after Japanese planes launched their attack on Pearl Harbor. The secretary of state had already heard the news by the time the ambassador arrived. After glancing at the message, an outraged Hull declared, "In all my fifty years of public service, I have never seen such a document that was more crowded with infamous falsehoods and distortions on a scale so huge that I never imagined until today that any government on this planet was capable of uttering them."[2] Then he ordered Nomura to leave his office. The ambassador did not learn about the attack—and the role he unknowingly played in preserving its secrecy—until he got back to the Japanese embassy.

Japanese pilot Mitsuo Fuchida watched the destruction of the battleship Arizona *from above. "A huge column of dark red smoke rose to 1,000 feet and a stiff shock wave rocked the plane," he remembered.*

The First Wave Begins

The Japanese warplanes arrived over their targets a little before the scheduled time of 8:00 A.M. Much of the first wave concentrated on attacking the various air bases on the island, rather than the ships in Pearl Harbor. These included the Army Air Force bases at Wheeler Field in the center of Oahu, at Hickam Field near the entrance to Pearl Harbor, at Bellows Field on the east coast of Oahu, and at Haleiwa Field on the northwest shore of Oahu; the Naval Air Stations at Kaneohe Bay on the northeast shore of Oahu and at Ford Island in the middle of Pearl Harbor; and the Ewa Marine Corps Air Station on the southwest shore of Oahu.

The Japanese knew that the success of their attack strategy depended on their ability to maintain control of the air space above Pearl Harbor. In order to destroy the Navy warships, they had to prevent American warplanes from getting off the ground. Once airborne, the U.S. military planes could either engage the Japanese planes in aerial combat or locate and attack the Japanese aircraft carriers waiting offshore.

At 7:51 A.M., one of the first bombs of the Japanese attack hit the Hawaiian Air Force fighter planes lined up in neat rows at Wheeler Field. Several

Much of the first wave of the Japanese attack focused on destroying the various air bases on Oahu.

planes caught on fire, and they were parked so close together that the fire soon spread to others nearby. Most of the 153 planes at Wheeler Field were destroyed in the first 15 minutes of the Japanese attack, and 27 Americans were killed.

Around the same time, Japanese planes bombed and strafed the Kaneohe Naval Air Station. They destroyed 27 seaplanes, or flying boats, that were tied to the docks or sitting on ramps. Only the three seaplanes that happened to be out on patrol at that time escaped damage. The attack took the lives of 18 Americans, some of whom were heroically trying to save the planes.

At 7:55 A.M., 17 Val dive bombers and 18 Zeros struck the Army Air Force Base at Hickam Field. Compared to the other air bases, Hickam Field was full of activity that morning. Crews were busy preparing for the arrival of the 11 B-17 Flying Fortress bombers from California, and a number of officers had come out to watch. The Japanese attack not only destroyed most of the 57 planes that were lined up wingtip to wingtip, but also caused extensive damage to the base's runways, hangars, armory, barracks, and mess hall. The Army suffered its worst losses of the Pearl Harbor attack at Hickam Field, with 182 men killed. The expected group of B-17s also arrived in the middle of the attack—unarmed, with minimal crews, and nearly out of fuel. Remarkably, though, most of them managed to land safely at Hickam or Bellows, and one set down on a nearby golf course.

The first few minutes of the Japanese attack also saw dive bombers swoop down on the Naval Air Station at Ford Island. Nearly half of the 70 planes at the airfield were destroyed, but only one American was killed. At 7:58 A.M., the officer on duty at the Ford Island command center, Lieutenant Commander Logan Ramsey, managed to inform the outside world that Hawaii was under attack. The shocking message "Air raid Pearl Harbor! This is no drill!"[3] reached top military officials in Washington, D.C., a few minutes later.

Battleship Row Is Hit Hard

Just minutes after the first bombs hit Wheeler Field, Japanese torpedo bombers began striking the U.S. Navy vessels anchored in Pearl Harbor. Since none of the Pacific Fleet's prized aircraft carriers were in port at the time, the Japanese pilots concentrated on attacking Battleship Row. They dropped their torpedoes into the shallow waters of the harbor, then watched as the deadly devices streaked toward the unprotected bellies of the American ships. One of the first torpedoes hit the *West Virginia* at 7:56, putting a gaping hole in her side. Some of her sailors had reported to their battle stations when they heard explosions coming from the airfield, and they fought hard until several more torpedo strikes managed to sink the ship.

Several Japanese torpedo bombers also attacked the ships moored on the north side of Ford Island, including the light cruiser *Raleigh* and the obsolete battleship *Utah*. The *Utah* had been dismantled and its topside covered with wooden decking to serve as a target ship. In the smoke and confusion of battle, some Japanese pilots mistook it for an aircraft carrier. The *Utah* capsized within minutes of the first torpedo hit, taking the lives of fifty-eight sailors (see "A U.S. Navy Crewman Remembers Chaos and Casualties," p. 179).

The battleship USS *Arizona* went down in flames after a Japanese bomb exploded the gunpowder and ammunition stored in the ship's forward magazine.

The next battleship to be sunk was the *Oklahoma*, which took the first of five torpedo hits at 7:55. Jinichi Goto, commander of the Japanese torpedo bombers, recalled scoring a direct hit on the vessel: "I saw that I was even lower than the crow's nest of the great battleship. My observer reported a huge waterspout springing up…. 'Atarimashita! [It hit!]' he cried."[4] U.S. Navy Commander J.L. Kenworthy was on board the *Oklahoma* when it came under attack. "I felt a very heavy shock and heard a loud explosion," he remembered, "and the ship immediately began to list to port [lean over to the left]. As I attempted to get to the conning tower over decks slippery with oil and water, I felt the shock of another very heavy explosion."[5] Kenworthy ordered his men to abandon ship, but many were not able to escape in time. When the *Oklahoma* rolled over eight minutes later, more than 400 sailors were trapped below deck.

Some of the worst destruction on Battleship Row was caused by bombs rather than torpedoes. The battleship *Arizona* avoided being hit by torpedoes because it was moored inside the repair ship *Vestal*. But at 8:08 A.M., it was hit by a 1,760-pound armor-piercing shell dropped from a high-level Kate bomber. The bomb struck the ship's forward magazine—a large compartment in the bow that held fifty tons of gunpowder and ammunition. The strike triggered a massive explosion that tore apart the front part of the *Arizona* and sent flaming debris, metal fragments, and human body parts raining down on nearby ships. Fuchida watched the destruction of the *Arizona* from above. "A huge column of dark red smoke rose to 1,000 feet and a stiff shock wave rocked the plane," he remembered. "It was a hateful, mean-looking red flame, the kind that powder produces, and I knew at once that a big magazine had exploded. Terrible indeed."[6]

The *Arizona* disaster took the lives of 1,177 sailors, or about half of the total number of Americans who died in the attack on Pearl Harbor. Only 337 crew members survived. Many of them were forced to jump overboard and swim through flaming oil and debris to reach shore. The fires from the *Arizona* burned for hours, filling the skies with thick black smoke.

The Second Wave Arrives

The first wave of the Japanese attack lasted only about thirty minutes. Then there was a brief lull before the second wave of warplanes arrived. Much of Oahu was in chaos during this lull in the attack. Military personnel rushed around trying to find and rescue survivors, treat the injured, and get ready in case of another air raid or a land invasion. By the time the second wave of Japanese planes began to attack at 8:54 A.M., American sailors and troops were ready to fight back. Some greeted the strike force with a barrage of antiaircraft fire, while others broke into locked ammunition caches and fired away with machine guns and small arms. The Air Force even managed to launch eleven fighter planes to engage in combat with the Japanese.

The increased American resistance and the smoke swirling around Pearl Harbor targets combined to limit the effectiveness of the second wave of the Japanese attack. The warplanes struck Hickam and Wheeler air bases again.

Following the second wave of the Japanese attack, the minelayer *Oglala* lies capsized, while the destroyer *Shaw* (left) and battleship *Nevada* burn in the background.

They also destroyed five planes at Bellows Field, which had suffered only minor damage in the first wave. Looking for new targets in the harbor, the second wave attacked the battleship *Pennsylvania* as it sat in dry dock, killing twenty-four men on board. The Japanese also did severe damage to the American destroyers *Cassin*, *Downes*, and *Shaw*.

A few American warships had used the time between attacks to start up their engines and get underway. They hoped to escape the confines of Pearl Harbor and reach the relative safety of open sea. Some of the most dramatic fighting took place when the battleship *Nevada* pulled away from its moorings and steamed toward the entrance to the harbor. Although a torpedo from the first wave had left a thirty-foot hole in her bow, the crew had managed to close off the damaged area and keep her afloat. As a moving target, though, the *Nevada* attracted a great deal of attention during the second wave. The Japanese were determined to sink her and block the entrance to Pearl Harbor. The *Nevada* took at least five direct hits but fought valiantly, shooting down two Japanese planes. Ultimately, the damage became too great and the battleship began to take on water. The crew managed to run her aground at Hospital Point, on the east side of the harbor entrance, to avoid blocking the main channel.

Casualties and Losses

Before the second wave of Japanese planes flew away at 9:45 A.M., Fuchida circled above Pearl Harbor to survey the damage. "I counted four battleships definitely sunk and three severely damaged, and extensive damage had also been inflicted on other types of ships," he recalled. "The seaplane base at Ford Island was all in flames, as were the airfields, especially Wheeler Field."[7] The last of the planes that had survived the attack arrived back on their aircraft carriers by 1:30 P.M.

The officers of the Japanese attack force debated about launching a third wave of planes before they sailed for home. Although they had successfully hit all of their primary targets, a few important secondary targets had remained untouched. For example, the Pearl Harbor installation included several "tank farms" that contained 4.5 million barrels of oil to fuel the U.S. Pacific Fleet. The base also featured extensive ship-repair facilities, which would help the Americans recover from the attack more quickly. Fuchida and other officers argued that that they should go back and finish the job.

But Nagumo decided to order the attack force back to Japanese waters. In defending this decision, he noted that the Japanese attack had achieved its main objective: it had inflicted enough damage to the U.S. Pacific Fleet to prevent it from interfering with Japanese expansion plans for at least six months. The admiral also pointed out that the attack force had suffered relatively few casualties. The Japanese had lost only 29 planes (9 in the first wave and 20 in the second)—or about 8 percent of the total launched—carrying 55 airmen. Japanese losses also included 1 submarine with its crew of 65 men, and all 5 midget subs with 9 crew members (see "The First Japanese Prisoner of War," p. 48).

In contrast, the American losses were tremendous—both in terms of lives and military capacity. A total of 2,388 Americans were killed during the

The First Japanese Prisoner of War

Ensign Kazuo Sakamaki was the pilot of one of the 78-foot-long, two-man Japanese midget submarines that took part in the attack on Pearl Harbor. Five midget subs made the journey across the Pacific to Hawaii attached to the backs of regular submarines. The midget subs were launched outside the harbor shortly before the attack began. Their mission was to sneak through the entrance and fire their torpedoes at American warships during the heat of battle. Since the battery-powered midget subs had a range of only eighteen miles underwater, however, they were not expected to be able to return to their mother ships afterward. Sakamaki and the other members of the Japanese midget sub force were fully prepared to die in the service of their country.

Unfortunately for Sakamaki, the gyrocompass on his submarine malfunctioned, making it nearly impossible for him to steer the vehicle. He struggled to control it, ran out of battery power, and ended up running aground on a coral reef without ever entering Pearl Harbor. To prevent his top-secret vessel from falling into American hands, Sakamaki tried to use explosive charges to destroy it. After he and his crewman leaped overboard, however, the fuse went out. The two men tried to swim back to

attack on Pearl Harbor, and another 1,178 were injured. The U.S. Navy suffered the highest losses, with 1,998 sailors killed, while the Army lost 233 soldiers and the Marines lost 109. In addition, 48 civilian (non-military) men, women, and children were killed in and around Honolulu during the attack. Although the Japanese only dropped one bomb on the city, it was hit by 39 American antiaircraft shells and countless spent bullets. The exploding shells tore the roofs off of several buildings and started fires that destroyed whole neighborhoods.

The Japanese attack sank or severely damaged 21 American warships. In addition, 188 warplanes were destroyed and 159 others damaged. None of the eight U.S. battleships that were moored in Pearl Harbor on December 7 escaped damage in the attack. The two that fared best were the *Maryland*, which was hit by two bombs but was protected from torpedoes by the *Okla-*

their submarine but became exhausted. His crewman drowned, while Sakamaki lost consciousness and eventually washed up on a beach.

Sakamaki woke up to find American soldiers standing guard over him. He became the first Japanese prisoner of war to be captured in the Pacific conflict. According to *bushido*—the warrior code of the Japanese samurai—any soldier who was captured alive dishonored himself, his family, and his country. Deeply humiliated, Sakamaki burned his face with cigarettes and demanded to be allowed to commit suicide, but his captors refused. Sakamaki spent the remainder of the war in prisoner-of-war camps on the American mainland. His midget sub was salvaged, examined by U.S. intelligence, and then put on public display to raise money for the U.S. war effort.

When the war ended, Sakamaki returned to Japan and took a job with Toyota. In 1969 he became president of the automaker's subsidiary in Brazil. He also wrote a memoir about his wartime experiences, which was published as *The First Prisoner* in Japan and as *I Attacked Pearl Harbor* in the United States. Sakamaki was reunited with his submarine in 1991, when he attended a historical conference in Texas to mark the fiftieth anniversary of the Pearl Harbor attack. He died on November 29, 1999, at the age of 81. He was survived by his wife and two children.

homa lying upside-down next to her; and the *Tennessee*, which was scarred by fires started by flaming debris from the *Arizona*, but was protected from torpedo damage by the sunken *West Virginia* alongside her.

As it turned out, though, all but three of the ships that were hit by Japanese bombs and torpedoes in the attack were later salvaged (the target ship *Utah* and the battleship *Arizona* were beyond repair and remained on the bottom of the harbor, while the battleship *Oklahoma* was raised but sold for scrap). The lightly damaged battleships *Maryland* and *Tennessee* returned to action by December 20, and the *Pennsylvania* set sail for California that same day to undergo repairs. Even the *West Virginia, California,* and *Nevada* eventually returned to fight in the Pacific War. In addition, Pearl Harbor remained a vital naval base because its fuel tanks and ship-repair facilities escaped damage in the attack.

Most importantly, the Japanese forces failed to locate and destroy the American aircraft carriers that operated out of Pearl Harbor. The devastating attack had proven that aircraft carriers were the key to modern naval warfare. When U.S. military leaders were forced to recognize this new reality, they still had carriers available to incorporate into their strategy. "Both services had not fully learned the lessons of the development of air power in respect to the defense of a navy and of a naval base," wrote Secretary of War Henry L. Stimson in his diary. "It was only through such a disaster that we could all in the nation learn what modern air power can do even in the high seas."[9]

Still, at a relatively low cost to the Japanese, the attack on Pearl Harbor had dealt a serious blow to the U.S. Pacific Fleet. In the coming months, Japan would take full advantage of this fact to expand its empire southward, conquering large areas of Asia and the Pacific islands. From a tactical standpoint, Yamamoto's plan worked brilliantly and achieved its objectives. As the admiral predicted, however, the victory would be short-lived.

Notes

[1] Quoted in Friedrich, Otto. "Day of Infamy." *Time,* December 2, 1991, p. 30.

[2] Quoted in Van der Vat, Dan. *Pearl Harbor: The Day of Infamy—An Illustrated History.* Toronto: Madison Press, 2001, p. 77.

[3] Quoted in Prange, Gordon W. *At Dawn We Slept: The Untold Story of Pearl Harbor.* New York: McGraw-Hill, 1981, p. 517.

[4] Quoted in Prange, *At Dawn We Slept,* p. 509.

[5] Quoted in Friedrich, p. 30.

[6] Quoted in Prange, Gordon W. *God's Samurai: Lead Pilot at Pearl Harbor.* Washington, D.C.: Brassey's, 1991, p. 35.

[7] Quoted in Harris, Nathaniel. *A Day That Made History: Pearl Harbor.* North Pomfret, VT: David and Charles, 1986, p. 32.

[8] National Park Service, USS Arizona Memorial, http://www.nps.gov/archive/usar/extendweb1.html.

[9] Quoted in Conn, Stetson, Rose C. Engelman, and Byron Fairchild. *Guarding the United States and Its Outposts.* Washington, D.C.: U.S. Army Center of Military History, 2000, p. 196.

Chapter Four

HEROISM AND HEARTBREAK

—⫘⫘⫘—

> I was scared to death.... In four years at sea I sat through seventy-eight air attacks, but nothing was as frightening as the attack on Pearl Harbor.
>
> —Warren K. Taylor, a sailor aboard the U.S. Navy hydrographic survey ship *Sumner*

The Japanese attack on Pearl Harbor is a well-documented event in American history. Through the years, hundreds of survivors have shared their memories of the unforgettable morning of December 7, 1941. The feelings of shock and disbelief, the atmosphere of panic and chaos, the incredible displays of courage, the dramatic stories of escape and rescue, and the tragic loss of young men in the service of their country—all have been described in vivid detail by those who experienced them firsthand. These accounts add a rich, highly personal element to broader discussions of the military strategies and political implications of the Pearl Harbor attack.

Shock and Disbelief

As the Japanese strike force approached an unsuspecting Pearl Harbor, the American soldiers and sailors stationed there were enjoying a quiet, leisurely Sunday morning. The Army and Navy granted regular leave time on Saturday nights, so many of the men had gone out the night before. Some of the most popular off-duty activities included going to bars or seeing variety shows in downtown Honolulu, or hanging around with friends on Waikiki Beach. When enemy planes appeared on the horizon shortly before 8:00 A.M., most American soldiers and sailors were in the midst of their morning routines. Some were eat-

American sailors watch for Japanese attack planes as the battleship *California* burns and the *Oklahoma* lies capsized.

ing breakfast, taking a shower, or getting dressed for church, while others were performing regular duties on board ships or in barracks.

On the stern of the battleship *Nevada,* a Navy band was playing "The Star-Spangled Banner" as part of a morning flag-raising ceremony. None of the gathered sailors reacted when the first Japanese planes roared overhead. It took a few moments for them to realize that it was an enemy attack rather than one of the air-raid drills that were staged periodically by the Army Air Force.

Rear Admiral William Rhea Furlong, the Navy's senior officer afloat that morning, was on board the minelayer *Oglala* at the north end of the harbor. When he saw a bomb drop out of a plane near Ford Island, he initially felt angry because he thought a careless American pilot had neglected to secure his weapon. Then the plane came closer and he saw a red circle on its side—the Rising Sun symbol of the Japanese Empire. Furlong yelled, "Japanese! Man your stations!" and ordered his radio operator to sound a general alarm, "All ships in harbor sortie [prepare for battle]."[1]

Colonel William J. Flood, commander of the Army Air Force base at Wheeler Field, was reading his morning newspaper when he began hearing strange sounds. He ran outside and was stunned to see Japanese planes "bombing and strafing the base, the planes, the officers' quarters and even the golf course. I could see some of the Japanese pilots lean out of their planes and smile as they zoomed by.... I could even see the gold in their teeth."[2]

The sense of disbelief was equally strong among the officers in charge of the Navy and Army forces on Oahu. Admiral Husband E. Kimmel, commander of the Pacific Fleet, heard about the Japanese attack while he was at home preparing for his weekly golf game with his army counterpart, General Walter C. Short. Kimmel ran out onto the neighboring lawn of his chief of staff, Captain John Earle, which offered a good view of Battleship Row. Earle's wife saw him there and said that his face was "as white as the uniform he wore."[3] The admiral watched in horror as the *Arizona* exploded and the *Oklahoma* capsized. "My main thought was the fate of my ships," he recalled, "to see what had taken place and then strike back at the Japs."[4]

Lieutenant Colonel George W. Bicknell also witnessed the destruction of the fleet from his home in the hills above Pearl Harbor. "Well, naturally, when you are looking out of your window on a peaceful Sunday morning and see a battleship blow up under your eyes, you are pretty apt to be surprised,"[5] he noted. Bicknell rushed to Army headquarters, where he ran into General Short. Short had heard explosions, so he asked Bicknell what was going on outside. When Bicknell told his commanding officer that he had just seen two battleships sunk by enemy planes, Short replied, "That's ridiculous!"[6]

Meanwhile, the frantic message "Air raid Pearl Harbor! This is no drill!" reached Washington, D.C., around 1:30 P.M. (8:00 A.M. in Hawaii). Military leaders in the nation's capital were nearly as shocked as those in Hawaii. "My God, this can't be true,"[7] Secretary of the Navy Frank Knox said upon receiving the message. One of the few people who did not express surprise was President Roosevelt. When he heard the news in the Oval Office, he remarked that a sneak attack on Hawaii seemed like "just the kind of unexpected thing the

Japanese would do." Then the president noted angrily that "at the very time they were discussing peace in the Pacific they were plotting to overthrow it."[8]

Panic and Chaos

Among the soldiers and sailors in Hawaii, initial feelings of shock and disbelief soon gave way to fear and confusion. As the first wave of the Japanese attack washed over Pearl Harbor's docked ships and airfields, the situation on the ground erupted into chaos. Men rushed to reach their battle stations in the midst of explosions, machine-gun fire, diving planes, flames, and screams.

Sergeant Nick Gaynos had just finished working the night shift in the radio building at Hickam Field. The Japanese planes began shooting up the airfield while he was walking back to his barracks. "All hell broke loose with the strafing of the wooden barracks by Zeros," he remembered. "The hangar line was ablaze with aircraft and fuel trucks, and smoke was belching from the hangars. I remember seeing bodies and walking wounded as I raced up the street.... The chaos and pandemonium of the first wave created an open season on all targets with constant low-level strafing and bombing."[9]

At the Kaneohe seaplane base, Private First Class James Evans was relaxing in his barracks when the attack started. "Suddenly someone came running into the barracks yelling, 'We're being attacked by the Japs!'" he recalled. "Panic prevailed as we scrambled for our rifles; ammunition was another story. The storeroom was locked and it took a few minutes to find the supply sergeant and get him to issue ammo without the proper authority."[10]

Many sailors shared this feeling of being caught off guard and unprepared for the enemy's arrival. Bill Speer had just stepped out of the shower on the light cruiser *Honolulu* when the first explosions rocked Pearl Harbor. He raced to the deck to see what was happening. "I saw a torpedo drop and our guns were firing before they'd even sounded general quarters. I ran to my battle station and went through the rest of that day without getting fully dressed," he remembered. "We could clearly see the *Arizona* and all of battleship row from our post. At one point we were all just standing there with tears in our eyes watching the devastation and feeling helpless, with nothing to be done about it."[11]

The Fleet Fights Back

The ships of the Pacific Fleet anchored in Pearl Harbor on December 7, 1941, began fighting back just a few minutes after the Japanese launched their air

54

A small boat pulls a survivor from the water near the burning battleship *West Virginia*.

attack. Few of the American ships had their engines running and were ready to move. Even sitting still, however, they were heavily armed—with a total of 353 large-caliber and 427 short-range weapons on board—and soon started sending up a barrage of antiaircraft fire. Midori Matsumura, pilot of a Japanese torpedo bomber in the first wave, remembered that "enemy aircraft fire had begun to come up very fiercely. Black bursts were spoiling the once beautiful sky."[12]

Some Navy officers and seamen put up a terrific fight against the Japanese, even though they were caught off guard and faced overwhelming force. Commander Cassin Young was captain of the *Vestal*, a repair ship that was moored next to the battleship *Arizona*. Young personally manned one of his ship's antiaircraft guns until the explosion of the *Arizona*'s forward magazine

The skies over Pearl Harbor fill with smoke from the burning battleship *Arizona* and shell bursts from the antiaircraft guns on other ships in the fleet.

blew him overboard into the flaming, debris-strewn water. He managed to swim back to the *Vestal*, covered head-to-toe in oil, only to find that someone had ordered his crew to abandon ship. Young corralled his men by yelling, "Get back aboard ship! You don't abandon ship on me!"[13]

With the huge blaze on the *Arizona* threatening to engulf the *Vestal*, Young decided to move his ship to a safer spot in the harbor. It took several bomb hits along the way, but he managed to beach it to keep it from sinking. Young received the Congressional Medal of Honor for his efforts.

Mervyn Bennion, captain of the battleship *West Virginia*, suffered a mortal wound early in the attack when a piece of shrapnel tore open his abdomen. An African-American cook on board the ship, Doris Miller (see

Miller biography, p. 136), carried the captain to a protected spot. Before he died, Bennion continued to monitor the battle and give orders as Japanese bombs and torpedoes rocked the battleship. Meanwhile, Miller—who, like most African-American military personnel at that time, had never received any weapons training—manned a machine gun on the deck and fired away at enemy planes for the duration of the attack. Bennion received the Medal of Honor posthumously for his bravery, while Miller became the first black man ever to win the Navy Cross.

Some sailors managed to keep up the fight even after their ships were destroyed. When the battleship *Nevada* began heading toward the entrance to the harbor, it went past the burning wreck of the *Arizona*. Three crewman from the doomed vessel swam over, were pulled aboard the *Nevada,* and manned one of her antiaircraft guns.

The Airfields Mount Some Resistance

Like the Pacific Fleet, the air bases and army barracks scattered around Oahu started to put up some resistance shortly after the Japanese attack began. As soon as he got over his initial shock, General Short ordered his men to their battle stations and set up a command post to oversee the defense of the island. Unfortunately, most of the Army's antiaircraft guns were not ready to fire at a moment's notice. In most cases, the ammunition had been locked away to protect against sabotage, and soldiers had to go collect it from centralized ordnance depots. Even so, two Army antiaircraft batteries managed to open fire by 8:30 A.M.

Until the big guns were ready, some Army soldiers fought back the best they could by firing machine guns, automatic rifles, or even pistols at the Japanese planes. At Schofield Barracks, a huge military housing complex near Wheeler Field, Lieutenant Stephen G. Saltzman grabbed a Browning automatic rifle (BAR) and started shooting. He and another soldier managed to hit a low-flying Japanese plane. It crashed onto a nearby highway and burst into flames. "Of the four aircraft which fell to Army guns during [Japanese air commander Mitsuo] Fuchida's first wave," one historian noted, "all succumbed to machine-gun or BAR fire when they screamed down to strafe within range of these relatively limited weapons."[14]

Navy pilots and crew members fought valiantly to save their planes at the Kaneohe seaplane base. Even though Chief Ordnanceman John W. Finn

The Japanese attack destroyed U.S. Army planes and hangars at Wheeler Field.

was surrounded by burning gasoline and got shot in the foot, he remained on the seaplane dock and continued firing a machine gun at enemy aircraft. He later received the Congressional Medal of Honor for his valiant stand.

At all of the airfields, pilots and crews desperately tried to get planes in the air to counter the Japanese attack. Although most of the planes on the ground were not armed and ready to fly immediately, there were exceptions. For instance, two Army pursuit squadrons had been dispatched to Bellows and Haleiwa airfields for gunnery practice the night before the attack. These planes had their weapons loaded and only needed to be fueled up before they could take off. They also happened to be located at outlying airfields which did not come under heavy Japanese attack.

All together, the American forces managed to get about a dozen planes into the air after the attack began. Two planes that took off from Bellows Field were shot down by the Japanese before they could gain altitude, however, and another American fighter plane was shot down by "friendly" antiaircraft fire in the confusion of the attack.

But some of the American planes that managed to take off engaged in daring aerial combat against the Japanese strike force, with remarkable success. Two Army Air Force pilots, Lieutenants Kenneth Taylor and George Welch, were on their way home from an all-night poker game when the attack began. They called ahead to have the flight crews at Haleiwa Field get their planes ready to go. They launched their speedy P-40 Tomahawk fighters at around 8:15 A.M., right into the middle of the Japanese attack. "We took off directly into them and shot some down," Welch recalled. "I shot down one right on Lieutenant Taylor's tail."[15]

In an hour and a half of combat, Taylor and Welch landed twice to get more fuel and ammunition. Both times they managed to take off again and rejoin the battle. The two pilots were credited with shooting down seven enemy planes, or about one-fourth of the total Japanese aircraft lost in the attack. They also prevented the Japanese from doing major damage to the airfield at Haleiwa.

Acts of Heroism

While some soldiers and sailors fought back, others worked to save the lives of their fellow men. The Japanese attack had plunged thousands of servicemen into a nightmarish world. Ships in Pearl Harbor were rocked by explosions, started taking on water, and capsized within a matter of minutes. Planes, hangars, and barracks at airfields suddenly turned into raging infernos. Yet even in the midst of all this chaos, some brave men managed to ignore the danger to themselves and rush to the aid of others in peril.

The battleship *Oklahoma* rolled over only eight minutes after the first Japanese torpedoes hit her hull. The ship's chaplain, Father Aloysius Schmitt, was below deck at the time. He calmly led a group of sailors up a series of inverted ladders to the lowest deck of the ship, found a watertight compartment, and locked the door from the outside. The men were saved the following day when rescuers cut through the *Oklahoma*'s bottom with welding torches.

Returning to the middle of the upside-down ship, Father Schmitt helped another group of sailors escape through a porthole. When he tried to climb through the porthole himself, he got stuck. He then insisted that the men outside push him back in so the porthole would remain open for others to use. Although Father Schmitt did not make it, he saved dozens of lives. He was awarded the U.S. Navy and Marine Corps Medal posthumously, and a destroyer escort was named after him.

Lieutenant Commander Samuel G. Fuqua, who performed equally heroic rescues aboard the flaming battleship *Arizona*, lived to tell the dramatic story of his experience. "I saw a Japanese plane go by, the machine guns firing, at an altitude of about 100 feet. As I was running forward on the starboard side of the quarter deck … I was apparently knocked out by the blast of a bomb," he remembered. "When I came to and got up off the deck, the ship was a mass of flames."[16]

Fuqua tried in vain to put out the fires, then sent some men to search unsuccessfully for the ship's captain. When it became clear that the *Arizona* could not be saved, Fuqua began directing the transfer of wounded sailors into small boats from the rear of the battleship. Several of his men remarked upon his ability to remain calm under pressure. "There were lots of men coming out on the quarterdeck with every stitch of clothing and shoes blown off, painfully burned and shocked," recalled Aviation Machinist's Mate D.A. Graham. "Mr. Fuqua was the senior officer on deck and set an example for the men by being unperturbed, calm, cool, and collected, exemplifying the courage and traditions of an officer under fire."[17] Fuqua received the Congressional Medal of Honor for his courageous efforts to help 100 injured men escape the burning *Arizona* and reach the hospital ship *Solace*.

Scenes of Heartbreak

The true extent of the devastation in Pearl Harbor only became clear after the last of the Japanese attack planes flew away at 9:45 A.M. (3:15 P.M. in Washington, D.C.). Able-bodied seamen took every available small craft out into the burning, debris-strewn waters to look for survivors. In most cases they found only dead bodies or body parts, which were stacked up on shore for later identification. Critically injured soldiers—many of them burned beyond recognition—swamped the base's hospitals and first-aid clinics, so mess halls and barracks were pressed into service as makeshift medical facilities.

In the confusing aftermath of the attack, the whereabouts and condition of many soldiers and sailors could not be determined for days or even weeks. Several cases of mistaken identity occurred, with heartbreaking consequences for the

More than 400 U.S. Navy crewmen lost their lives when the battleship *Oklahoma* rolled over during the Japanese attack. Their bodies were not recovered until the ship was raised in 1943.

men's families. Seaman John Andrew Rauschkolb, assigned to the battleship *West Virginia,* was presumed dead after his ship sank. The Navy sent a telegram to his family in Illinois informing them of his death, and they held a memorial service in his hometown. In reality, though, Rauschkolb was alive and well. He had jumped overboard before the *West Virginia* went down, swum underneath a layer of burning oil to the *Tennessee,* and then joined a team of firefighters. Although he eventually was able to get in touch with his family, his mother never recovered from the shock of the erroneous death notice, and she died a month later.

Rescue and recovery operations continued for days, and sometimes weeks, after the attack. A few of these efforts had happy results. Several groups of sailors who were trapped inside the *Oklahoma* when it capsized managed to signal their whereabouts by banging "SOS" on the bulkhead in Morse code. A total of 32 survivors were eventually pulled to safety after rescuers cut holes in the hull. After struggling with rising water and stale air for more than a day, First Electronics Mate Irvin H. Thesman remembered the moment of his rescue as "a deep, powerful feeling,... like being dug up out of your own grave."[18]

For every positive outcome, however, there were heartbreaking tragedies. One of the most frustrating failed rescue attempts took place on the battleship *West Virginia*. Six sailors who were trapped inside the sunken ship managed to survive for more than two weeks after the attack. Despite repeated efforts, however, they were never located. "They sent divers down fourteen times to find those guys," said Richard Fiske, a Marine bugler who served on the ship. "Finally, around December 18 or 19, they had to stop looking. They did the best they could, but they just couldn't find them." The men died shortly before Christmas, but their bodies were not recovered until June 18, 1942, when the *West Virginia* was raised and taken to dry dock. "They were in the last watertight compartment we opened," Fiske noted. "I often wonder what they were thinking about. Their lives were cut so short and they never had a chance to realize their dreams."[19]

Rumors and Tension

As American soldiers and sailors tried to find survivors and help the wounded in the wake of the Pearl Harbor attack, they also struggled to prepare for further hostilities with the Japanese. Many military officials believed that the air strike was only the first part of a larger Japanese plan to take over Hawaii. They worried that more planes—or even transport ships carrying troops for a land invasion—might appear at any moment. They took a number of precautions, including establishing a curfew; evacuating the families of military personnel to the mainland; and issuing a mandatory blackout, which required all lights to be turned off at night or windows covered to prevent light from being visible (see "A High School Student Describes How the Attack Changed Her Life," p. 184).

The widespread sense of fear and dread created a very tense atmosphere on Oahu in the days following the attack. Rumors flew around the island about sightings of hostile ships on the horizon, Japanese invasion forces landing by parachute, and sabotage of water supplies and other facilities by sympa-

Following the Pearl Harbor attack, thousands of Japanese Americans were rounded up and taken to internment camps for the duration of the war.

thetic locals. Young, inexperienced soldiers who were assigned to guard duty at night often ended up shooting at anything that moved, including wildlife, civilians, and each other. Sailors were similarly quick on the trigger, and several fishing boats were accidentally destroyed in the weeks following the attack.

The aircraft carrier USS *Enterprise* nearly came under fire from American forces as it returned to port in the tension-filled period following the attack. Captain John E. Lacouture remembered when his destroyer, which was patrolling the waters around Oahu, almost attacked one of its own: "I had the watch at about four or four-thirty in the morning, five o'clock, just as dawn was breaking, and all of a sudden I see a big shape of a carrier through my goggles, sort of off Barbers Point, and I immediately go to general quarters,

The Internment of Japanese Americans

Large numbers of Japanese and other Asian immigrants began arriving in the United States in the late 1800s. Many settled along the Pacific Coast and made important contributions to the settlement of the West as farmers, miners, and railroad workers. Many whites resented Asian immigrants, however, and these views influenced public policy. During the 1920s the U.S. Congress put a halt to virtually all Asian immigration, and the U.S. Supreme Court ruled that Japanese immigrants already living in the United States were not eligible to become citizens or own American land.

Following the attack on Pearl Harbor, many people viewed Japanese Americans with suspicion. They questioned their loyalty to the United States and worried that they might spy for Japan or sabotage the American war effort. These fears intensified in early 1942, when Japan conquered large parts of Asia and the Pacific and Japanese soldiers committed atrocities against American prisoners of war.

In the spring of 1942, the U.S. government responded by expelling people of Japanese descent from the West Coast. Some were deported, and about 112,000 ethnic Japanese were sent to inland internment camps for the duration of the war. This total included about 40,000 individuals who had been born in Japan and were unable to obtain U.S. citizenship, and about 70,000 individuals of Japanese descent who had been born in the United States and were American citizens. These people were rounded up and taken away on short notice, often with no possessions other than

man the guns, man the torpedo tubes, get ready to fire the torpedoes, and about that time the carrier puts a searchlight up and shows the American flag flying. That was the *Enterprise* just as I was about to launch torpedoes."[20]

The tense period following the attack was particularly difficult for the many people of Japanese descent living on Oahu. Rumors spread that they had provided aid to the strike force, perhaps by cutting arrows into fields of sugarcane to direct the planes toward their targets. Other rumors suggested that they were guilty of spying, sabotage, or other forms of disloyalty. "Other ethnic groups looked upon us as the enemy, not to be trusted," recalled Ronald Oba, the clothes they were wearing. Their homes, businesses, bank accounts, and other assets were seized and sold by government authorities.

Norman Mineta, a Japanese American who went on to represent California in the U.S. Congress and serve in the cabinets of two U.S. presidents, spent the war years living in bleak internment camps surrounded by barbed wire and armed guards. "I was ten years old and wearing my Cub Scout uniform when we were packed onto a train in San Jose," he recalled. "Our own government put a yoke of disloyalty around our shoulders. But throughout our ordeal, we cooperated with the government because we felt that in the long run, we could prove our citizenship."

Some critics claimed that the internment of Japanese Americans was unwarranted and unlawful. They pointed out that the U.S. Constitution protects American citizens against arbitrary arrest and imprisonment, and they argued that holding Japanese Americans prisoner without bringing legal charges against them violated their individual rights and liberties. Some also noted that no evidence of spying by Japanese Americans had ever been found, and that internment had not been pursued against German Americans or Italian Americans. Although these arguments made little difference during the war, the U.S. government eventually apologized and paid reparations to the Japanese Americans who were victimized by the internment policy.

Source: Quoted in Friedrich, Otto. "A Time of Agony for Japanese Americans." *Time*, December 2, 1991. Available online at http://www.time.com/time/magazine/article/0,9171,974371,00.html.

the son of Japanese immigrants who lived in the village of Aiea on Oahu. "Our village elders soon got together to burn or destroy anything to do with Japan: photos of the Emperor, flags, swords, and even shortwave radios that could be turned into transmitters. Still, the police on the sugar plantation where we lived led the FBI into Japanese homes."[21] Many Japanese Americans were subjected to questioning in the days and weeks after the attack. Some had their cameras, radios, and newspapers taken away, while others were shipped off to internment camps on the U.S. mainland for the duration of the war (see "The Internment of Japanese Americans," p. 64).

Assigning Blame

Almost as soon as the attack ended, U.S. political and military officials started asking how the Japanese could have planned and executed such a major operation without their knowledge. Humiliated and outraged, they could not believe that Pearl Harbor—one of the strongest military outposts in the world—had failed to anticipate and prepare for such an attack. They immediately began investigating the situation to find out who should be held responsible.

"The United States services were not on the alert against the surprise air attack on Hawaii," declared Secretary of the Navy Frank Knox. "This fact calls for a formal investigation."

As the top naval commander in the Pacific, Kimmel knew that he would take the blame for the destruction of his fleet. Even while the attack was going on, the admiral felt a deep sense of responsibility and regret that made him wish he could follow the age-old sea captain's tradition and go down with his ship. As Kimmel stood watching the devastation from the window of his headquarters, a spent machine-gun bullet smashed through the glass and hit him lightly in the chest. He picked it up thoughtfully and told his aide, "It would have been merciful had it killed me."[22]

The day after the attack, President Roosevelt sent Secretary of the Navy Frank Knox to Hawaii to find out why the American forces had been caught completely off guard. Knox arrived in Honolulu on December 11 and discussed the matter with Kimmel and Short. In his report to Roosevelt, Knox noted that "There was no attempt by either Admiral Kimmel or General Short to alibi [explain] the lack of a state of readiness for the air attack. Both admitted they did not expect it, and had taken no adequate measures to meet one if it came."[23]

Knox also recommended that the president launch a formal investigation. "The United States services were not on the alert against the surprise air attack on Hawaii. This fact calls for a formal investigation which will be initiated immediately by the President. Further action is, of course, dependent on the facts and recommendations made by this investigating board. We are all entitled to know it if (A) there was any error of judgment which contributed to the surprise, (B) if there was any dereliction of duty prior to the attack."[24]

Roosevelt ordered the first of many official inquiries into the Pearl Harbor attack on December 18. The committee, chaired by Supreme Court Justice Owen J. Roberts, spent several weeks gathering testimony and then issued its report in January 1942. It concluded that both Kimmel and Short were guilty of dereliction of duty—a willful failure to perform their expected duties due to negligence or inefficiency. Being convicted of such a serious offense in military law was a crushing blow to these two career officers, who prided themselves on their commitment to duty. They both lost their rank and were relieved of their commands.

Air Corps Lieutenant General Delos C. Emmons was appointed to replace Short as commander of Oahu's ground and air defenses. The new commander of the Pacific Fleet was Admiral Chester W. Nimitz (see Nimitz biography, p. 139), who would prove himself to be a bold and brilliant strategist in the coming war against Japan. In the short term, however, Nimitz found that his most pressing task involved restoring the pride and confidence of the men who had endured the attack on Pearl Harbor. "All of these staffs were in a state of shell shock," he recalled, "and my biggest problem at the moment was morale. These officers simply had to be salvaged."[25]

Finally, in an effort to make sure that such breakdowns in Army-Navy communications did not happen again, Roosevelt reorganized the overall command structure of the American armed forces. He created the Joint Chiefs of Staff to oversee and coordinate the operations of the different branches of the armed services.

Notes

[1] Quoted in Prange, Gordon W. *At Dawn We Slept: The Untold Story of Pearl Harbor.* New York: McGraw-Hill, 1981, p. 506.

[2] Quoted in Prange, *At Dawn We Slept,* p. 523.

[3] Quoted in Prange, *At Dawn We Slept,* p. 507.

[4] Quoted in Prange, *At Dawn We Slept,* p. 511.

[5] Quoted in Prange, *At Dawn We Slept,* p. 507.

[6] Quoted in Prange, *At Dawn We Slept,* p. 526.

[7] Quoted in Prange, *At Dawn We Slept,* p. 527.

[8] Quoted in Sherwood, Robert E. *Roosevelt and Hopkins: An Intimate History.* New York: 1948, p. 430.

[9] Quoted in Van der Vat, Dan. *Pearl Harbor: The Day of Infamy—An Illustrated History.* Toronto: Madison Press, 2001, p. 89.

[10] Quoted in Van der Vat, p. 69.

[11] Quoted in National Park Service (NPS), USS Arizona Memorial site. "Survivors Relive December 7, 1941." Available online at http://www.nps.gov/historyculture/survivors-relive.htm.

[12] Quoted in Prange, *At Dawn We Slept,* p. 508.

[13] Quoted in Prange, *At Dawn We Slept,* p. 514.

[14] Prange, *At Dawn We Slept,* p. 527.

[15] Quoted in Prange, *At Dawn We Slept,* p. 534.

[16] Quoted in Wallin, Homer N. *Pearl Harbor: Why, How, Fleet Salvage and Final Appraisal.* Washington, D.C.: Government Printing Office, 1968, pp. 297-327. Available online at "Reports by Survivors of Pearl Harbor Attack," Department of the Navy, Navy Historical Center, http://www.history.navy. mil/docs/wwii/pearl/survivors2.htm.

[17] Quoted in Wallin, pp. 297-327.

[18] Quoted in Prange, *At Dawn We Slept,* p. 563.

[19] Quoted in NPS, "Survivors Relive December 7, 1941."

[20] "Oral Histories of the Pearl Harbor Attack, 7 December 1941: Captain John E. Lacouture, USN." Department of the Navy, Naval Historical Center, June 8, 2001. Available online at http://www.history. navy.mil/faqs/faq66-3d.htm.

[21] Oba, Ronald. "December 7, 1941: What I Saw at Pearl Harbor." *Time,* March 31, 2003, p. A22.

[22] Quoted in Prange, *At Dawn We Slept,* p. 516.

[23] Quoted in Conn, Stetson, Rose C. Engelman, and Byron Fairchild. *Guarding the United States and Its Outposts.* Washington, D.C.: U.S. Army Center of Military History, 2000, p. 194.

[24] Quoted in Prange, *At Dawn We Slept,* p. 589.

[25] Quoted in Prange, Gordon W. *Pearl Harbor: The Verdict of History.* New York: McGraw-Hill, 1986, p. 537.

Chapter Five

THE "SLEEPING GIANT" WAKES UP

—⟨⟩—

We have awakened a sleeping giant and instilled in him a terrible resolve.

—Isoroku Yamamoto, Japanese admiral who conceived the Pearl Harbor attack

The Japanese attack on Pearl Harbor united the American people toward a common cause in a way that no other event in the nation's history ever had. Initial feelings of shock and grief quickly gave way to righteous anger and a burning desire for revenge. Abandoning two decades of isolationism, the United States declared war against Japan and began working to repair and rebuild the Pacific Fleet.

In the meantime, though, Japan continued moving forward with its ambitious plan to take control of large parts of Asia and the Pacific. Before the smoke had cleared from the skies above Hawaii, Japanese forces had invaded British and Dutch colonies in southeast Asia and launched air attacks against other U.S. military outposts in the Pacific. For the first six months of the war, the Japanese offensive appeared unstoppable. But in the spring of 1942, a rapidly recovering U.S. Navy won a string of hard-fought sea battles to give American morale a much-needed boost.

America Rallies to the Cause

The American people first became aware of the Japanese attack on Pearl Harbor about an hour after it started. It was an ordinary Sunday afternoon on the U.S. mainland. Since television was still in the early stages of development, many families were gathered around their radios listening to broadcasts of news, music, drama, and football games. The major radio networks began breaking into their regular programming at 2:26 P.M. Eastern time with news bulletins about the attack. The CBS network already had a news program called *The World Today* scheduled to begin at 2:30, so it was the first to provide full commentary and analysis.

The news that the United States had come under attack was met with a combination of shock, bewilderment, grief, outrage, and anger. Most people recognized that the country now had no choice but to go to war, and that the coming months would require great sacrifices from all Americans. "Dead and crippled Americans, sunken American ships, and incinerated American planes conveyed a message that the most obtuse could not fail to read," explained historian Gordon W. Prange. "The Axis did indeed cherish lethal intentions toward the United States; no compromise could be reached with this evil; the good life would be impossible in the Americas if they should be squeezed like lemons between a Nazi Europe and a Japanese Asia. Here was an enemy worth the cost of battle and a cause worth the best every American adult could bring to it—even life itself."[1]

On December 8, at 12:29 P.M. in Washington, D.C., Roosevelt addressed a joint session of Congress to request a formal declaration of war against Japan (see "Roosevelt Requests a Declaration of War with Japan," p. 189). Millions of Americans listened on the radio as the president began with the famous words, "Yesterday, December 7, 1941—a date which will live in infamy—the United States was deliberately attacked by the naval and air forces of the Empire of Japan." Congress granted his request by a vote of 82-0 in the Senate and 388-1 in the House of Representatives (see "The U.S. Congress Declares War," p. 191).

The following day, Roosevelt outlined the historic challenge facing the nation in one of his regular radio addresses to the American people, known as Fireside Chats (see "Roosevelt Calls the American People to Action," p. 192). The president emphasized the danger that Axis aggression posed to the security of the United States and the world. He acknowledged that he expected a long war, but expressed confidence that America and its allies would eventually prevail. Then he explained how every U.S. citizen must play a role in aiding the war effort and securing peace. "We are now in this war. We are all in it—all the way. Every single man, woman, and child is a partner in the most tremendous undertaking of our American history," he declared. "The United States does not consider it a sacrifice to do all one can, to give one's best to our Nation, when the Nation is fighting for its existence and its future life."[2]

Roosevelt's message resonated with the American people. Still reeling from the news of the attack, most were glad to be called to participate in the upcoming war effort. "Overnight, isolationists became converts to intervention, stirred in part by the eloquent call to service from Franklin Roosevelt and in part by the great tidal wave of gung-ho patriotism that swept across the land," noted journalist Tom Brokaw. "Pearl Harbor had enraged and unified a country, committing the United States to a common goal."[3]

Rallying around the slogan "Remember Pearl Harbor," the American people committed themselves to the

President Franklin D. Roosevelt signed declarations of war against Japan, Germany, and Italy in the days following the Pearl Harbor attack.

war effort in every possible way. Millions of men rushed to join the armed forces. Factories across the country hired more workers and ran assembly lines around the clock to make boats, planes, guns, and uniforms for the troops. The wartime production created shortages of some consumer goods—especially rubber, gasoline, meat, oils, and sugar—but the American people readily accepted rationing of these items or simply found ways to do without. Many families started "Victory Gardens" in their yards or neighborhoods, figuring that growing their own vegetables helped make more food available for the troops. Other civilians volunteered as air-raid wardens to make sure homes and businesses observed blackout rules at night. Even children helped out by collecting bottles, scrap metal, and rubber to be recycled.

The impact of the Pearl Harbor attack on the American people—and the immediate and whole-hearted commitment to war that it produced—convinced some observers that Japan had made a terrible strategic mistake. Even

The attack on Pearl Harbor united the American people behind the war effort. This poster—showing the heads of Axis leaders Emperor Hirohito of Japan, Adolf Hitler of Germany, and Benito Mussolini of Italy on the body of a snake—reflects the mood of the time.

Admiral Isoroku Yamamoto, who had come up with the Japanese attack plan, worried that Pearl Harbor had merely "awakened a sleeping giant." The surprise nature of the attack—which most Americans viewed as an unethical, dishonorable, and treacherous act—contributed to the strong desire for revenge. Literally overnight, the United States shifted from reluctant support of its European allies to an unprecedented focus of national energy toward wartime goals.

British Prime Minister Winston Churchill recognized that the full commitment of the American people could determine the outcome of the war. The day after the Japanese attack, Churchill recalled feeling a deep sense of relief that the United States would now enter the conflict. "We had won the war," he stated. "England would live."[4] On December 11, Japan's fellow Axis Powers, Germany and Italy, declared war on the United States. Although German Chancellor Adolf Hitler had hoped to complete his conquest of Russia before America entered the war, he was still pleased about the Japanese attack. He figured that it would force the United States to concentrate its military strength in the Pacific, so the Americans would not be able to send so much money, food, weapons, and other supplies to help the Allies in Europe.

Japan Presses Its Advantage in the Pacific

Japan did not wait to see how America would react to the attack on Pearl Harbor. Knowing that they had limited the U.S. Pacific Fleet's ability to respond, Japanese leaders immediately began implementing their larger plan to dominate Asia and the Pacific. One part of this plan, called the Southern Operation, involved conquering territory in southeast Asia to gain access to land and raw materials. The second part of the plan involved capturing islands throughout the Pacific to create a defensive perimeter around the expanded Japanese Empire. Japanese leaders estimated that it would take the United States at least a year to recover the naval capacity it had lost in the Pearl Harbor attack. By that time, they believed that they could establish a chain of military bases capable of controlling a 4,000-mile-wide stretch of territory from Wake Island in the central Pacific to Burma on the border of India.

This strategy led Japan to attack numerous targets in the Pacific, including U.S. air bases on the Pacific islands of Guam and Wake, at the same time it bombed Pearl Harbor. Wake Island was an important stopover for American military planes traveling from Hawaii to the Philippines. Its defenses consisted of a garrison of 450 U.S. Marines and one squadron of fighter planes. They managed to repel the initial Japanese attack on December 8, sinking two Japanese destroyers in the process. But the Japanese returned on December 23 with two aircraft carriers and overwhelmed the American defenses. The first wave of Japanese conquests also included Guam, which was not fortified under a 1922 treaty with Japan. George McMillan, a U.S. Navy Captain who served as governor of the territory, surrendered on December 10 when he learned that 5,000 Japanese troops were preparing to land on the island.

Within 24 hours of the Pearl Harbor attack, the Japanese had also launched an invasion of Thailand and landed troops in the British colonies of Hong Kong and Malaya (now Malaysia). Japan desperately wanted to control Malaya's valuable natural resources. The British possession supplied half the world's rubber and one-third of its tin. But the colony was protected from a sea invasion by the British naval base at Singapore, a diamond-shaped island at the end of the Malay Peninsula.

> *"Yesterday, December 7, 1941—a date which will live in infamy—the United States was deliberately attacked by the naval and air forces of the Empire of Japan."*

Japanese leaders used a two-part plan to capture Singapore. First, they sent ground troops southward through the jungles and rubber plantations of the Malay Peninsula. Second, they used planes launched from French Indochina (now Vietnam, Cambodia, and Laos) to attack the British naval defenses. Although Great Britain could not spare too many forces from the fight against Germany, British leaders had sent a new battleship, the HMS *Prince of Wales,* and a heavy cruiser, the HMS *Repulse,* to defend Singapore. In another demonstration of the superiority of air power on the high seas, however, both ships were sunk by Japanese torpedo bombers, at a cost of 840 British lives. The destruction of these ships meant that no Allied battleships remained in operation in the Pacific west of Hawaii.

Immediately afterward, the Japanese launched a land invasion of Singapore. Rather than attacking the British fort from the sea, however, they came from the unprotected jungle side. The British were so confident that no enemy forces could make it through to Singapore by land that the huge guns defending the fort did not even turn around in that direction. British General Arthur Percival surrendered on February 15, 1942, a short time after Japanese forces cut off Singapore's water supplies. The fact that Percival's 85,000-man army lost to an enemy force that numbered around 30,000 served as a further embarrassment for the British.

The Bataan Death March

Only a few short hours after the Pearl Harbor attack, Japanese planes had also attacked a U.S. air base in the Philippines. The United States had gone to great lengths to fortify this chain of islands in case war broke out with Japan. It had even sent General Douglas MacArthur (see MacArthur biography, p. 131), a famous military hero of World War I, to command the American forces and train and equip a Filipino army.

Although MacArthur had heard about the attack on Pearl Harbor, he made some of the same mistakes that had cost the American military dearly in Hawaii. For example, he left most of his planes in plain sight on the airfield, where they made perfect targets for Japanese pilots. "Instead of encountering a swarm of enemy fighters, we looked down and saw some 60 enemy bombers and fighters neatly parked," recalled Saburo Sakai, pilot of a Zero fighter. "They squatted there like sitting ducks. Our accuracy was phenomenal. The entire air base seemed to be rising into the air with the explosions. Great fires erupted, and smoke boiled upward."[5] The attack killed 80 Americans, destroyed 100 planes, and gave an enormous boost to Japanese efforts to seize the Philippines.

On December 22, the Japanese took advantage of the lack of American air defenses to land 40,000 troops on Luzon, the northernmost island in the Philippines. They moved quickly to capture the capital city of Manila. MacArthur ordered the American and Filipino troops who had been stationed there to make a tactical retreat to the mountainous Bataan peninsula east of the city. Military leaders in Washington, D.C., had promised to send air support as soon as possible, so MacArthur planned to wait until it arrived.

Instead, in January 1942 Roosevelt ordered MacArthur to leave the Philippines and go to Australia to take command of U.S. forces there. As the Japanese had advanced southward through the Pacific, the Australian government had threatened to recall its troops from Africa to defend against a possible attack at home. Allied leaders felt that the Australian troops were needed to fight the Germans in Africa, though, so they made a deal to send MacArthur to oversee the defense of Australia. The famous general left the Philippines reluctantly, knowing that it would appear as if he had abandoned his troops. "I'm leaving over my repeated protests," he told his men. "If I get through to Australia, you know I'll come back as soon as I can with as much as I can. In the meantime you've got to hold."[6] After arriving in Australia, MacArthur famously vowed that "I shall return" to liberate the Philippines.

As many as 20,000 Allied prisoners died in the Bataan Death March, when Japanese troops forced them to walk 65 miles in extreme heat without food or water. In this photo, some of the prisoners carry their fallen comrades in makeshift stretchers.

MacArthur's remaining 70,000 troops in the Philippines, which were placed under the command of Lieutenant General Jonathan Wainwright, held off the Japanese for several months. By the time they surrendered on May 6, 1942, the American and Filipino soldiers had run out of food and medicine. They were weak and exhausted, and many were suffering from tropical diseases. Nevertheless, their Japanese captors forced them to march 65 miles across the Bataan peninsula to prisoner-of-war camps north of Manila.

Since surrender was considered dishonorable in Japanese culture, the Japanese treated their prisoners very badly. They made them walk through terrible heat with no food or water. Many died from dehydration or exhaustion along the way, and many others were killed if they stumbled or tried to drink. As many as 20,000 U.S. and Filipino soldiers died in what has become known to history as the Bataan Death March. The atrocities committed in the Philippines convinced many Americans that the Japanese were vicious and inhumane and deserved no mercy.

The Doolittle Raid Lifts American Spirits

In February 1942 the list of Japanese conquests in Asia and the Pacific grew to include Borneo, the site of valuable oil fields in the Dutch East Indies (now Indonesia). To take control of this territory, the Japanese defeated an Allied naval force that included American, Australian, and Dutch ships. The rapid string of victories expanded the Japanese Empire to the greatest size in its history. In fact, Japan controlled nearly one-seventh of the world's territory. Many people felt that the Japanese were unstoppable and worried that they might attack Australia, India, Alaska, or Hawaii next.

As the American people grew increasingly discouraged with the news from the Pacific, U.S. leaders came up with a daring plan to attack the Japanese capital of Tokyo. They hoped to demonstrate that Japan was still vulnerable to attack, despite all of its recent conquests. They also wanted to reassure the American people and give them a reason for hope. The plan involved launching 16 Army Air Force long-range B-25 bombers from an aircraft carrier about 500 miles off the coast of the Japanese home islands. The man chosen to lead the air raid was Lieutenant Colonel James H. Doolittle, who had become famous as a stunt pilot in the 1930s.

Doolittle's attack force took off from the U.S.S. *Hornet* on April 18, 1942. The 16 planes faced no resistance on the way to Tokyo, and successfully dropped their bombs on military and industrial targets. Since the bombers were too large to land back on the aircraft carrier, though, they had to continue flying toward U.S.-friendly areas of China afterward. Three of the planes crashed, and eight pilots and crew members were captured by Japanese soldiers, but 71 of the 80 Americans involved in the raid survived.

The Doolittle Raid damaged around 90 buildings and killed an estimated 50 people in Tokyo and nearby cities. Japanese leaders dismissively called it the "Do-Nothing Raid" because it had caused so little physical damage. But it had important repercussions for both Japan and the United States. On the American side, the Doolittle Raid gave the American people and U.S. military

An American B-25 bomber takes off from the deck of the USS *Hornet* to participate in the famous Doolittle Raid on Tokyo, Japan.

forces a much-needed infusion of positive news that led to a big increase in morale. For his leadership of the attack, Doolittle received the Congressional Medal of Honor and was promoted to brigadier general.

On the Japanese side, the air raid caused great embarrassment for military and government leaders. They had told the Japanese people that an enemy force could never get through the defensive perimeter they had established and attack Japan directly. After the Doolittle Raid, Japanese leaders became convinced that they needed to strengthen and expand their defenses in the Pacific. They decided to push the Southern Operation even further to the south and west. But they also called several squadrons of fighter planes back from the Pacific War to defend the home islands. This shift left fewer aircraft available for Japan's offensive campaigns.

The Battle of the Coral Sea

The first area the Japanese targeted following the Doolittle Raid was Port Moresby in New Guinea, an important Allied port located off the northeast coast of Australia. Japanese leaders believed that capturing Port Moresby would allow them to isolate MacArthur's forces and eliminate a potential staging area for Allied offensive operations in the southern Pacific. But U.S. Navy code breakers intercepted Japanese messages about the coming attack. Allied leaders decided to make a stand at Port Moresby because of its strategic importance to the defense of Australia and New Zealand.

Less than five months after the Pearl Harbor attack had devastated the Pacific Fleet, the U.S. Navy managed to send a large force to head off the Japanese offensive. It included 2 aircraft carriers, the U.S.S. *Yorktown* and *Lexington,* with 141 planes aboard, as well as 11 destroyers and 5 cruisers. These forces, under the command of Rear Admiral Frank J. Fletcher, engaged the Japanese Combined Fleet in the Coral Sea on May 4, 1942. It marked the first time in the history of naval warfare that an entire sea battle took place without the opposing fleets ever coming within sight of one another. Instead, the battle was fought by planes launched from aircraft carriers as the American and Japanese ships maneuvered between 100 and 200 miles apart.

Based only upon damage reports, the Battle of the Coral Sea could be considered a draw. Japanese bombs ignited huge fires on the carrier *Lexington,* forcing her crew to abandon ship. But U.S. planes damaged the Japanese carrier *Shokaku* and sank the light carrier *Shoho.* Upon scoring the fatal hit on the *Shoho,* American pilot Robert Dixon sent a famous radio message back to his ship: "Dixon to carrier, scratch one flattop."[7] The Japanese lost 80 aircraft in combat, while the Americans lost 74.

In the end, however, the battle was an important triumph for the United States and its allies. For the first time since the start of the Pacific War, they had managed to stop a Japanese advance. The transport ships full of Japanese troops were forced to turn around and abandon their attempt to capture Port Moresby. This result showed both sides that the Japanese were not invincible.

President Franklin D. Roosevelt (center) chose General Douglas MacArthur (left) and Admiral Chester W. Nimitz to lead the American forces fighting in the Pacific.

The Battle of Midway

The next Japanese effort to expand its defenses centered around a tiny but strategically vital U.S. naval base called Midway. Located in the central Pacific, about 1,200 miles northwest of Pearl Harbor, Midway consisted of two small islands with a harbor and an airfield. Despite its small size, Admiral Yamamoto argued that capturing Midway should be a key element of the Japanese strategy. He believed that taking control of the island would not only shore up the Japanese defensive perimeter, but would also give his fleet a land base from which to attack Hawaii or even California. Yamamoto came up with an elaborate plan to lure the U.S. Pacific Fleet into a trap at Midway in hopes of destroying it once and for all.

Yamamoto's plan involved more than 200 ships and 250 aircraft. One part of this fleet steamed toward the Aleutian Islands off the coast of Alaska in the northern Pacific. Their main job was to create a diversion to draw the American Navy's attention away from the real target. At the same time, Japan sent four aircraft carriers, two battleships, and a dozen troop transports to Midway. This part of the fleet was charged with bombing the island defenses to clear the way for landing a ground invasion force.

Finally, Yamamoto's plan called for a third part of the fleet, including one carrier and seven battleships, to sit quietly a few hundred miles off Midway. When the U.S. Navy responded to the attack on Midway by sending ships to the rescue from Pearl Harbor, this group would be ready to ambush them. "After attacking Midway by air and destroying the enemy's shore-based air strength to facilitate our landing operations, we should still be able to destroy any enemy task force which may choose to counterattack,"[8] noted Admiral Chuichi Nagumo, commander of the second group of Japanese ships. Yamamoto led the third group himself aboard the *Yamoto*, the largest battleship in the Japanese fleet.

Shortly before Yamamoto launched the attack on Midway, however, U.S. Navy code breakers led by Commander Joseph J. Rochefort cracked the secret Japanese military code known as JN-25 (see "Cracking the Japanese Secret Code," p. 82). They were able to give Admiral Chester W. Nimitz, commander of the Pacific Fleet, all the details of Yamamoto's attack plan. Nimitz used this valuable information to set his own trap for the Japanese.

Although he knew it was risky to leave Hawaii undefended, Nimitz decided to send every available ship to Midway to help fend off the Japanese attack—including all three aircraft carriers at his disposal. At first he had only two healthy aircraft carriers, the *Enterprise* and the *Hornet,* because the *Yorktown* had suffered serious damage in the Battle of the Coral Sea. The *Yorktown* had managed to limp back to Pearl Harbor, but repair crews told Nimitz it would take three months to repair the carrier. The admiral refused to accept this situation and ordered his men to complete the repairs in three days. A 1,500-member crew worked around the clock to patch up the *Yorktown,* and she sailed off with the rest of the American task force to join in the defense of Midway. Under the command of Admiral Raymond Spruance, this fleet of 76 ships and 300 planes reached Midway ahead of the Japanese.

Importantly, the task force at Midway did not include any battleships—partly because most of them had been damaged in the Pearl Harbor attack,

Cracking the Japanese Secret Code

The leader of the team of U.S. Navy code breakers who uncovered the Japanese plot to attack Midway was Commander Joseph John Rochefort. Born in 1898 in Dayton, Ohio, he enlisted in the Navy at the age of twenty after earning a degree from Stevens Institute of Technology. Prior to U.S. involvement in World War II, his career included fourteen years at sea and nine years in assignments relating to foreign intelligence and cryptanalysis (code breaking). Rochefort received his first assignment in cryptanalysis in 1925 because one of his commanding officers knew that he enjoyed doing crossword puzzles. His training included a year in Tokyo studying the Japanese language.

In early 1941 Rochefort was sent to Hawaii to take command of Station Hypo, a code breaking center in the basement of naval headquarters at Pearl Harbor. U.S. military code breakers had already built a machine that was capable of deciphering the Japanese secret code used for diplomatic messages. Unfortunately, the sheer volume of information transmitted by the Japanese made it difficult for Rochefort and other analysts to predict the attack that occurred on December 7, 1941. "I can offer a lot of excuses," he said later, "but we failed in our job. An intelligence officer has one job, one task, one mission—to tell his commander, his superior, today what the Japanese are going to do tomorrow."

Following the declaration of war against Japan, Rochefort and his team worked around the clock trying to break the Japanese Fleet General Purpose Code, known as JN-25, that the enemy used to send operational orders to its navy. The code breakers punched thousands of intercepted messages onto computer cards and analyzed the data for possible clues to

and partly because Nimitz recognized the shift toward carrier-based naval warfare. "In the new style of naval warfare, which admirals around the world were just beginning to learn, aircraft carriers were supreme," explained one historian. "They could destroy anything but were highly vulnerable, so the key was to find and attack the enemy's carriers."[9]

the code. But every time they got close to unraveling the mystery, the Japanese changed the code.

Rochefort and his team finally succeeded in breaking JN-25 in March 1942. From that time on, they could read Japanese naval communications. Rochefort himself sometimes reviewed, analyzed, and reported to top Navy commanders on the contents of over 100 messages per day. On May 14, Station Hypo intercepted a message indicating that a Japanese attack was in the works for early June. The target of the attack was a Pacific air base with the code name AF. Rochefort believed that AF referred to Midway, but he needed confirmation in order to convince military leaders to take action. He asked radio operators at Midway to send a test message saying that a water treatment plant had failed. A few days later—just as Rochefort had hoped—a coded Japanese message made reference to this information, which revealed that AF was actually Midway.

Knowing when and where the Japanese attack would occur allowed Admiral Chester W. Nimitz to get the U.S. Pacific Fleet in position for an ambush. Thanks to Rochefort and the code breakers, the American Navy scored a major victory in the Battle of Midway. Rochefort retired from the military in 1947 but returned to active duty for three years during the Korean War. He did not receive any public recognition for his work until after his death in 1976. Posthumous honors include the Navy Distinguished Service Medal (1985), the Presidential Medal of Freedom (1986), and induction into the National Security Agency Hall of Fame (2000).

Source: Quoted in Budiansky, Stephen. *Battle of Wits: The Complete Story of Codebreaking in World War II.* Converted for the Web as "Midway: A Man on a Mission." Available online at http://worldwar2history.info/Midway/mission.html.

Springing the Trap

On the morning of June 4, 1942, an unsuspecting Nagumo launched his attack on Midway. Planes from the four Japanese aircraft carriers started off by conducting a bombing raid on the island's airfield. Midway's outdated air-

American Dauntless dive bombers fly above a sinking Japanese aircraft carrier during the Battle of Midway.

craft proved to be no match for the Japanese, and all but two of the 26 Marine fighters were destroyed. But American forces on the ground were ready, and they put up a barrage of antiaircraft fire that took down 67 of the first wave of 108 Japanese planes.

As the rest of the Japanese planes returned to their carriers, Spruance decided to spring the trap. He launched planes from all three of his aircraft carriers against the Japanese fleet. The battle began badly for the Americans, as the first wave of Devastator torpedo bombers was torn apart by Japanese anti-aircraft fire and speedy Zero fighters. Only one of the initial 41 U.S. planes survived the attack. In the meantime, though, 49 American Dauntless dive bombers arrived on the scene without being noticed by the Japanese. These planes dove quickly from an altitude of 15,000 feet down to 1,500 feet and then released their bombs. They avoided the enemy's defenses and sank three of the four Japanese aircraft carriers within a matter of minutes.

The remaining Japanese carrier, the *Hiryu*, was shrouded in mist during the first wave of the American attack and managed to escape attention. The *Hiryu* struck back with an aerial assault that sank a U.S. destroyer and the hastily repaired carrier *Yorktown*. A short time later, however, U.S. planes from the *Enterprise* located and sank the *Hiryu*. Yeoman Jack Adams, a sailor who had abandoned ship as the *Yorktown* was sinking and ended up on a life raft, heard the results of the battle after he was rescued. "We learned that four of the enemy carriers had been sunk," he recalled. "The Japanese lost all their planes and most of their aircrew, either in combat or for sheer lack of a place to land…. This was the victory we needed."[10]

Upon learning that Nagumo's attack force had been defeated, Yamamoto had no choice but to retreat in order to save his remaining ships. The battle had cost Japan nearly 300 warplanes and 3,000 men, including many experienced pilots. Although the United States lost the *Yorktown* and 147 aircraft, it was far more capable than Japan of replacing its losses. Now fully geared up for wartime production, the industrial giant could produce more new ships in a year than had been in the entire Japanese Combined Fleet at the beginning of the war.

The Battle of Midway was a tremendous victory for the United States, and it marked a key turning point in the Pacific War. Even though the American forces were badly outnumbered, superior military intelligence gave them the advantage. They not only turned back a major Japanese offensive, but caused enough damage to put Japan on the defensive. From this point on, in fact, Japan never won a major battle in the Pacific War. British Prime Minister Winston Churchill summed up the impact of the American victories in the battles of the Coral Sea and Midway: "At one stroke, the dominant position of Japan in the Pacific was reversed," he wrote. "The annals of war at sea present no more intense, heart-shaking shock than these two battles, in which the qualities of the United States Navy and Air Force and of the American race shone forth in splendor."[11]

The only negative outcome of the Battle of Midway was that the diversionary Japanese force did gain control over the westernmost islands in the Aleutian chain: Adak, Amchitka, Kiska and Attu. Although these barren and remote outposts were located about 1,000 miles off the coast of Alaska, many Americans expressed anxiety after learning about their capture. The United States and Canada responded by sending 100,000 troops to fight in the Aleutians. They recaptured Adak in August 1942, Amchitka in January 1943, and Attu in May 1943. Two months later, Japan withdrew its occupation forces from Kiska.

Notes

[1] Prange, Gordon W. *Pearl Harbor: The Verdict of History.* New York: McGraw-Hill, 1986, p. 541.

[2] Roosevelt, Franklin D. "Address to Congress Requesting a Declaration of War with Japan," December 8, 1941, and "Fireside Chat," December 9, 1941. In Woolley, John T., and Gerhard Peters, *The American Presidency Project.* Available online at http://www.presidency.ucsb.edu/ws/?pid=16053 and http://www.presidency.ucsb.edu/ws/?pid=16056.

[3] Brokaw, Tom. "A Generation's Trial by Fire." *Newsweek,* May 14, 2001, p. 58.

[4] Quoted in Harris, Nathaniel. *A Day That Made History: Pearl Harbor.* North Pomfret, VT: David and Charles, 1986, p. 59.

[5] Quoted in Friedrich, Otto. "Down but Not Out." *Time,* December 2, 1991. Available online at http://www.time.com/time/magazine/article/0,9171,974392,00.html.

[6] Quoted in Campbell, James. *The Ghost Mountain Boys.* New York: Crown, 2007.

[7] Quoted in Friedrich, "Down but Not Out."

[8] Quoted in Budiansky, Stephen. *Battle of Wits: The Complete Story of Codebreaking in World War II.* Converted for the Web as "Midway: Ambush the Ambushers." Available online at http://world-war2history.info/Midway/ambush.html.

[9] Friedrich, "Down but Not Out."

[10] Quoted in Klam, Julie. *World War II Chronicles: The Rise of Japan and Pearl Harbor.* North Mankato, MN: Byron Preiss, 2003, p. 45.

[11] Quoted in Friedrich, "Down but Not Out."

Chapter Six

VICTORY IN THE PACIFIC

The Japanese began the war from the air at Pearl Harbor. They have been repaid many fold.

—President Harry S. Truman, in a press release announcing that the United States had dropped an atomic bomb on Japan, August 6, 1945

After halting Japanese expansion in the Battle of Midway, the Allies launched an offensive strategy known as "island hopping." They used amphibious (combined air, land, and sea) assaults to capture a series of island bases in the Pacific. These victories eventually brought American bombers within range of Japan. The Japanese suffered a series of defeats in 1943 and 1944 that steadily reduced their ability to make war. By the time the war reached traditional Japanese territory at Iwo Jima and Okinawa, the enemy turned to increasingly desperate measures to inflict damage and casualties on the Allies. These Japanese tactics convinced President Harry S. Truman that a ground invasion of Japan would cost millions of lives. He chose instead to end the war quickly by using a powerful new weapon—the atomic bomb.

America Takes the Offensive at Guadalcanal

The Allied victories in the battles of the Coral Sea and Midway were important in stopping Japanese momentum and increasing the confidence of American forces. Still, U.S. military leaders recognized that they had a great deal of work to do to dislodge the Japanese from all the territory they had captured in Asia and the Pacific. During the first few months of the Pacific War, the Japanese had established a strong defensive perimeter that extended thousands of miles from their home islands. They had built ports and airfields and dug fortifications into hillsides on island chains stretching across the Pacific, including the Marshalls, Gilberts, Carolines, Marianas, and Solomons. In addition, the Japanese still maintained superior naval strength in the Pacific.

But the American victories at sea in the spring of 1942 convinced U.S. leaders to try to seize the initiative. "Although the Coral Sea and Midway engagements did not give the Americans undisputed access to the South Pacific," noted one historian, "they did bring the naval balance of forces close enough that the Americans could realistically consider an amphibious operation."[1]

That operation began on August 7, 1942—eight months to the day after the Japanese attack on Pearl Harbor—at Guadalcanal, an island in the Solomon chain just north of Australia. Fairly large at 90 miles long and 25 miles wide, Guadalcanal was a tropical jungle full of forbidding 8,000-foot peaks, steep ravines, and rushing streams. Allied leaders chose to invade it because of its strategic importance. The Japanese had established a military base there that threatened to disrupt Allied shipping, communication, and troop transports to and from Australia.

As with other amphibious operations in the Pacific War, the Guadalcanal offensive began with intensive bombing and shelling of Japanese positions by Allied naval vessels and carrier-based planes. This advance bombing was intended to "soften" the Japanese defenses and make it possible to bring ground troops ashore. Next came the landing of assault forces, led by U.S. Marines, in small boats, tanks, and other vehicles that could move through shallow water. The Marines fought their way inland from the beach under heavy enemy fire, knocked out Japanese defensive positions, and established a protected area for further landings of troops and equipment. Then the Allied forces continued pushing across the island, often engaging in close combat with enemy soldiers, in a brutal campaign that dragged on for months. On Guadalcanal, the American invasion force not only fought against the Japanese, but also struggled to deal with extreme heat and humidity, heavy rains, swarming insects, and tropical diseases.

The battle for Guadalcanal also included a series of naval battles between the American and Japanese fleets during the fall of 1942. The U.S. Pacific Fleet lost three valuable aircraft carriers in these battles. In August, the U.S.S. *Saratoga* was put out of commission for three months after it was hit by a torpedo. The Japanese sank the *Wasp* in September, followed by the *Hornet* in

The bodies of Japanese defenders lie on the beach at Guadalcanal in the Solomon Islands while U.S. Marines take stock of the situation.

October, leaving the *Enterprise* as the only American carrier available for action in the Pacific. But Japan suffered huge losses as well. The Japanese lost 24 ships and 600 aircraft and experienced pilots in these clashes.

By the time the Allied forces finally captured Guadalcanal in February 1943, the six-month battle had claimed 1,600 American and 25,000 Japanese lives. The loss of one of its defensive perimeter islands was a major blow for Japan. It was also an important victory for the United States and its allies. Although it came at a high cost, the successful counteroffensive taught them valuable lessons about amphibious warfare and helped them prepare for the next phase of the Pacific War.

The Allies Pursue an "Island-Hopping" Strategy

In the spring of 1943, Allied leaders met in Washington, D.C., to discuss military strategy. Most still wanted to concentrate on fighting against Germany. They hoped to end the war in Europe before committing large amounts of naval power and troop strength to the Pacific War. But some military leaders, like U.S. General Douglas MacArthur, argued that defeating Japan should be America's top priority. He viewed the war in Europe as a distraction that prevented the United States from focusing on the only enemy that had attacked it directly.

In the end, Allied leaders agreed that it was necessary to fight the war on both fronts. But the demands of the war in Europe did affect the strategy that the United States employed against Japan in the Pacific. Since they could not get all the ships, planes, troops, and equipment they wanted, U.S. military leaders had to scale back their offensive maneuvers. They came up with a plan to attack only the Japanese positions that had great strategic value, while bypassing many other territories held by enemy forces. By capturing several key islands in the Pacific, they believed that they could isolate other Japanese-held islands and cause them to "wither on the vine" without supplies or reinforcements from the homeland.

> *On Guadalcanal and other Pacific islands, the American invasion force not only fought against the Japanese, but also struggled to deal with extreme heat and humidity, heavy rains, swarming insects, and tropical diseases.*

This Allied plan became known as "island hopping." The idea was to move quickly across the Pacific toward the Japanese home islands, launching amphibious assaults to capture strategically located islands along the way, and then using each captured island as a base from which to attack the next one. The island-hopping strategy created some controversy, because it violated the usual military rule that said forces on the offensive should secure an entire area before moving forward. But some experts felt that it represented an innovative approach to breaking through Japan's defenses. "The Japanese defensive perimeter was strong only if the United States chose to attack each fortified island," noted one historian. "If the majority of islands was bypassed and only selected islands of primary strategic importance were taken, the Japanese perimeter would collapse."[2]

The Allies launched the island-hopping campaign, formally known as Operation Cartwheel, on July 1, 1943. The overall forces were broken down into different commands based on geographic area: Admiral Chester W. Nimitz took charge of forces in the central and northern Pacific; Admiral William "Bull" Halsey commanded those in the southern Pacific; General Douglas MacArthur led the troops in Australia and New Guinea; and British Admiral Lord Mountbatten controlled the Allied efforts in India, Burma, and Southeast Asia. These separate commands forced the Japanese to spread out their defenses and fight on many fronts.

As at Guadalcanal, the Allied offensive operations involved both ground combat on little-known Pacific islands and sea battles against the Japanese fleet. The U.S. Navy developed two types of aircraft carriers to participate in the island-hopping campaign. Fleet carriers held between 80 and 100 planes and were primarily used to locate and destroy Japanese vessels. Smaller escort carriers were primarily used to support amphibious landings and to accompany supply shipments and troop transports.

Another U.S. Navy innovation that proved invaluable to the island-hopping strategy was the "special service fleet." Previous naval operations had required warships to return to their home port for fuel, supplies, or repairs after every sea battle. But the development of special service fleets allowed the U.S. Pacific Fleet to perform maintenance while at sea. These groupings of repair ships, fuel tankers, supply barges, tugs, hospital ships, and floating dry docks functioned collectively like a naval base to keep the warships ready for combat. They made it possible for the Allies to advance steadily toward Japan.

Allies Sweep Across the Central Pacific

One of the first targets of the island-hopping campaign was the Gilbert chain in the central Pacific, southwest of Hawaii. The main Japanese stronghold was on a tiny island—only two miles long and 600 yards wide—called Betio in the Tarawa Atoll. A garrison of 4,500 highly trained Japanese troops was stationed there to defend the island's airstrip. They had built so many fortifications that the Japanese commander in the Gilberts boasted that a million men could not capture Tarawa in a hundred years.

In fact, it took 5,600 U.S. Marines about three days to secure Betio. Following a period of preparatory bombing to soften the Japanese defenses, the Marines started coming ashore on November 20, 1943. Unfortunately, some of their landing craft became stuck on a coral reef, forcing the soldiers to wade through the surf under heavy enemy fire. As they moved inland, the Marines

Ships of the U.S. Pacific Fleet bombard an island in the Palau chain in preparation for a Marine landing, 1944.

found that the Japanese defenders had dug protected caves and bunkers into hillsides. The U.S. troops had to eliminate these strongholds one by one, using grenades, flamethrowers, or hand-to-hand combat. About 1,000 Marines were killed and another 3,000 were wounded in the fierce fight for Tarawa.

After securing the Gilberts, Allied forces moved northwest to capture the Marshall and Caroline islands in early 1944. The next target of the island-hopping campaign was the Mariana chain to the northwest. The Marianas consisted of three main islands—Saipan, Tinian, and Guam. All three contained airfields that could enable American long-range bombers to reach Japan. For this reason, the Japanese sent a large naval force, featuring nine aircraft carriers and 500 planes, to Saipan in June 1944. But the American naval forces were so dominant that the ensuing battle became known as the "Great Marianas Turkey Shoot." Led by U.S. Navy Hellcat fighters, which matched up favorably with Japanese Zeros, American planes shot down 450 enemy aircraft while losing only 29 of their own.

On the evening of June 20, an American carrier task force under the command of Admiral Marc Mitscher discovered the location of the Japanese carriers. Knowing that the enemy had few planes left, the admiral launched 200 aircraft in pursuit. These planes destroyed three Japanese carriers, a battleship, and a cruiser. But the mission ended badly for the American flyers, as 80 of them had trouble locating and landing on the American aircraft carriers as darkness fell. Mitscher listened helplessly over the ship's radio as pilot after pilot either ran out of fuel and went down in the open ocean, or misjudged the landing and crashed into the carrier deck.

Despite such tragic setbacks, the fight for the Marianas was an important success for the Allies. The Japanese never recovered from the loss of so many planes and experienced pilots, and it left them in a weaker position to defend their other island territories. In addition, the capture of Saipan and Tinian gave U.S. bombers access to airfields within range of the Japanese home islands. A short time later, the Allies launched a bombing campaign that devastated many Japanese ports, cities, and factories.

Meanwhile, the Allies also went on the offensive in Europe, successfully landing 156,000 troops on the beaches of Normandy, France, on June 6, 1944. Although the Allied forces suffered heavy casualties in the invasion, it eventually led to the liberation of France. The Allies began reclaiming territory held by the Germans and pushing the enemy forces back toward Germany, just as they were doing against Japan in the Pacific.

MacArthur Returns to the Philippines

The Allied capture of the Marianas also cleared the way for General Douglas MacArthur and Admiral William "Bull" Halsey to move into the Philippines in 1944. MacArthur had been determined to return to the Philippines ever since he had been ordered to leave his troops behind and go to Australia in early 1942. While MacArthur's forces had fought their way from Port Moresby westward across the northern coast of New Guinea, Halsey's fleet had fought its way northwest from Guadalcanal through the Solomon and

General Douglas MacArthur (center) followed through on his promise to return to the Philippines in 1944.

Admiralty islands. By the fall of 1944, they were ready to come together for a combined land and sea assault on the Philippines.

The U.S. plan for recapturing the Philippines involved landing troops on the southernmost island of Leyte, then moving north toward the main island of Luzon and the capital of Manila. When MacArthur's forces landed on Leyte on October 20, 1944, the Japanese sent a fleet of ships to repulse the invasion. A few days later, one of the largest naval battles in history took place in

Leyte Gulf. Once again, air power proved to be the key to a victory at sea. The lack of aircraft and experienced pilots on board the Japanese carriers put them at a serious disadvantage. In many cases, American dive bombers and torpedo bombers were able to attack the Japanese ships at will. The lopsided battle cost Japan four aircraft carriers, three battleships, and nineteen other vessels. Embarrassed and discredited by the defeat, General Hideki Tojo resigned from his post as prime minister of Japan.

As MacArthur's forces marched northward toward Luzon, which was defended by an estimated 250,000 Japanese troops, some military strategists questioned the general's strategy. They argued that MacArthur should forget about Luzon and instead try to capture Formosa, an island to the north that held greater strategic value because it was closer to Japan. But the stubborn, opinionated general had sworn to return to the Philippines to help the men of his original command—many of whom were being held prisoner by the Japanese—and there was no way to change his mind.

The invasion of Luzon began on January 9, 1945. MacArthur had 200,000 American and Australian troops at his disposal, as well as Halsey's task force for air and naval support. To the surprise of Allied commanders, the initial landing force of 68,000 Marines did not face any resistance. They moved quickly across the island and surrounded Manila by the end of the month. The city was held by 17,000 elite Japanese troops who engaged the Americans in street warfare. But their resistance was not enough to stem the Allied tide. MacArthur entered Manila on February 23, and by March 3 his forces had secured the capital.

The Battle of Iwo Jima

By mid-1944, the Allies were making such good progress in the Pacific that U.S. military leaders started planning for an eventual invasion of Japan. Although they had begun conducting bombing raids on the Japanese home islands from air bases in the Marianas, only the long-range B-29 Superfortress bombers were capable of making the 3,000-mile roundtrip flight. The distance prevented the B-29s from carrying a full payload of heavy explosives and also restricted the use of fighter plane escorts. American planners decided that they needed to establish bases closer to the Japanese home islands in order to bomb Japan more effectively and protect the ships that would eventually transport troops for an invasion.

The most obvious choice for such a base was Iwo Jima, a small volcanic island located about 700 miles from Japan along a direct flight path from the Marianas. Other than its valuable airfield, which the Japanese used to harass the American B-29s on their way to and from bombing raids, it had little to offer the Allies. Iwo Jima was a remote, barren, rocky place that smelled like rotten eggs. In fact, its name meant "Sulphur Island" in Japanese. "Iwo Jima was a rude, ugly sight," recalled Lieutenant David N. Susskind, who arrived on the troopship *Mellette*. "Only a geologist could look at it and not be repelled."[3] Still, the Allies knew that capturing Iwo Jima would deal en enormous psychological blow to the enemy.

Admiral Nimitz's fleet began bombing Iwo Jima heavily from offshore in November 1944. Many sailors were heartened to see old, familiar battleships like the *Nevada*—which had been raised from the bottom of Pearl Harbor—taking part in the naval attack. After several weeks of preparatory bombing, American planners felt confident that most of the Japanese defenses had been destroyed, and they expected the invasion forces to meet with little opposition.

But the 27,000 Japanese troops holding Iwo Jima were led by General Tadamichi Kuribayashi, a fifth-generation samurai warrior and an experienced and innovative commander. Under his command, the Japanese had dug an extensive network of defensive fortifications into the island's soft, volcanic rock. This network of 1,500 rooms, connected by sixteen miles of tunnels, allowed the Japanese forces to remain hidden underground throughout the bombing. The fortifications also made it extremely difficult to dislodge the Japanese soldiers when the Allies launched their ground invasion of the island. "Masked gun positions provided interlocking fields of fire, miles of tunnels linked key defensive positions, every cave featured multiple outlets and ventilation tubes," one historian noted. "The Americans would rarely see a live Japanese on Iwo Jima until the bitter end."[4]

A force of 30,000 U.S. Marines landed on Iwo Jima on February 19, 1945. They faced a series of difficulties from the beginning of the invasion. A number of landing craft ran into a coral reef offshore, overturned in the surf, or got stuck in the loose sand near the beach. Many of those that made it on shore were ripped apart by enemy fire or hidden land mines. Some soldiers recalled that the large number of damaged vehicles made the landing zone look like a salvage yard. In the midst of this chaos, it took the first wave of Marines about forty-five minutes to get from their transports to the beach. As they waded slowly through mounds of volcanic ash, they were exposed to

U.S. Marines plant an American flag at the top of Mount Suribachi during the Battle for Iwo Jima in February 1945.

heavy fire from Japanese troops hidden in caves, underground bunkers, and small concrete shelters known as "pillboxes."

Once ashore, the Marines' first priority was to capture Mount Suribachi, a dormant volcano that loomed over the beach. It took three days of bloody fighting to dislodge the Japanese defenders from their dug-in positions. On February 23—the same day that MacArthur entered Manila—an exhausted but triumphant group of Marines raised an American flag on top of Mount Suribachi. A photographer for the Associated Press, Joe Rosenthal, happened to capture the moment on film. This famous picture became an important fund-raising and recruiting tool for the U.S. military, as well as a symbol of the courage and patriotism of American soldiers.

> *"Among the Americans who served on Iwo Island, uncommon valor was a common virtue," said U.S. Navy Admiral Chester W. Nimitz.*

The battle for Iwo Jima lasted for another month after the capture of Mount Suribachi, however. Kuribayashi demanded that his troops fight to the death, and the Japanese soldiers obeyed this command. The Marines made a slow, tension-filled advance across the island, often coming under fire from hidden enemy troops. As they moved forward, they used flamethrowers, hand grenades, and explosive charges to destroy hundreds of underground bunkers. By the time Iwo Jima was declared secure on March 26, 6,800 Americans had lost their lives, 25,000 had been wounded, and 3,000 had broken down from combat fatigue. An impressive 24 servicemen who fought at Iwo Jima received the Congressional Medal of Honor for bravery, prompting Admiral Nimitz to remark, "Among the Americans who served on Iwo Island, uncommon valor was a common virtue." His words were engraved at the base of the U.S. Marine Corps War Memorial—a bronze sculpture of the flag-raising created by artist Felix de Weldon—in Arlington, Virginia.

The Battle of Okinawa

Even before the invasion of Iwo Jima had been completed, U.S. military leaders began preparing to launch an amphibious assault on their next target: Okinawa. This island was located 370 miles south of Japan, along a direct flight path from the Philippines. It offered the Allies a number of strategic advantages, including several airfields and natural harbors. American officials felt that Okinawa would provide an excellent staging ground for the naval fleets, air forces, and ground troops that would be needed to mount an invasion of the Japanese home islands.

On March 14, 1945, U.S. naval forces began bombing Okinawa to soften its defenses. During the two weeks of preparatory bombing, as well as the nearly three months of ground combat, the American ships faced a constant threat of suicide attacks by Japanese planes. As Japan's position grew increasingly desperate, its leaders resorted to sending young, untrained pilots known as *kamikazes* to crash their planes into enemy ships (see "Japanese Kamikazes," p. 100). "Their only hope was to make the war so costly for the Americans that an honorable peace could be made before the homeland was invaded,"[5] explained one historian. Some soldiers aboard the U.S. ships felt so helpless in the face of kamikaze attacks that they preferred to take their chances against the Japanese on land instead.

U.S. Marines began landing on the beaches of Okinawa on April 1, 1945. As in earlier island warfare, they faced Japanese forces hidden in elaborate systems of bunkers and tunnels. Once again, the Marines advanced slowly—sometimes gaining only about 100 yards of territory per day—against the entrenched and determined enemy troops. Some of the fiercest fighting took place on the south end of the island, where the Japanese had established a strong defensive line at a medieval structure called Shuri Castle. The Allies finally broke through and captured Okinawa on June 22. Although 12,000 Americans died in the battle, this number paled in comparison to the 70,000 Japanese soldiers and 100,000 civilians who were killed.

While the battle raged on Okinawa, the American forces were saddened to hear that President Franklin D. Roosevelt died of a brain hemorrhage on April 12. His vice president, Harry S. Truman, took over as commander in chief. A few weeks later, the fighting forces in the Pacific and the American people were thrilled to learn that the Allies had emerged victorious in Europe. In early 1945, Allied forces had fought their way toward Germany from the west while Russian troops applied pressure from the east. When they moved into Poland, the Allied forces discovered the Nazi concentration camps where millions of Jews had been murdered in the Holocaust. As the Allied troops neared the German capital of Berlin in late April, Nazi leader Adolf Hitler decided to kill himself rather than be captured. Germany officially surrendered on May 8, known as Victory in Europe or V-E Day. Japan thus lost its main ally, while the United States gained the ability to focus its full attention on the Pacific theater.

Japanese Kamikazes

By 1945 Allied forces were sweeping across the Pacific toward the Japanese home islands. Japan was on the defensive and starting to get desperate. Much of its once-formidable navy had been destroyed, and thousands of its experienced pilots had been lost in combat. Japanese leaders decided that their only hope was to make the war so costly for the Allies that they would grow tired of fighting and negotiate a peace agreement.

The main weapon that remained in Japan's arsenal was the fanatical commitment of its soldiers. In nearly every ground battle on remote Pacific islands, Japanese troops proved that they were willing to die for their country. When cornered with no chance of escape, they often made desperate *banzai* rushes to try to kill as many enemy soldiers as possible before they died. Many others committed *hara-kiri* (ritual suicide) rather than suffer the indignity of surrendering or being captured.

As Allied naval forces moved into Japanese waters, Japanese leaders came up with a new tactic that took advantage of their soldiers' commitment. With few experienced pilots and no time to fully train new ones, they created a force of *kamikaze* ("divine wind") pilots. These novice fliers were very young—sometimes just teenagers—but they were eager to sac-

Japan Refuses to Give Up

As soon as they took control of Iwo Jima and Okinawa, the United States and its allies began using the islands' airfields to pummel Japan with bombs. Some of the attacks used incendiary bombs that started huge fires in Japanese cities. On March 9, for instance, an incendiary attack destroyed 95 percent of the capital city of Tokyo, or sixteen square miles of homes, offices, and factories. An estimated 100,000 people were killed, and millions more fled the city to hide in the surrounding mountains and countryside. Similar raids hit sixty-seven Japanese cities before the end of the war.

Meanwhile, Allied naval forces moved further into Japanese waters. American minelayers placed explosive devices in Japanese harbors, while Allied submarines patrolled the shorelines and shipping lanes. These efforts rifice their lives for their country. They were trained to take off in older planes that were filled with bombs, and then crash their aircraft into enemy ships in a way that would cause the most damage. They left airfields in Japan without enough fuel to return and carried out suicide missions against the American fleet.

During the last few months of the Pacific War, the U.S. Navy faced a constant threat of kamikaze attacks. The Japanese used this tactic with devastating results during the battle of Okinawa, sinking 16 Allied vessels, damaging 150 more, and taking the lives of 5,000 American sailors. "The Kamikaze would become the nightmare of American naval personnel," noted one historian. "Their fanatical determination made it virtually impossible to stop them with conventional air and naval defense tactics. Kamikaze attacks would wreak more damage on American task forces than any of the previous surface engagements. Perhaps most important, when combined with the Banzai land attack psychology, the Kamikaze indicated the lengths to which the Japanese intended to go to stop the American advance toward the Japanese Home Islands."

Source: Welsh, Douglas. *The USA in World War II: The Pacific Theater.* New York: Galahad Books, 1982, p. 50.

cut off the supply of raw materials between the Japanese islands, causing extreme shortages of food and fuel and bringing industry to a standstill.

American bombers even dropped pamphlets on Japanese cities that explained the dire circumstances facing the nation and encouraged the Japanese people to give up. But Japanese leaders continued to resist calls to surrender. In fact, they seemed prepared to accept the terrible losses that an Allied invasion of the home islands would bring, in hopes that fighting one last "decisive" battle might enable them to end the war on more favorable terms. "We can no longer direct the war with any hope of success," acknowledged the *War Journal of the Imperial Headquarters.* "The only course left is for Japan's one hundred million people to sacrifice their lives by charging the enemy to make them lose the will to fight."[6]

Japan's refusal to consider surrendering weighed heavily on the minds of Allied leaders as they tried to figure out the best way to end the Pacific War. The fierce battles for Iwo Jima and Okinawa, and the Japanese use of kamikaze pilots, convinced President Truman that Japan was determined to fight to the bitter end, regardless of the cost. He worried that an Allied invasion of the Japanese home islands could cost up to one million American lives.

Truman Drops the Atomic Bomb

These concerns led Truman to consider using a newly developed weapon—the atomic bomb—to end the war against Japan more quickly. The idea of harnessing the energy of the tiny particles known as atoms was first suggested by the famous physicist Albert Einstein in 1939. President Roosevelt and British leader Winston Churchill agreed to collaborate on a top-secret project to use this energy to create a powerful explosive device. Known as the Manhattan Project, it was carried out by a group of top scientists and engineers from the United States and Great Britain under the leadership of physicist J. Robert Oppenheimer. Only a few top government officials in both countries knew about the project. In fact, Truman did not learn about the development of the atomic bomb until after he took office. On April 25, 1945, Secretary of War Henry Stimson informed the new president that the United States now possessed "the most terrible weapon ever known in human history."[7]

Scientists successfully tested the first atomic bomb in the desert near Alamagordo, New Mexico, on July 16. Truman and his advisors then debated about the morality of using such a powerful weapon against Japanese cities, where many of the people affected would be civilians, including women and children. For a while, Truman considered telling Japanese leaders about the atomic bomb. He hoped that the mere threat of using it would persuade them to give up. In the end, though, the president made the grave decision to use the atomic bomb if Japan did not agree to the Allied terms of surrender.

On July 26, Truman and other Allied leaders issued the Potsdam Declaration, a document that outlined the terms of unconditional surrender that Japan must accept in order to end the war. It demanded that Japan agree to: completely disarm and disband its military forces; submit to a period of military occupation; remove all leaders responsible for the nation's imperialist aggression from positions of authority and influence in government; limit the boundaries of its sovereignty to the four main Japanese islands of Honshu,

A mushroom cloud rises over Nagasaki, Japan, after a U.S. plane dropped an atomic bomb on August 9, 1945.

Hokkaido, Kyushu, and Shikoku; and turn over war criminals for prosecution by the Allies.

Although these conditions were tough, the Potsdam Declaration also contained language that was designed to make the agreement more acceptable to the Japanese. For instance, the Allies promised to support democracy and industry in the new Japan. But the document ended by presenting Japanese leaders with an ultimatum. If they did not agree to the terms and surrender, it would result in "the inevitable and complete destruction of the Japanese armed forces and just as inevitably the utter devastation of the Japanese homeland." Japanese leaders chose to ignore this threat and refused to accept the Potsdam Declaration.

When this last attempt at a diplomatic solution fell through, Truman approved the use of an atomic bomb. On August 6, 1945, an American B-29 Superfortress bomber called the *Enola Gay,* piloted by Colonel Paul Tibbets, left the airbase at Tinian in the early morning hours. The plane arrived over its target, the Japanese city of Hiroshima, and dropped the bomb known as "Little Boy" at 8:11 A.M. The detonation reduced 80 percent of the city's buildings to rubble within seconds. An estimated 70,000 people were killed instantly, and the number eventually reached 200,000 as others succumbed to injuries or radiation poisoning.

Since only three enemy planes had appeared on radar (the *Enola Gay* was accompanied by two other planes carrying scientific and photographic equipment to record the explosion), Japanese leaders initially dismissed rumors that Hiroshima had been destroyed in an air raid. Before long, though, workers at the Japanese Broadcasting Corporation noticed that Hiroshima's radio station had suddenly gone off the air. Then military leaders who tried to contact the army control center in Hiroshima got no response, so they sent a reconnaissance plane to investigate. The crew saw a huge, mushroom-shaped cloud of smoke and confirmed that the city had been destroyed by a huge explosion. "Practically all living things, human and animal, were literally seared to death," a Tokyo radio station reported.

A short time later, President Truman announced to the world that the United States had dropped an atomic bomb on Japan. He warned Japanese leaders that "if they do not now accept our terms they may expect a rain of ruin from the air, the like of which has never been seen on earth." Still, Japanese government officials refused to consider an unconditional surrender. They discussed imposing several conditions, including no occupation of the Japanese home islands by Allied forces, assuming responsibility for their own disarmament, and preserving the status of the Emperor as the sacred ruler of Japan. They even considered approaching Russian leader Joseph Stalin and asking him to mediate a peace agreement on their behalf.

The response from Stalin came in loud and clear on August 8, when Russia rejected the neutrality agreement it had signed in 1941 and declared war on Japan. The following day, Russian troops launched an offensive into Manchuria, a disputed region of China that had been the first target of Japanese expansion. As Japanese leaders absorbed the fact that they faced attack from another side, the United States dropped a second atomic bomb, dubbed

A Japanese delegation prepares to sign the official instrument of surrender during a ceremony on board the battleship USS *Missouri,* September 2, 1945.

"Fat Man," on the city of Nagasaki. It was delivered by a B-29 bomber called *Bockscar* flown by Major Charles W. Sweeney. Detonating with the explosive power of twenty-one kilotons of dynamite, and producing heat up to 7,000 degrees Fahrenheit, it flattened every structure within a mile radius in the old port city and resulted in the immediate death of about 70,000 people.

Japan Surrenders

The combination of the Russian offensive and the threat of more atomic bombs finally convinced Emperor Hirohito to take action. The Japanese ruler asked officials in his government to end the war. Hard-line military leaders still resisted the idea of unconditional surrender, though, and they engaged in a tense power struggle with officials who wanted to accept the Allied terms. Finally, on August 14, Japanese leaders formally agreed to surrender, although they did request that the Emperor be allowed to remain on his throne.

Shortly after receiving word from Japan, a triumphant President Truman announced that World War II was over, and the Allies had prevailed (see "President Harry S. Truman Announces the End of the War," p. 203). He proclaimed a national holiday to celebrate the Victory over Japan, or V-J Day. The American people greeted the news with great joy and relief. Spontaneous celebrations took place across the country and around the world. Many people felt proud that the country had punished Japan for the attack on Pearl Harbor. "Although the United States was caught unprepared for war, its resources and the grim determination of the American people in a time of crisis carried the nation to ultimate victory,"[8] declared one historian.

U.S. Secretary of War Henry Stimson described the atomic bomb as "the most terrible weapon ever known in human history."

On August 15 in Tokyo, Emperor Hirohito addressed the Japanese people over the radio to announce that the hostilities had ended in his country's defeat. He ordered all Japanese citizens to cooperate with the Allied occupation of Japan. Until this time, Japanese leaders had not shared much information with the public about the nation's dwindling prospects in the war. The news of the surrender thus came as a terrible shock to many Japanese. They were a proud and patriotic people with a strong warrior tradition, so many felt disgraced by the surrender.

Over the next two weeks, the Allies celebrated their victory, recovered prisoners of war, and prepared for the occupation of Japan. Representatives of the Japanese government formally signed the instrument of surrender in a special ceremony held on September 2, 1945, aboard the battleship USS *Missouri* in Tokyo Bay (see "Japan Surrenders," p. 200). General MacArthur, as the Supreme Commander of the Allied Powers, presided over the simple, half-hour ceremony.

Accompanied on the deck of the ship by Admirals Nimitz and Halsey, MacArthur made a gracious speech in which he expressed hope for a peaceful and prosperous future: "It is my earnest hope, and indeed the hope of all mankind, that from this solemn occasion a better world shall

106

emerge out of the blood and carnage of the past—a world dedicated to the dignity of man and the fulfillment of his most cherished wish for freedom, tolerance, and justice."[9]

Notes

1 Anderson, Charles R. "Guadalcanal." Brochure prepared for the U.S. Army Center of Military History, 2003. Available online at http://www.history.army.mil/brochures/72-8/72-8.htm.
2 Welsh, Douglas. *The USA in World War II: The Pacific Theater.* New York: Galahad Books, 1982, p. 38.
3 Quoted in Alexander, Joseph H. "Closing In: Marines in the Seizure of Iwo Jima." From *Marines in World War II Commemorative Series,* National Park Service, War in the Pacific National Historical Park, Guam. Available online at http://www.nps.gov/archive/wapa/indepth/extContent/usmc/pcn-190-003131-00/index.htm.
4 Alexander, "Closing In: Marines in the Seizure of Iwo Jima."
5 Welsh, p. 57.
6 Quoted in Frank, Richard B. *Downfall: The End of the Imperial Japanese Empire.* New York: Penguin, 1999, p. 89.
7 Quoted in Burr, William, ed. "The Atomic Bomb and the End of World War II." National Security Archive, George Washington University, 2005. Available online at http://www.gwu.edu/~nsarchiv/NSAEBB/NSAEBB162/index.htm.
8 Welsh, p. 63.
9 Quoted in "MacArthur's Speeches: Surrender Ceremony on the U.S.S. Missouri," *PBS: The American Experience.* Available online at http://www.pbs.org/wgbh/amex/macarthur/filmmore/reference/.

Chapter Seven
LEGACY OF PEARL HARBOR

The impact of Pearl Harbor was such that an entire generation of Americans tended to regard December 7, 1941, as the
beginning of a new era in world history.

—Gordon Prange, *At Dawn We Slept*

The legacy of the Japanese attack on Pearl Harbor extended far beyond the
end of World War II. The crisis—and America's response to it—had an
enduring impact on the nation's position in the world, its outlook on
world events, and its foreign policy decisions for decades to come. While conducting research for a book published sixty years after the attack, historian Dan
Van der Vat recalled being struck "by how deeply the disaster had penetrated
the American psyche despite the overwhelming U.S. victory in 1945, and how
powerful it remains as a folk memory, with demonstrable influence on the foreign and defense policy of past and present Washington administrations."[1]

The United States Becomes a Superpower

The end of World War II ushered in a period of fast-paced and far-reaching change in the United States and around the world. "The bombs that hit
Pearl Harbor unleashed forces that produced a quarter century of the vastest
changes the world has ever known," noted a *U.S. News and World Report* article published on the twenty-fifth anniversary of the Japanese attack. "Since
that morning, man has tamed atoms, moved into space, surged ahead in
unprecedented prosperity in many parts of the world. Empires have vanished,
maps changed, centers of power shifted. And a whole new set of problems has
replaced the problems of the past."[2]

The Marine Corps War Memorial in Arlington, Virginia, features a bronze statue of the famous flag-raising on Iwo Jima during the Pacific War.

In the midst of all these changes, though, the United States emerged as an undisputed world power. One reason for this emergence was that, other than the Japanese attack on Pearl Harbor, no major battles took place on American soil during World War II. While many nations in Europe and Asia saw their cities, factories, and infrastructure destroyed, the United States largely escaped physical damage. In addition, wartime production had a positive impact on the U.S. economy. The high unemployment and widespread poverty of the Great Depression gave way to an industrial boom once the nation entered the war. Following the Pearl Harbor attack, American factories worked around the clock to produce ships, planes, tanks, guns, uniforms, and other materials for the Allied war effort. By the end of the war, the nation had built 80,000 ships and 300,000 planes, and millions of Americans had found high-paying manufacturing jobs that raised their standard of living.

Of course, the American people did make sacrifices. About 16 million Americans served in the armed forces during World War II, and about 400,000 were killed and another 500,000 wounded. But the Allied victory allowed the families of these soldiers to take pride in the fact that their loved ones had helped stop fascism and spread democracy in the world. The United States demonstrated its military and industrial strength and emerged from the conflict with tremendous international prestige and respect. In this way, as one historian noted, "today's military, economic, and cultural superpower was born"[3] through the Pearl Harbor attack.

Investigations and Blame

Although the war ended in an Allied victory, interest in the causes and consequences of the Pearl Harbor attack remained high among U.S. government officials and the American people. A total of six official investigations took place during and after the war. The most extensive was convened by the Congressional Pearl Harbor Joint Committee on November 15, 1945. After reviewing the results of previous inquiries and collecting 30 volumes of transcribed testimony, the committee released a 500-page report—with 15,000 additional pages of documentation and exhibits—on July 20, 1946.

Like the other investigations, the committee found that the officers responsible for defending Pearl Harbor had made errors in judgment and failed to prepare for a possible attack. The report placed some of the blame on military planners in Washington, but ultimately held Admiral Husband E.

Kimmel and General Walter C. Short accountable. "It can fairly be concluded that there was a complete failure in Hawaii of effective Army-Navy liaison [coordination] during the critical period ... and no integration of Army and Navy facilities and efforts for defense. Neither of the responsible commanders really knew what the other was doing with respect to essential military activities," the report concluded. "No one in authority appreciated the danger to which Pearl Harbor was exposed and consequently the Army and Navy commanders ... were preoccupied with training activities to the exclusion of adequate alertness against attack."[4]

By the time the Congressional Joint Committee issued its report, a number of conspiracy theories had surfaced to explain the American forces' lack of advance warning or preparation for the attack. Some critics, who eventually became known as revisionists, claimed that President Roosevelt or British Prime Minister Winston Churchill knew about the Japanese plans beforehand and allowed the attack to happen in order to increase public support for the United States to enter World War II. Some even suggested that the Roosevelt administration intentionally used diplomatic means—such as placing the embargo on oil and gasoline—to lure Japan into a confrontation. Questions and controversies continued to swirl around the Pearl Harbor attack for many years, but none of the official investigations ever uncovered solid evidence to support the revisionist point of view.

> *"No one in authority appreciated the danger to which Pearl Harbor was exposed and consequently the Army and Navy commanders ... were preoccupied with training activities to the exclusion of adequate alertness against attack."*

In the wake of its investigation, the U.S. Congress passed several laws that were intended to prevent the nation from falling victim to a similar sneak attack in the future. One such law, the National Security Act of 1947, established the Central Intelligence Agency (CIA) to oversee the collection and evaluation of spy information about other countries. Centralizing foreign intelligence gathering was supposed to help eliminate some of the breakdowns in communication, misinterpretation of signals, and problems comparing information from different sources that had enabled the Japanese to achieve tactical surprise.

Unfortunately, some of the same problems occurred sixty years later. The CIA came under intense criticism in 2001 for failing to predict or prevent the September 11 terrorist attack that destroyed the World Trade Center towers in New York City and damaged the Pentagon building in Washington, D.C.

Many analysts pointed out similarities between the 9/11 attack and Pearl Harbor. Both attacks were carried out by enemies who felt contempt for the United States and resented an American military presence in their region of the world, for instance, and both attacks shocked and outraged the American people and united them against a common enemy. "Four commercial jetliners, three of them hitting their intended targets, changed our view of the world on September 11, 2001, just as surely as did the bombs falling from Japanese planes on December 7, 1941,"[5] noted one historian.

The Occupation and Reconstruction of Japan

As the United States continued to deconstruct the events surrounding Pearl Harbor after the war, it also engaged in a military occupation of Japan. Led by General Douglas MacArthur as Supreme Commander of the Allied Powers (SCAP), the main goal was to make sure that the defeated nation never again posed a threat to its neighbors, to the United States, or to world peace. During the first stage of the occupation, therefore, MacArthur dismantled Japan's armed forces and military production capacity. He also removed thousands of people who had supported the policy of imperialist aggression from positions of power in government and industry. A number of top Japanese officials were put on trial for war crimes, and Hideki Tojo and six others were executed. Emperor Hirohito and his family agreed to cooperate with the occupation forces, so they escaped punishment.

Another important aspect of the occupation involved helping Japan recover from the war. Two million Japanese soldiers had lost their lives in the conflict, and most major cities in Japan had suffered significant damage from Allied bombing, particularly Hiroshima and Nagasaki. Transportation and communication networks had been disrupted throughout the Japanese home islands, and few areas had working electricity or sanitation. Millions of Japanese citizens were displaced or homeless, and they suffered from severe shortages of food and other basic necessities. By the end of 1945 MacArthur had 350,000 U.S. troops stationed in Japan, and many of them were involved in providing food and humanitarian aid to the Japanese people.

The next step in the occupation involved introducing democratic reforms to Japan's government and culture. MacArthur oversaw the creation of a new constitution that took effect on May 3, 1947. It stripped away all of the emperor's political authority and established an elected parliament, or

More than sixty years later, interest in the Pearl Harbor attack remained high in both the United States and Japan. In this 2008 photo, a Japanese delegation from Nagaoka City—birthplace of attack planner Isoroku Yamamoto—pays their respects during a visit to the USS *Arizona* memorial.

Diet, instead. The constitution also formally renounced war and gave many new civil rights and liberties to the Japanese people. For example, all citizens over the age of twenty received the right to vote—including women for the first time in the nation's history. Japan's first modern prime minister, Shigeru Yoshida, was elected on April 10, 1946.

Many other reforms focused on redistributing property and wealth to the Japanese people. MacArthur took land away from wealthy landlords and gave it to the small farmers who worked on it. He also gave industrial workers more power by allowing them to form trade unions. These economic changes helped individual citizens become more independent and participate in the new democracy. The occupation forces used their control of Japan's newspapers and radio stations to promote the changes and explain basic democratic principles to the Japanese people.

Although many Japanese felt saddened by the defeat and occupation of their country, most citizens accepted the changes that MacArthur instituted. Years of hardship and struggle during the war had left them disillusioned with the policies of the imperialist government, so they tended to be open to new ways of thinking. Of course, the occupation was unpopular in some respects. Some people resented its censorship of Japanese radio and newspapers. Other Japanese citizens angrily charged that the U.S. military authorities allowed—or even encouraged—prostitution to grow in Japanese cities. On the whole, however, the occupation was considered highly successful. MacArthur's supporters point out that most of the political and economic reforms made during that time have remained in place to the present day. In addition, Japan has maintained a peaceful, democratic government and a close alliance with the United States.

Japanese leaders signed the San Francisco Peace Treaty on September 8, 1951. When it took effect on April 28, 1952, the treaty ended seven years of foreign occupation and made Japan an independent nation once again. By this time, Japan's economy was in the midst of a remarkable recovery. Its Gross National Product (the total value of goods and services produced) increased from $1.3 billion in 1946 to $290 billion in 1972. Although the 1973 oil crisis took a heavy toll, Japanese leaders responded by shifting toward high-technology industries. Before the decade ended, Japan had become the world's leading manufacturer of televisions, calculators, and cameras, as well as a highly successful automobile producer.

The Cold War

As the United States came into its own as a world power, the nation also went through a period of self-examination and appraisal following World War II. American leaders wanted to learn from the Pearl Harbor attack in order to avoid making the same mistakes again in the future. One of the main lessons they internalized was that the nation always needed to remain vigilant and be prepared for a surprise preemptive strike. They decided that it was not safe for the United States to stand idly by while its enemies expanded their geographic and political reach. This view led to changes in U.S. foreign policy and national defense priorities that affected the whole world for the next fifty years.

One major change was in the relationship between the United States and its former ally, the Soviet Union. Although the two powerful nations had worked together to defeat Germany during World War II, many people on both sides suspected that the alliance would be temporary. After all, the countries had competing political philosophies and conflicting national goals and interests.

Adding to the potential for disagreement, the United States and the Soviet Union faced very different situations at the end of the war. While the United States emerged with little physical damage and a booming economy, the Soviet Union suffered greatly from the war's horrors. The long fight against Germany took the lives of 25 million Russians and destroyed 70,000 cities and towns. All across the Soviet Union, homes, farms, factories, roads, and railroad lines lay in ruins. Soviet leader Joseph Stalin felt that his country deserved to be repaid for the enormous sacrifices it made to help the Allied war effort. He grew angry when the United States seemed to dictate the terms of peace.

As the victorious Allies started working to recover and rebuild, the United States and the Soviet Union argued over how to deal with defeated Germany and Japan. Both nations were determined to protect their own interests and expand their spheres of influence around the world. This led to a period of intense military buildup and political rivalry known as the Cold War.

The first phase of the Cold War played out in Germany. Immediately after the war ended, Germany was divided into four zones occupied by troops from the United States, Great Britain, France, and the Soviet Union. The capital city of Berlin—located in the middle of the Soviet-occupied section of Germany—was also divided into four zones. Within a short time, the first three occupying powers combined their zones to form West Germany and West Berlin, while the Soviets continued to control East Germany and East Berlin.

The political rivalry between the United States and the Soviet Union prevented them from agreeing on a plan to reunify Germany. The situation grew tense in 1948-49, when Stalin established a blockade around Berlin. By cutting off outside access to the city, he hoped to force the United States and its allies to give up their claims on West Berlin. U.S. leaders responded by sending B-29 bombers to airlift supplies into the city. Many people feared that the standoff would escalate into war. Stalin ultimately backed down and lifted the blockade, but Berlin and Germany remained divided into the communist East and democratic West for decades.

The Cold War also led to armed conflicts in a number of small, developing nations that were collectively known as the Third World. At the end of World War II, some European powers tried to reclaim their former colonies in Asia, Africa, and Eastern Europe. But the turmoil of the war weakened the colonial powers and encouraged the people of these exploited nations to rise up and seek independence. Although some former colonies attempted to establish democratic governments, many others saw the rise of socialist or communist movements.

"Seldom if ever has a war ended leaving the victors with such a sense of uncertainty and fear," said the famous journalist Edward R. Murrow, "with such a realization that the future is obscure and that survival is not assured."

The postwar foreign policy of the United States emphasized "containment," or stopping the spread of communism to new parts of the world. American leaders wanted to prevent Third World countries from aligning themselves politically and economically with the Soviet Union. Meanwhile, the Soviets tried to keep the United States from installing pro-American governments in Third World nations. If one of the Cold War enemies provided funding or military equipment to a Third World government that supported its basic interests, the other would usually offer supplies to an anti-government faction. This situation led to wars in Korea, Vietnam, Angola, Afghanistan, and other countries from the 1950s onward. Before long, the entire world was divided into two opposing camps, based on whether they aligned themselves with the United States or the Soviet Union.

All of this political and military maneuvering took place against the backdrop of new developments in weapons technology. President Truman's decision to use atomic bombs against Japan ushered in the Atomic Age, and some observers argued that the world became less safe. "Seldom if ever has a war ended leaving the victors with such a sense of uncertainty and fear," said the famous journalist Edward R. Murrow, "with such a realization that the future is obscure and that survival is not assured."[6]

The Soviet Union detonated its first atomic bomb in 1949. From that time onward, the Cold War enemies entered a nuclear arms race. Both countries tried to build enough nuclear capacity to destroy the other. The eventual result was a tenuous balance of power, in which the possibility of deadly retaliation—known as "mutual assured destruction"—deterred both sides from launching a first strike.

Over time, the high cost of continually building new, advanced weapons systems took a heavy toll on the inefficient Soviet economy. In the late 1980s, protests erupted in Poland and other nations aimed at ending Soviet control over eastern Europe. Soviet authority crumbled in East Germany as well, and in 1990 all of Germany was reunited under a single, democratic government for the first time since World War II. As Soviet leaders looked on in disbelief, communist governments fell from power in several other countries. The Cold War finally ended in 1991, when the Soviet Union broke apart and its former members became independent states.

Remembering Pearl Harbor

"Remember Pearl Harbor" became a rallying cry for the American people during World War II. It also became an influential concept underlying U.S. foreign policy during the Cold War. Even in the twenty-first century, as President Roosevelt famously predicted, the date December 7, 1941, continues to "live in infamy." All across the country, Americans still honor the date by lowering flags to half-mast and observing moments of silence. The steady level of interest in understanding the attack and remembering its victims is also evident in the 1.5 million people who travel to Hawaii to visit the USS *Arizona* Memorial each year.

The memorial is a 184-foot-long structure spanning the midsection of the famous battleship that still lies at the bottom of Pearl Harbor. Architect Alfred Preis designed the unusually shaped white building, which is only accessible by boat. "Wherein the structure sags in the center but stands strong and vigorous at the ends, [it] expresses initial defeat and ultimate victory," Preis explained. "The overall effect is one of serenity. Overtones of sadness have been omitted to permit the individual to contemplate his own personal responses."[7]

This photograph of modern-day Pearl Harbor shows the aircraft carrier USS *Carl Vinson* pulling into port, with the USS *Arizona* Memorial in the foreground and the retired battleship USS *Missouri* in the center.

Funded by private donations, the USS *Arizona* Memorial was dedicated in 1962 and became a national park in 1980. It serves as a tomb for most of the 1,177 crew members who died when the battleship exploded (229 bodies were removed immediately after the attack), as well as a shrine for all the American servicemen who lost their lives in World War II.

An average of 4,500 visitors arrive at the memorial by tour boat each day, making it the most visited historic site in the country. Looking through the windows of the observation room, they can see the outline of the battleship beneath the surface, as well as turrets and anchor points still above water. The names of the victims of the Pearl Harbor attack are engraved in marble inside.

Decades of exposure to salt water and its status as an artificial reef for a community of fish and aquatic plants have taken a serious toll on the *Arizona*. Its hull has corroded and its upper decks have begun to collapse. Although oil has been leaking out in a slow but steady stream for years, environmentalists worry that the ship's deterioration might lead to the sudden release of up to a half-million gallons still trapped inside. Hoping to avoid an environmental disaster in Pearl Harbor, some people argue that the *Arizona* should undergo major preservation and repairs. But others claim that the ship should remain undisturbed out of respect for the Americans who lost their lives on December 7, 1941.

Notes

[1] Van der Vat, Dan. "Pearl Harbor Revisited." *History Today,* June 2001, p. 2.

[2] "25 Years After Pearl Harbor—An Attack That Remade the World," *U.S. News and World Report,* December 12, 1966, p. 47.

[3] Van der Vat, Dan. *Pearl Harbor: The Day of Infamy—An Illustrated History.* Toronto: Madison Press, 2001, p. 160.

[4] Quoted in Prange, Gordon W. *Pearl Harbor: The Verdict of History.* New York: McGraw-Hill, 1986, p. 397.

[5] O'Connell, Kim A. "The Ship That Bleeds." *National Parks,* November-December 2001, p. 18.

[6] Quoted in "The Atomic Age: From Fission to Fallout." *CNN Specials: The Cold War.* Available online at http://www.cnn.com/SPECIALS/cold.war/experience/the.bomb/history.science/.

[7] Quoted in National Park Service, "USS Arizona Memorial." Available online at http://www.nps.gov/archive/usar/extendweb1.html.

BIOGRAPHIES

Mitsuo Fuchida (1902-1976)
Japanese Naval Officer
Lead Pilot in the Japanese Attack on Pearl Harbor

Mitsuo Fuchida was born in Nara Prefecture, Japan, on December 2, 1902. He entered the Japanese Naval Academy at Eta Jima in 1921. Fuchida soon became interested in flying and began training as a pilot. He gained combat experience in the 1930s by providing air support for Japan's invasion of China. Fuchida demonstrated such tremendous skill and courage as a flyer that he was selected to become an instructor at the Naval Staff College.

In 1939 Fuchida was stationed on the aircraft carrier *Akagi*. He became acquainted with Isoroku Yamamoto, the commander in chief of the Japanese Combined Fleet, during this time. Fuchida found that Yamamoto shared his belief that carrier-based air power represented the future direction of naval warfare. Yamamoto used this belief as the basis for a daring plan to attack the U.S. Pacific Fleet at Pearl Harbor, Hawaii.

As this plan took shape in 1941, Fuchida was the most experienced pilot in the Japanese navy, with over 3,000 hours of flight experience. He had also impressed his superior officers with his calm demeanor and strong leadership skills. As a result, Fuchida was chosen to be the lead pilot in the attack on Pearl Harbor. "Fuchida had a very strong fighting spirit—his best quality," recalled Minoru Genda, one of the planners of the attack. "He was also a gifted leader with the ability to understand any situation and react to it quickly. He was not only our best flight leader but a good staff man as well—cooperative, with a clear head. The success of the Pearl Harbor attack depended on the character and ability of its flight leader, and that is why Fuchida was selected for the job."[1]

Leads the Attack on Pearl Harbor
In the months leading up to the attack, Fuchida oversaw the training of the Japanese pilots who would take part in the air raid. He put his pilots

through hours of low-level flying drills and horizontal bombing practice. By the time the Japanese carrier task force set sail for Hawaii on November 26, 1941, Fuchida had developed a crack team of pilots.

On the morning of December 7, the Japanese carriers reached Hawaiian waters and launched their planes. Fuchida led the first wave of 183 planes in a Nakajima B5N2 "Kate" bomber. As they neared the coast of Oahu at 7:40 A.M., Fuchida fired a flare to inform his pilots that they had achieved complete surprise and should proceed according to plan. Nine minutes later, with all the planes in attack formation, the commander told his pilots, "To, to, to!" (short for *totsugekiseyo,* which means "charge"). Fuchida also ordered his radio operator, Norinobu Mizuki, to send a famous message to be relayed back to Tokyo: "Tora, tora, tora!" This code word, meaning "tiger," informed Japanese military planners that their strategy had succeeded in catching the Americans off guard.

The first wave of the Japanese attack devastated the American air bases on Oahu and the ships of the U.S. Pacific Fleet anchored in Pearl Harbor. Fuchida recalled watching with excitement as his pilots bombed and torpedoed the American warships lined up on Battleship Row. "Like a hurricane out of nowhere, my torpedo planes, dive bombers, and fighters struck suddenly with indescribable fury," he wrote. "As smoke began to billow and the proud battleships, one by one, started tilting, my heart was almost ablaze with joy."[2]

Fuchida remained in the air above Oahu while the second wave of 167 Japanese planes continued the attack. Then he circled above Pearl Harbor to survey the damage before returning to his ship. "I counted four battleships definitely sunk and three severely damaged, and extensive damage had also been inflicted on other types of ships," he recalled. "The seaplane base at Ford Island was all in flames, as were the airfields, especially Wheeler Field."[3] Back on the deck of the *Akagi,* Fuchida found more than twenty holes in his plane from American antiaircraft fire.

The Pearl Harbor attack severely crippled U.S. military capacity in the Pacific while costing the Japanese only twenty-nine planes and fifty-five air crew. Fuchida argued that the Japanese should launch a third wave of planes to destroy fuel-storage tanks, ship-repair facilities, and other targets that had escaped damage. His superior officers decided that it would be too risky, however, and sailed back toward Japan.

Upon returning home, Fuchida was greeted as a national hero. He was even invited to meet Japan's sacred ruler, Emperor Hirohito, and tell him about the attack in person. Fuchida considered an audience with the emperor to be the highest possible honor for a Japanese citizen.

Becomes a Christian Missionary

In 1942 Fuchida continued leading carrier-based air raids against Allied targets in the Pacific. He was on board the *Akagi* during the Battle of Midway, but he was unable to fly because he was recovering from emergency surgery to remove his appendix. Fuchida disobeyed doctors' orders and went up on deck just as the ship came under attack by American bombers. He was thrown into the air by an explosion and broke both ankles when he landed.

For the remainder of the war Fuchida served as a staff officer and taught at the Naval Staff College. On August 5, 1945, he attended a military conference in Hiroshima. Fuchida was scheduled to stay over, but Japanese navy officials called him back to Tokyo. The next day, U.S. warplanes dropped an atomic bomb on the city, reducing 80 percent of the buildings to rubble and killing an estimated 70,000 people.

Japan surrendered to end the war on September 2, 1945. When the Japanese military was disbanded during the Allied occupation of Japan, Fuchida turned to farming to feed his family. In 1948, while getting off a train in Tokyo to testify in a war-crimes trial, Fuchida was handed a pamphlet that changed his life.

It was written by a Free Methodist missionary named Jacob DeShazer. DeShazer was a former member of the U.S. Army Air Force who bombed Tokyo in 1942 as part of the famous Doolittle Raid. After parachuting to the ground when his plane ran out of fuel, DeShazer was captured by Japanese troops. He spent forty months in a prisoner-of-war camp being starved and tortured by Japanese soldiers. During this ordeal, he converted to Christianity, forgave his captors, and promised to return to Japan as a missionary.

Fuchida felt drawn to the message of forgiveness in DeShazer's pamphlet. He began reading the Bible and soon converted to Christianity. Fuchida felt that he had survived several close calls during the war because he was meant to do something important with his life. He joined DeShazer's mission and dedicated himself to spreading a message of hope and forgiveness. "Christianity has opened my eyes," he declared, "and I hope through Christ to help the young people of Japan learn a great love for America."[4]

Fuchida's spiritual awakening led him to reassess the war and his role in it. "I would give anything to retract my actions … at Pearl Harbor, but it is impossible," he noted. "Instead, I now work at striking the death-blow to the basic hatred which infests the human heart and causes such tragedies. And that hatred cannot be uprooted without assistance from Jesus Christ."[5]

Fuchida published several books and articles based on his wartime experiences. One of these works, 1951's *Midway: The Battle That Doomed Japan*, tells the story of the decisive battle from the Japanese perspective. Fuchida also served as the subject of a biography by World War II historian Gordon W. Prange called *God's Samurai: Lead Pilot at Pearl Harbor*. Fuchida died of complications from diabetes on May 30, 1976, in Kashiwara, Japan.

Sources

Fuchida, Mitsuo, and Masatake Okumiya. *Midway: The Battle that Doomed Japan—The Japanese Navy's Story*. Annapolis, MD: U.S. Naval Institute Press, 2001.

Prange, Gordon W., Donald Goldstein, and Katherine V. Dillon. *God's Samurai: Lead Pilot at Pearl Harbor*. Washington, D.C.: Potomac Books, 2003.

Seamands, David. "The Kamikaze of God." *Christianity Today*, December 3, 2001. Available online at http://www.christianitytoday.com/ct/2001/december3/7.58.html.

Notes

[1] Prange, Gordon W. *At Dawn We Slept: The Untold Story of Pearl Harbor*. New York: McGraw-Hill, 1981, p. 196.

[2] Fuchida, Mitsuo. "From Pearl Harbor to Calvary." Available online at http://www.biblebelievers.com/fuchida1.html.

[3] Quoted in Harris, Nathaniel. *A Day That Made History: Pearl Harbor*. North Pomfret, VT: David and Charles, 1986, p. 32.

[4] "Pearl Harbor Pilot a Missionary." *New York Times*, October 31, 1952, p. 17.

[5] Fuchida, "From Pearl Harbor to Calvary."

Husband E. Kimmel (1882-1968)
U.S. Navy Admiral
Commander of the U.S. Pacific Fleet during the
Pearl Harbor Attack

Husband Edward Kimmel was born in Henderson, a small town in northwestern Kentucky, on February 26, 1882. His father, Manning Marius Kimmel, graduated from the U.S. Military Academy at West Point, fought in the Civil War, and later became a civil engineer. His mother, Sibbella Lambert Kimmel, was a homemaker.

Throughout his youth, Kimmel always wanted to follow in his father's footsteps and make a career in the military. He was deeply disappointed when he was not accepted to West Point. After attending Central University in Kentucky for a year, however, Kimmel received an appointment to the U.S. Naval Academy in Annapolis, Maryland, in 1900. He graduated near the top of his class in 1904. Kimmel continued his education at the Naval War College in Newport, Rhode Island, where he became an expert in ordnance and gunnery on the heavily armed battleships that were then being built for the U.S. Navy.

Over the next decade, Kimmel served tours of duty on several ships and gradually moved up in rank. In 1912 he married Dorothy Kinkaid, the daughter of an admiral. They eventually had three sons, Manning, Thomas, and Edward. When the United States entered World War I in 1917, Kimmel was sent to England to help the British Navy improve its gunnery techniques. After the war ended in 1918, Kimmel returned to active duty in the United States. His assignments included serving as commander of a destroyer division and as captain of the battleship *New York*. He also held several prestigious posts in the office of the chief of naval operations in Washington, D.C. In 1937 Kimmel was promoted to the rank of rear admiral.

On February 1, 1941, President Franklin D. Roosevelt formally divided the U.S. Fleet into Atlantic and Pacific divisions. Most Navy resources were focused on the Atlantic Fleet, which was dedicated to stopping the German submarines known as U-boats that disrupted transatlantic shipping of supplies to the Allied forces fighting World War II in Europe. Somewhat to his surprise, Kimmel was named commander in chief of the Pacific Fleet, head-quartered in Pearl Harbor, Hawaii. Navy officials bypassed several admirals with more seniority in order to give Kimmel the job.

Fails to Prepare for the Japanese Attack

At the time Kimmel took charge of the Pacific Fleet, its main purpose was to act as a deterrent against Japanese aggression. Japanese military leaders wanted to expand their territory and build an empire in Asia and the Pacific. U.S. leaders viewed Japan as a growing threat, and many believed that the two nations would eventually go to war. But President Roosevelt wanted to avoid war with Japan as long as possible in order to concentrate on helping the Allies defeat Germany. He held diplomatic negotiations with Japan while also building up the nation's defenses in the Pacific.

By the fall of 1941, many U.S. military leaders felt that war with Japan was imminent, but they did not specifically express concerns about an attack on the center of U.S. Pacific defenses in Hawaii. Instead, most believed that Japan would target areas of southeast Asia or the Pacific that were not well defended. When diplomatic negotiations between the United States and Japan broke down on November 27, Kimmel received a "war warning" from Navy officials in Washington, D.C., suggesting that they expected a Japanese attack on the Philippines, Thailand, or Borneo.

Kimmel and his Army counterpart in Hawaii, General Walter C. Short, put a few measures in place to increase Pearl Harbor's defenses in case of a Japanese attack. They agreed to operate an Army radar station for longer periods each day and take precautions to prevent sabotage by local people of Japanese descent. But they did not believe the threat of attack was great enough to put their forces on full alert, place protective torpedo nets around the ships in Pearl Harbor, or increase aerial patrols of likely attack routes.

As a result, Kimmel and all of the sailors under his command were caught off guard on the morning of December 7, 1941, when Japanese planes launched a surprise attack on Hawaii. The attack devastated the Pacific Fleet, sinking or severely damaging 21 warships. The air raid also took the lives of 2,388 Americans. Nearly 2,000 of those killed were members of the U.S. Navy under Kimmel's command.

Held Responsible for Pearl Harbor

As the top U.S. naval commander in the Pacific, Kimmel knew that he would primarily take the blame for the destruction of his fleet. Roosevelt ordered the first of many official inquiries into the Pearl Harbor attack on December 18. The committee, chaired by Supreme Court Justice Owen J. Roberts, spent several weeks gathering testimony and then issued its report in January 1942. It concluded that both Kimmel and Short were guilty of dereliction of duty—a willful failure to perform their expected duties due to negligence or inefficiency.

Being convicted of such a serious offense in military law was a crushing blow to Kimmel, who prided himself on his commitment to duty. Both he and Short lost their rank and were relieved of their commands. Kimmel retired from the Navy on March 1, 1942. For the remainder of the war, he worked for a marine engineering firm in New York. One of his main accomplishments in this position was developing a drydock system that was used to repair ships in the Pacific.

After the war ended, Kimmel repeatedly requested a public hearing on the events surrounding the Pearl Harbor attack. He received one before the U.S. Congress in 1945. During this hearing, Kimmel insisted that he took all reasonable precautions to defend the Pacific Fleet based on the information he was given by military leaders in Washington. He claimed that he failed to prepare adequately because he was not kept up to date on all the developments in U.S.-Japanese relations that affected his situation. "My belief is that General Short and I were not given the information available in Washington and were not informed of the impending attack because it was feared that action in Hawaii might deter the Japanese from making the attack," he explained. "Our president had repeatedly assured the American people that the United States would not enter the war unless we were attacked. The Japanese attack on the fleet would put the United States in the war with the full support of the American people."[1]

Kimmel spent the rest of his life trying to clear his name. After he died on May 14, 1968, several members of his family took up his crusade. The debate over the Pearl Harbor attack—and the extent of Kimmel's responsibility for what happened—has raged ever since. His supporters claim that he was made a scapegoat to cover up the failures of people higher up in the chain of command. Many others, however, argue that as the officer in charge of the fleet at Pearl Harbor, Kimmel was ultimately accountable for the results of the attack. "Kimmel and Short should have been ready, period," declared historian Donald Goldstein. "They weren't the only ones responsible, but the man on the bridge has to be the one [to take the blame]."[2]

Sources

"Admiral Husband E. Kimmel." *National Geographic,* "Beyond the Movie: Pearl Harbor," 2001. Available online at http://plasma.nationalgeographic.com/pearlharbor/ngbeyond/people.

Beach, Edward L. *Scapegoats: A Defense of Kimmel and Short at Pearl Harbor.* Annapolis, MD: Naval Institute Press, 1995.

Holloway, James L. III. "Pearl Harbor Scapegoat." *Washington Post,* October 6, 2000.

Prange, Gordon W. *At Dawn We Slept: The Untold Story of Pearl Harbor.* New York: McGraw-Hill, 1981.

Notes

[1] Quoted in Manion, Dean Clarence. "An Interview with Admiral Kimmel." *Journal of Historical Review,* originally broadcast in 1958. Available online at http://www.ihr.org/jhr/v11/v11p495_Manion.html.

[2] Quoted in Curry, Andrew. "Blamed for Pearl Harbor." *U.S. News and World Report,* June 4, 2001, p. 46.

Douglas MacArthur (1880-1964)
U.S. Army General
Leader of Allied Forces in the Pacific during
World War II

Douglas MacArthur was born in Little Rock, Arkansas, on January 26, 1880. His father, Arthur MacArthur Jr., was a career officer in the U.S. Army who received the Congressional Medal of Honor for his heroism during the Civil War. His mother, Mary Pinkney Hardy (known as Pinky), took care of Douglas and his older brother, Arthur III.

MacArthur spent his youth on the western frontier, where his father led groups of soldiers who were assigned to protect white settlers from hostile Indians. He had fond memories of growing up at Army outposts in remote parts of Kansas, New Mexico, and Texas. "It was here I learned to ride and shoot even before I could read or write—indeed, almost before I could walk or talk,"[1] he recalled in his book *Reminiscences.*

MacArthur did not take academics seriously until 1893, when he entered West Texas Military Academy in San Antonio. His good grades and family connections helped him earn an appointment to the U.S. Military Academy at West Point, New York, in 1899. MacArthur became one of the top students in the school's history and graduated first in his class in 1903.

Upon receiving a commission in the U.S. Army, MacArthur was sent to the Philippines, a chain of islands in the western Pacific. He arrived shortly after the people of the Philippines had mounted a U.S.-backed rebellion against Spanish colonial rule. In 1904 MacArthur was sent to Japan to serve as a military aide to his father. He also got an opportunity to tour other parts of Asia, and he became convinced that his destiny lay in the Far East.

A Rising Star in the Army

Over the next dozen years, MacArthur received a variety of assignments and rose quickly through the military ranks. In 1906 he served as a White House military aide to President Theodore Roosevelt. After joining the general staff of the War Department in 1913, MacArthur became the first public relations officer for the Army. In this role, he helped promote and increase public acceptance of a military draft.

When the United States entered World War I in 1917, MacArthur was promoted to colonel and sent to Europe. He took command of the Rainbow Division, an elite unit made up of National Guard troops from various states. MacArthur quickly proved himself to be a bold and courageous leader. He fought in several major battles, won numerous combat medals, and became famous for his willingness to face danger.

After the war ended, MacArthur was promoted to brigadier general and named superintendent of West Point. In four years at the helm of the famous military academy (1919-1922), he made many important changes and reforms. His achievements included modernizing the curriculum, raising admissions criteria and academic standards, and requiring students to participate in sports. MacArthur married Louise Cromwell Brooks in 1922, but the couple divorced in 1929.

The following year MacArthur moved to Washington, D.C., to become the Chief of Staff of the U.S. Army under President Herbert Hoover. The United States had entered the Great Depression, a severe economic crisis marked by high rates of poverty and unemployment and the failure of countless American banks, businesses, and farms. In June 1932, 10,000 desperate military veterans and their families gathered in Washington to ask Congress to authorize early payment of their war bonuses. These "bonus marchers" camped out in tents and shacks. Worried about social unrest and the spread of communist ideas, Hoover ordered MacArthur to disperse the protesters. MacArthur attacked the group with tanks and troops and burned their shantytown to the ground. His brutal treatment of the peaceful protesters created controversy and harmed his reputation.

In 1935 President Franklin D. Roosevelt sent MacArthur back to the Philippines to help the nation prepare for full independence. He worked to develop a Filipino army that could defend the island chain's 2,000 miles of coastline. In 1937 MacArthur married Jean Marie Faircloth, and they soon had a son, Arthur IV. MacArthur retired from the army and remained in the Philippines with his family. Over the next few years, however, political and military tensions increased steadily between the United States and Japan. Japanese leaders wanted to expand their territory and build an empire in Asia and the Pacific. Recognizing the growing threat posed by Japan, Roosevelt recalled MacArthur to active duty in July 1941 and named him commander of U.S. forces in the Far East.

Leads the Pacific Campaign in World War II

Tensions between the United States and Japan erupted into war on December 7, 1941, when Japanese planes launched a devastating attack on the American military base at Pearl Harbor, Hawaii. Only a few short hours after the Pearl Harbor attack, Japanese planes also attacked Clark Field, a U.S. air base in the Philippines. Although MacArthur had heard about the attack on Pearl Harbor, he left most of his planes in plain sight on the airfield, where they made perfect targets for Japanese pilots. The attack on Clark Field destroyed 100 planes, killed 80 Americans, and gave an enormous boost to Japanese efforts to seize the Philippines.

Japanese troops landed in the Philippines on December 22 and quickly captured the capital city of Manila. MacArthur ordered the American and Filipino troops who had been stationed there to make a tactical retreat to the mountainous Bataan peninsula east of the city and wait for reinforcements. In January 1942, however, Roosevelt ordered MacArthur to leave the Philippines and go to Australia to command U.S. forces there. The famous general left the Philippines reluctantly, knowing that it would appear as if he had abandoned his troops. After making a daring escape to Australia with his family, MacArthur famously vowed that "I shall return" to liberate the Philippines. MacArthur's remaining 70,000 troops surrendered on May 6, 1942. Their Japanese captors forced them to march sixty-five miles across the Bataan peninsula to prisoner-of-war camps north of Manila. As many as 20,000 U.S. and Filipino soldiers died along the way in what has become known to history as the Bataan Death March.

As battles raged throughout the Pacific, MacArthur's forces fought their way across the northern coast of New Guinea. The general also launched a series of well-planned amphibious assaults in the Admiralty and Solomon Islands from 1942 to 1944. Throughout this time, MacArthur continually pushed U.S. leaders to dedicate more troops and equipment to the Pacific campaign.

On October 20, 1944, MacArthur fulfilled his promise to return to the Philippines. His troops landed on the southernmost island of Leyte, then moved north toward the main island of Luzon. After four months of fighting that took the lives of 10,000 American soldiers, MacArthur triumphantly entered the capital city of Manila on February 23, 1945.

Although Allied forces made similar gains throughout Asia and the Pacific in 1945, Japanese leaders refused to surrender. Rather than mounting a costly invasion of Japan, President Harry S. Truman decided to drop two atomic bombs on Japanese cities in August. The devastating results finally convinced Japan to give up the fight. World War II officially ended on September 2, 1945, when MacArthur formally accepted the Japanese surrender in a simple ceremony aboard the battleship *Missouri* in Tokyo Bay.

Heads the Postwar Occupation of Japan

After the war ended, MacArthur made what many people consider to be his greatest contribution to world history. As Supreme Commander of the Allied Powers (SCAP), he oversaw the postwar occupation and reconstruction of Japan. MacArthur made major changes to the nation's government and society to ensure that Japan never again posed a threat to world peace. He dismantled the Japanese military, redistributed land to poor farmers, increased civil liberties and women's rights, and created a new constitution and democratic government. MacArthur performed his duties with a combination of firmness and empathy that gained the respect and cooperation of the Japanese people. Japan emerged from the occupation in 1952 to become a peaceful, democratic nation, a major industrial power, and a dependable ally of the United States.

When war broke out in Korea in 1950, MacArthur was appointed commander of the United Nations forces sent to help democratic South Korea resist a takeover by communist North Korea. He launched a risky but brilliant attack at Inchon, a port city near the South Korean capital of Seoul, that pushed North Korean forces back to the Yalu River. MacArthur assured U.S. leaders and his troops that the conflict would be over soon. But then Chinese communist forces joined the fight and forced MacArthur to retreat.

Angry and determined, MacArthur publicly declared that the United States should go to war with China. He also made other inflammatory statements that contradicted the Truman administration's goals and strategies. The president decided that MacArthur had exceeded his authority and relieved him of command in April 1951. Upon returning to the United States, the famous general received a great deal of public sympathy and support. He even considered running for president. But MacArthur's popularity faded when he suggested dropping atomic bombs on North Korea and China.

After serving his country for 50 years, MacArthur left the public eye and became a private citizen. "I now close my military career and just fade away—an old soldier who tried to do his duty as God gave him the light to see that duty,"[2] he declared. In 1952 he accepted a job as chairman of the board of Remington Rand Corporation, a military supplier. After struggling with poor health for several years, MacArthur died on April 5, 1964.

Sources

"General Douglas MacArthur." *The American Experience,* PBS. Available online at http://www.pbs. org/wgbh/amex/macarthur/peopleevents.

MacArthur, Douglas. *Reminiscences.* New York: McGraw-Hill, 1964.

Schlesinger, Arthur Jr., and Richard H. Rovere. *The MacArthur Controversy and American Foreign Policy.* New York: Noonday, 1965.

Whan, Vorin E. Jr. *A Soldier Speaks: Public Papers and Speeches of General of the Army Douglas MacArthur.* New York: Praeger, 1965.

Notes

[1] MacArthur, Douglas. *Reminiscences.* New York: McGraw-Hill, 1964.

[2] Whan, Vorin E. Jr. *A Soldier Speaks: Public Papers and Speeches of General of the Army Douglas MacArthur.* New York: Praeger, 1965.

Doris Miller (1919-1943)
Cook on the Battleship West Virginia *during the Pearl Harbor Attack*
First African-American Recipient of the Navy Cross

Doris Miller, known as Dorie, was born in Waco, Texas, on October 12, 1919. His parents, Conery and Henrietta Miller, were farmers. He had three brothers, one of whom served in the U.S. Army. Miller attended Moore High School in Waco, where he played fullback on the football team. Hoping for an opportunity to travel and earn some money, he enlisted in the U.S. Navy in September 1939.

Although the official policy of the U.S. military allowed African Americans to serve their country, in those days most black servicemen were placed in segregated units under the command of white officers. Since white military leaders considered black soldiers unfit for combat, the units generally were assigned support tasks like cooking, cleaning, or transporting supplies. "When Franklin Delano Roosevelt was president in 1932, he opened up the Navy again to blacks, but in one area only: they were called mess attendants, stewards, and cooks," recalled Clark Simmons, who served as a mess attendant on the USS *Utah* during the Pearl Harbor attack. "The Navy was so structured that if you were black, this was what they had you do in the Navy—you could only be a servant."[1]

Miller was initially assigned the rank of Mess Attendant, Third Class. He was later promoted to Mess Attendant, Second Class and First Class, then to Cook, Third Class. After completing basic training in Norfolk, Virginia, Miller was assigned to the ammunition ship USS *Pyro*. In January 1940 he was transferred to the battleship USS *West Virginia*. Taking advantage of his physical size and strength, Miller soon became the ship's heavyweight boxing champion.

Heroism during the Pearl Harbor Attack

Miller was on board the *West Virginia* on the morning of December 7, 1941, when Japanese planes launched a surprise attack on the U.S. Pacific

Fleet at Pearl Harbor in Hawaii. His ship was anchored on Battleship Row, located on the southeastern shore of Ford Island in the middle of the harbor, along with six other heavily armed battleships. Beginning closest to the harbor entrance, there was the USS *California* by itself, the *Oklahoma* anchored outside of the *Maryland,* the *West Virginia* moored outside of the *Tennessee,* the *Arizona* on the inside of the *Vestal* (a repair ship), and the *Nevada* by itself.

Miller was below deck collecting laundry when the first Japanese torpedo slammed into the hull of the *West Virginia* at 7:56 A.M. He ran to his battle station—an antiaircraft battery magazine (ammunition storage area) in the middle of the ship—but found that the area had been wrecked by the torpedo. Then Miller went up on deck to try to find a way to contribute.

An officer ordered Miller to help carry wounded crew members to safe places where they could receive medical attention. One of the men Miller aided was the ship's captain, Mervyn Bennion, who was mortally wounded when a piece of shrapnel tore into his abdomen. After being patched up by a medic, Bennion remained alert and directed the ship's defenses until he finally succumbed to his injury.

Meanwhile, Miller found an unmanned 50-caliber antiaircraft machine gun and began firing away at the attacking planes. Even though the cook had never received weapons training, he quickly figured out how to operate the gun. "It wasn't hard. I just pulled the trigger and she worked fine. I had watched others with these guns," he recalled. "I guess I fired her for about fifteen minutes. I think I got one of those Jap planes. They were diving pretty close to us."[2]

The *West Virginia* was hit by five torpedoes and two bombs during the Japanese attack. The ship took on water, caught on fire, and sank to the bottom of the harbor, taking the lives of 130 crew members. Miller stayed on the deck and continued firing until he was ordered to abandon ship.

On May 27, 1942, Miller received the Navy Cross "for distinguished devotion to duty, extraordinary courage, and disregard for his own safety during the attack on the Fleet in Pearl Harbor." During the ceremony to present the medal, Admiral Chester W. Nimitz remarked that "This marks the first time in this conflict that such high tribute has been made in the Pacific Fleet to a member of his race and I'm sure that the future will see others similarly honored for brave acts."[3]

Dies in Combat in the Pacific

After his ship was destroyed at Pearl Harbor, Miller was assigned to the USS *Indianapolis*. He fought in the Pacific for a year and then returned to the West Coast in November 1942. The following spring he was assigned to the escort carrier USS *Liscome Bay* and returned to sea to participate in the Allied "island-hopping" campaign.

In November 1943 aircraft from the *Liscome Bay* supported the U.S. Marine landing on Tarawa Atoll in the Gilbert Islands. On November 24 the carrier was hit by a torpedo from a Japanese submarine. The impact ignited a magazine containing bombs for the ship's aircraft, causing a terrific explosion. The *Liscome Bay* sank within minutes, taking the lives of 646 American sailors, including Miller. The U.S. Navy named a ship in his honor, the frigate USS *Miller*, in 1973.

Sources

"Cook Third Class Doris Miller, USN." Department of the Navy, Navy Historical Center, 2007. Available online at http://www.history.navy.mil/faqs/faq57-4.htm.

"Ship's Cook Third Class Doris Miller." *National Geographic,* Beyond the Movie: Pearl Harbor, 2001. Available online at http://plasma.nationalgeographic.com/pearlharbor/ngbeyond/people.

Notes

[1] Quoted in "Ship's Cook Third Class Doris Miller." *National Geographic,* Beyond the Movie: Pearl Harbor, 2001. Available online at http://plasma.nationalgeographic.com/pearlharbor/ngbeyond/people.

[2] Quoted in "Cook Third Class Doris Miller, USN." Department of the Navy, Navy Historical Center, 2007. Available online at http://www.history.navy.mil/faqs/faq57-4.htm.

[3] Quoted in "Cook Third Class Doris Miller, USN."

Chester W. Nimitz (1885-1966)
U.S. Navy Admiral
Commander of the U.S. Pacific Fleet in World War II

Chester William Nimitz was born on February 24, 1885, in Fredericksburg, a small settlement of German immigrants on the plains of central Texas. His father, Chester Bernhard Nimitz, was a drover who led cattle drives in the West. He died before his son was born. Chester's mother, Anna Henke Nimitz, remarried when Chester was six years old. Her new husband was William Nimitz, the younger brother of her late husband. The family moved to Kerrville, Texas, where they managed a hotel.

Young Chester was a good student who always dreamed of a military career. He hoped to earn an appointment to the U.S. Military Academy at West Point, New York, but no positions were available. Instead, he received an appointment to the U.S. Naval Academy at Annapolis, Maryland. Nimitz entered the academy in 1901, at the age of fifteen, before he had graduated from Tivy High School (he finally received his diploma forty years later, after he had become an admiral). Although Nimitz got seasick the first time he went out on a sailboat, he excelled at Annapolis. He graduated seventh in his class of 114 cadets in 1905.

Assigned to the battleship *Ohio* in the Asiatic Fleet, Nimitz spent his first three years in the U.S. Navy touring the Pacific. In 1907 he was promoted to ensign and took command of a series of vessels, including the gunboat *Panay* and the destroyer *Decatur.* In July 1908 the *Decatur* ran aground on a mudbank in the Philippines. Nimitz faced a court martial for "hazarding" the ship, but he escaped punishment because the Navy had provided him with poor navigational charts.

Upon returning to the United States, Nimitz became involved in the development of early submarines. Part of this assignment involved traveling to Germany to study the design of diesel engines. Following his promotion to lieutenant in 1912, Nimitz took command of several subs operating in the

Atlantic, including the *Snapper, Narwhal,* and *Skipjack.* In 1913 he received a medal for heroism after jumping overboard to save the life of a drowning seaman. Nimitz also married Catherine Vance Freeman that year. They raised a family that included three daughters, Catherine, Mary, and Nancy, and one son, Chester Jr.

Rises through the Ranks of the Navy

During World War I, Nimitz served as an aide to Rear Admiral Samuel Robinson, the commander of the Allied submarine force. He was stationed in Connecticut, where his job involved getting Navy submarines ready for battle in the Atlantic. After the war ended in 1918, Nimitz served as executive officer of the battleship *South Carolina.* In 1920 he was promoted to commander and sent to Hawaii, where he helped build a submarine base at Pearl Harbor.

In 1922 Nimitz returned to the mainland to attend advanced training courses at the Naval War College. He felt that this training helped prepare him for what he would face during the Pacific War. "The enemy of our games was always Japan," he recalled, "and the courses were so thorough that after the start of World War II, nothing that happened in the Pacific was strange or unexpected."[1] In 1926 Nimitz became an instructor in Naval Science and Tactics in the new Naval Reserve Officers' Training Program at the University of California at Berkeley.

Promoted to captain in 1927, Nimitz returned to sea as commander of Submarine Division 20 and later as captain of the heavy cruiser *Augusta.* In 1935 he went to Washington, D.C., to work in the Bureau of Navigation. Three years later, following a promotion to rear admiral, Nimitz took over as chief of the bureau. By this time, World War II had begun in Europe and the United States faced a growing threat from Japan in the Pacific. The U.S. Congress responded by approving a billion-dollar naval construction program. Nimitz took charge of recruiting, training, and assigning personnel for the newly built ships. He also got a good overview of naval operations and became a trusted advisor to a number of political and military leaders, including President Franklin D. Roosevelt.

Takes Charge after the Pearl Harbor Attack

On December 7, 1941, Japanese planes attacked the U.S. military base at Pearl Harbor, devastating the Navy's Pacific Fleet. The following day, the

United States declared war on Japan and entered World War II. Upset that American forces were caught off guard at Pearl Harbor, President Roosevelt removed Admiral Husband E. Kimmel from command of the Pacific Fleet. Then, bypassing twenty-eight officers with more seniority, he named Nimitz as the new commander in chief of the Pacific Fleet. "Tell Nimitz to get the hell out to Pearl and stay there till the war is won," the president ordered Secretary of the Navy Frank Knox.

Upon arriving in Hawaii, Nimitz worked hard to restore the pride, confidence, and morale of the men who had endured the attack on Pearl Harbor. He also faced a difficult task in rebuilding the ships, planes, and facilities that had been destroyed. Since the eight battleships that had been anchored in Pearl Harbor suffered a great deal of damage, Nimitz was forced to reassess the composition of the Pacific Fleet. He decided to center his strategy around the aircraft carriers that had escaped damage in the attack. This decision proved to be key to the Allied victory in the Pacific War.

In early 1942 Nimitz took command of the Pacific Ocean Area, which included the Pacific Fleet as well as selected ground and air units. In effect, this change divided control of the Allied Pacific forces between Nimitz and U.S. Army General Douglas MacArthur. In contrast to the colorful and outspoken general, the admiral was "soft-spoken and relaxed, a team player, a leader by example rather than exhortation,"[2] according to one historian. Nimitz also proved to be a bold and brilliant naval strategist. Over the next three years he directed the largest military campaign in history, employing 2 million men, 5,000 ships, and 20,000 planes in a theater of operations that encompassed 65 million square miles.

Wins the Pacific War

Nimitz remained calm and confident during the first six months of the war, even as the Japanese conquered vast expanses of territory in the Pacific. By May 1942 he felt that his fleet was sufficiently recovered to make a defensive stand at Port Moresby in New Zealand. The United States and its allies successfully turned back a Japanese assault in the Battle of the Coral Sea, which was fought entirely by planes launched from aircraft carriers. It marked the first time in history that an entire naval battle took place without the opposing fleets coming in direct contact with one another.

In June 1942 Nimitz used reports from U.S. military code breakers to gain information about Japanese plans for an attack on Midway, a small but strategically important island in the Pacific. Although Allied ships were badly outnumbered, they used the element of surprise to hand the enemy a decisive defeat in the Battle of Midway. This battle marked a turning point in the Pacific campaign by putting Japan on the defensive.

In 1943 Nimitz launched an ambitious offensive campaign known as "island hopping" in the central Pacific. Over the next year the Allied forces under his command advanced steadily toward Japan. They launched amphibious assaults on selected islands of strategic importance, while bypassing others that were heavily fortified by the Japanese. They used the captured islands as bases to continue moving forward across thousands of miles of ocean.

In December 1944 Nimitz was promoted to the newly created rank of fleet admiral. Over the next six months, Allied forces under his command captured the islands of Iwo Jima and Okinawa, bringing them within a few hundred miles of Japan. Nimitz and other Allied leaders began developing a strategy for an invasion of Japan. Hoping to end the war more quickly, however, President Harry S. Truman decided to drop two atomic bombs on Japanese cities. The mass destruction convinced Japanese leaders to surrender to end World War II.

Representatives of the Allied Powers and Japan signed the official instrument of surrender on September 2, 1945, aboard the battleship *Missouri* in Tokyo Bay. General MacArthur presided over the ceremony, and Nimitz signed the document as the official representative of the U.S. government.

After the war ended, Nimitz became the chief of naval operations, making him the highest-ranking officer in the U.S. Navy. During his two years in this post, he mostly oversaw the demobilization of the forces that had fought in World War II. In 1949 Nimitz retired and moved to California, where he served as a regent of the University of California at Berkeley. He also became a goodwill ambassador for the United Nations and gave speeches across the country. After suffering a series of strokes, Nimitz died on February 20, 1966, at his home on Yerba Buena Island near San Francisco. He was buried at Golden Gate National Cemetery.

Sources

"Fleet Admiral Chester W. Nimitz." National Museum of the Pacific War. Available online at http://www.nimitz-museum.org/nimitzbio.htm.

"Fleet Admiral Chester William Nimitz." Washington, D.C.: Department of the Navy, Naval Historical Center. Available online at http://www.history.navy.mil/faqs/faq36-4.htm.

Nimitz, Chester W., with E.B. Potter. *Triumph in the Pacific.* 1963.

Potter, E.B. *Nimitz.* Annapolis, MD: Naval Institute Press, 1976.

Notes

[1] Quoted in "Admiral Chester W. Nimitz," *The American Experience,* PBS. Available online at http://www.pbs.org/wgbh/amex/macarthur/peopleevents.

[2] Spector, Ronald. Quoted in "Admiral Chester W. Nimitz." *The American Experience,* PBS.

Franklin D. Roosevelt (1882-1945)
President of the United States during the Attack on Pearl Harbor

Franklin Delano Roosevelt was born on January 20, 1882, in Hyde Park, a wealthy community just north of the city of Poughkeepsie in New York State. His parents were James Roosevelt, a railroad industry executive, and Sara (Delano) Roosevelt. Both parents came from families of wealth and privilege, so young Franklin received a wide array of educational and travel opportunities as he was growing up. He attended the finest schools and frequently traveled with his family to Europe and other exciting parts of the world. His mother was an overprotective, controlling presence throughout these years, but Roosevelt nonetheless grew into a self-confident and independent-minded young man.

In 1900 Roosevelt enrolled at Harvard University, where he became editor of the school newspaper. He also became romantically involved at Harvard with his cousin, Eleanor Roosevelt (niece of Theodore Roosevelt, who was president of the United States at the time). Franklin graduated from Harvard in 1904, and he married Eleanor one year later despite his mother's strong disapproval. In 1906 they had the first of five children. That same year, Roosevelt enrolled at Columbia Law School. Two years later—before actually earning a degree from Columbia—Roosevelt passed the New York state bar exam and took a job with a high-profile Wall Street law firm.

In 1910 Roosevelt won a seat in the state senate as a Democrat. Two years later, he accepted an appointment to serve as undersecretary of the Navy in the administration of Woodrow Wilson. Roosevelt spent the next several years in that post. By all accounts he performed his duties with great skill and dedication during World War I, when the nation's armed forces were mobilized to fight in Europe.

A Rocky Personal Life

In the fall of 1918, Eleanor Roosevelt discovered that her husband was having a romantic affair with Lucy Mercer, a former employee of the family.

She initially threatened to divorce her husband, but Franklin vowed to end the affair—a promise he later broke—and Eleanor agreed to remain with him. Their marriage never fully recovered from this crisis, however.

In 1920 Democratic presidential nominee James M. Cox selected Roosevelt to be his vice presidential running mate. The Republican ticket of Warren G. Harding and Calvin Coolidge ultimately triumphed in the presidential election later that fall, but Roosevelt's spirited campaigning made him one of the most prominent Democratic leaders in the country.

In August 1921, though, Roosevelt was stricken with polio, a viral disease that in its most severe forms can cause paralysis. Roosevelt lost the use of his legs because of the disease, and he was forced to rely on a wheelchair or heavy crutch-like braces for the rest of his life. But he refused to let his physical problems derail his political dreams, and in 1928 he waged a successful campaign for the governorship of New York State.

Giving Hope during the Great Depression

A few months after Roosevelt moved into the governor's mansion, the United States was hit by a terrible economic depression. The Great Depression swept around the globe, triggering huge increases in poverty, joblessness, business closings, and hunger. Roosevelt acted quickly to establish state programs that helped frightened New York citizens with housing, food, clothing, and job hunting assistance. His efforts attracted national attention, and in the summer of 1932 Roosevelt became the Democratic nominee for president.

Roosevelt faced Republican incumbent Herbert Hoover in the 1932 election. Hoover's ineffective response to the Great Depression had made him unpopular with many Americans, so Roosevelt easily cruised to victory with 57.4 percent of the popular vote. Roosevelt began his presidency on March 4, 1933, by assuring his fellow citizens that "the only thing we have to fear is fear itself." He then moved quickly to battle the economic problems that were battering the country. Roosevelt approved an ambitious agenda of new government programs and policies to help desperate farmers, ailing banks, and unemployed workers survive the nation's serious economic troubles. His administration also advanced programs and initiatives to get the American economy rolling again. These various Roosevelt programs came to be known collectively as "The New Deal."

The efforts of the president and his allies did not restore the United States to full economic health. But many historians believe that Roosevelt's

New Deal kept the country from collapsing during the 1930s. The majority of Americans agreed, which was why Roosevelt was re-elected three times—in 1936, 1940, and 1944 (the Twenty-Second Amendment to the U.S. Constitution, which limited presidents to two four-year terms, did not become law until 1951). Not all Americans liked him, of course. Roosevelt and his New Deal programs were slammed by conservatives and big business executives, for example, who thought the president's policies were anti-business. But their hostility was not enough to overcome the strong support that Roosevelt received from America's poor and working-class voters.

A Decisive Response to Pearl Harbor

When World War II erupted in 1939, Roosevelt knew that most Americans did not want to become directly involved. He managed to provide military and economic aid to Great Britain and the other Allied powers fighting against Nazi Germany, but even this indirect assistance was condemned by isolationists. During this period, political tensions increased steadily between the United States and Japan. Japan's military government wanted to conquer new territory in Asia and the Pacific in order to gain access to natural resources and build an empire. Already struggling to support the Allies in the face of strong isolationist sentiments, Roosevelt used a variety of diplomatic means to avoid war with Japan.

On December 7, 1941, however, Japan launched a surprise air attack against the U.S. Pacific Fleet in Pearl Harbor, Hawaii. The devastating attack shocked and angered the American people and united the country in support of going to war. After learning of the Pearl Harbor attack, Roosevelt delivered an emergency address to the American people and the U.S. Congress. He angrily described the assault as a "date which will live in infamy" and asked Congress to pass a declaration of war against Japan. Congress quickly did so, and within a week the United States was officially at war with Japan's allies, Germany and Italy, as well.

Over the next three years Roosevelt spent most of his time and energy on the war. As he stated at one point, "the war effort must come first and everything else must wait." With this in mind, he supervised America's transformation into the "arsenal of democracy"—a mighty industrial machine capable of turning out huge numbers of tanks, fighter planes, rifles, battleships, and other military equipment to fight the Axis Powers. This wartime

146

production enabled the United States to emerge from its long economic depression, and it gave American and Allied forces the resources they needed to simultaneously wage war in both Europe and the Pacific. Roosevelt's determination to achieve victory in the war, though, also led him to adopt unconstitutional policies such as censorship of U.S. media and internment of thousands of loyal Japanese-Americans in detention camps.

The war's momentum turned decisively in favor of the Allied powers in 1944, thanks to major U.S.-led victories in Europe and a series of hard-fought triumphs over Japanese forces in the Pacific. In February 1945 Roosevelt met with British Prime Minister Winston Churchill and Soviet leader Joseph Stalin to discuss various political and economic issues that would have to be addressed after Germany and Japan were defeated. But Roosevelt did not live to see Germany's surrender on May 7, 1945, or Japan's surrender on August 14, 1945. He died suddenly of a massive cerebral brain hemorrhage on April 12. His vice president, Harry S. Truman, was quickly sworn in as the nation's thirty-third president, and it was Truman who served as America's commander-in-chief during the war's closing weeks.

Sources

Freidel, Frank. *Franklin D. Roosevelt: A Rendezvous with Destiny.* Boston: Little, Brown, 1990.

Goodwin, Doris Kearns. *No Ordinary Time: Franklin and Eleanor Roosevelt, The Home Front.* New York: Simon & Schuster, 1994.

Hunt, John G., ed. *The Essential Franklin D. Roosevelt.* New York: Gramercy Books, 1995.

Leuchtenberg, William E. *The FDR Years: On Roosevelt and His Legacy.* New York: Columbia University Press, 1995.

O'Neill, William L. *A Democracy at War.* New York: Free Press, 1993.

Walter C. Short (1880-1949)
U.S. Army Lieutenant General
Commander of Hawaiian Ground and Air
Defenses during the Pearl Harbor Attack

Walter Campbell Short was born on March 30, 1880, in Fillmore, Illinois. He was the fifth of six children born to Hiram Spait Short, a medical doctor, and his wife, Sarah Minerva (Stokes) Short. After earning a degree from the University of Illinois in 1901, Short taught mathematics for a year at the Western Military Academy. His forty-year career in the U.S. Army began when he received a commission in 1902.

Short held a variety of assignments and gradually moved up through the ranks of the military. He spent his first five years in the Army with the 25th Infantry Division based in Fort Reno, Oklahoma. While there he met George C. Marshall, who became Chief of Staff of the Army in World War II. In 1907, Short was posted to the Philippines for a year. Upon returning to the United States, he served in California, Nebraska, and Alaska. In 1914, Short was promoted to commander of the 12th Infantry Division at Fort Sill, Oklahoma. He also married Isabel Dean that year. The marriage produced a son, Walter Dean Short.

When the United States entered World War I in 1917, Short was sent to France with the Army's 1st Infantry Division. He fought in several major battles and received the Distinguished Service Medal for training machine gunners and developing machine gun tactics. After the war ended, Short served in the training section of the Army General Staff. In 1920 he was promoted to major, and two years later he published a textbook called *Employment of Machine Guns*. Short attended the Army War College, graduating in 1925, and then served as instructor at the Army General Staff School and Army Infantry School. By 1938, when he was promoted to brigadier general, Short was widely considered to be one of the top training officers in the U.S. Army.

Takes Command of Hawaiian Defenses

In February 1941, Marshall promoted Short to lieutenant general and gave him command of the Army's Hawaiian Department. Pearl Harbor, on the Hawaiian island of Oahu, served as the base of the U.S. Navy's Pacific Fleet. Short's job was to coordinate the ground and air defense of the fleet at anchor and the various airfields and other military installations on the island. By all accounts, he was thorough and industrious in performing his duties as he understood them.

At the time Short received his command, political and military tensions were high between the United States and Japan. The Japanese military government wanted to expand its territory and build an empire in Asia and the Pacific. U.S. leaders viewed Japan as a growing threat, and many believed that the two nations would eventually go to war. But few people thought that the Japanese would dare to attack Hawaii. Instead, most predicted that Japan would target areas of southeast Asia or the Pacific that were not well defended.

When diplomatic negotiations between the United States and Japan broke down on November 27, Short received a "war warning" from the Army chief of staff in Washington, D.C. Although Marshall suggested that "hostile action [was] possible at any moment," he also ordered Short not to do anything to "alarm civil population or disclose intent."[1] Short interpreted the message to mean that he should increase defensive measures in a limited way that would not be noticeable to local residents.

As a result, Short and his Navy counterpart, Admiral Husband E. Kimmel, took only a few extra precautions against a possible Japanese attack on Pearl Harbor. For instance, they agreed to operate a new Army radar station for a few hours each day to scan for enemy ships and planes. Short also took steps to protect military equipment and facilities from possible sabotage by local people of Japanese origin. Instead of being tucked away in hangars, for instance, military planes were parked close together out in the open so they would be easier to guard. In addition, guns and ammunition were locked safely away so they would not be stolen.

Short and the soldiers under his command were caught off guard on the morning of December 7, 1941, when Japanese planes launched a surprise attack on Hawaii. The attack devastated the Pacific Fleet at anchor as well as the Army Air Force planes lined up wingtip-to-wingtip at the island's airfields. Many servicemen found their efforts to fight back hampered by a lack of available weapons and ammunition. A total of 2,388 Americans lost their lives in the attack, including 233 Army soldiers.

Held Responsible for Pearl Harbor

The Japanese attack on Pearl Harbor shocked and outraged the American people. Many demanded to know why U.S. military forces had not been better prepared to defend against the attack. President Franklin D. Roosevelt ordered the first of many official inquiries into the Pearl Harbor attack on December 18. The committee, chaired by Supreme Court Justice Owen J. Roberts, spent several weeks gathering testimony and then issued its report in January 1942. It concluded that both Short and Kimmel were guilty of dereliction of duty—a willful failure to perform their expected duties due to negligence or inefficiency.

Being convicted of such a serious offense in military law was a crushing blow to Short, who prided himself on his commitment to duty. Both he and Kimmel lost their rank and were relieved of their commands. Short retired from the Army on March 1, 1942. He then took a job as a traffic manager for Ford Motor Company in Dallas, Texas. He worked there until poor health forced him to retire in 1946.

After the war ended, the U.S. Congress held a series of public hearings into the Pearl Harbor attack. In his testimony, Short admitted that he had made errors in judgment that contributed to his troops' lack of preparation for the attack. But he also argued that Marshall and other officials had withheld important information that would have allowed him to be better prepared. Although the Congressional inquiry conceded that Marshall's orders to Short had been vague and contradictory, it still held Short primarily responsible.

Short died of heart failure on March 9, 1949. He was buried at Arlington National Cemetery. Ever since his death, members of his family have lobbied unsuccessfully for the return of his rank. "One may sympathize with Short, understand his motives, and agree that Washington did not give him all the facts in its possession," historian Gordon W. Prange concluded. "But these things cannot mitigate the fact that Short failed in the event for which his whole professional life had been a preparation."[2]

Sources
Beach, Edward L. *Scapegoats: A Defense of Kimmel and Short at Pearl Harbor.* Annapolis, MD: Naval Institute Press, 1995.

"Lieutenant General Walter C. Short." United States Army, Pacific, "History—Commanding Gener-
als." Available online at http://www.usarpac.army.mil/history/cgbios/cg_short.asp.
Prange, Gordon W. *At Dawn We Slept: The Untold Story of Pearl Harbor.* New York: McGraw-Hill,
1981.

Notes

[1] Quoted in Conn, Stetson, Rose C. Engelman, and Byron Fairchild. *Guarding the United States and
Its Outposts.* Washington, D.C.: U.S. Army Center of Military History, 2000, p. 178. Available online
at http://www.history.army.mil/books/wwii/guard-us/ch7.htm.
[2] Prange, Gordon W. *Pearl Harbor: The Verdict of History.* New York: McGraw-Hill, 1986.

Isoroku Yamamoto (1884-1943)
Commander in Chief of the Imperial Japanese Combined Fleet
Mastermind behind the Surprise Attack on Pearl Harbor

Isoroku Yamamoto was born as Isoroku Takano on April 4, 1884, in Nagaoka, Honshu Province, Japan. He was the sixth son born to Teikichi Takano, a schoolteacher, and his wife Mineko. His father, who came from a long line of samurai warriors, gave him a first name meaning fifty-six in Japanese because that was his age when Isoroku was born. Isoroku changed his last name to Yamamoto as an adult, when—according to a longstanding Japanese tradition—he was adopted by a wealthy, upper-class family that did not have a male heir.

In 1900, at the age of sixteen, Yamamoto enrolled in the Japanese Naval Academy at Eta Jima. He graduated seventh in his class in 1904. The following year, Yamamoto went to sea aboard the cruiser *Nisshin*. He fought in a famous naval battle at Tsushima, a strait between Japan and Korea. The Japanese fleet, under the command of one of the world's great admirals, Heihachiro Togo, won a decisive victory over the Russian Navy. Yamamoto was wounded in the battle and lost two fingers on his left hand.

Over the next decade, Yamamoto served aboard a variety of ships. His naval training took him to ports in Korea, China, the United States, and Australia. He also received officers' training at the Navy Staff College at Tsukiji, graduating in 1916. Later that year, Yamamoto married Reiko Mihashi, the daughter of a dairy farmer from Honshu Province. The marriage produced two sons and two daughters. But family life did not hold much appeal for Yamamoto. He loved gambling and often stayed out all night playing high-stakes games of poker, bridge, and billiards. On the quieter side, he also enjoyed practicing calligraphy and writing poetry.

Opposes War with the United States

In 1919 Yamamoto went to the United States to attend Harvard University. He spent two years there studying business, with a focus on the oil industry. Upon returning to Japan in 1921 he was promoted to commander and served as an instructor at the Naval Staff College in Tokyo. In 1924 Yamamoto received his first major command at a new naval aviation training center northeast of Tokyo. Placing a strong emphasis on discipline and teamwork, he created a program that trained an elite group of pilots for the Japanese Navy.

In 1926 Yamamoto went to Washington, D.C., for a two-year assignment at the Japanese embassy. He spent this time assessing the size, strength, and level of preparedness of the American military. After returning home in 1928, Yamamoto became commander of the aircraft carrier *Akagi*, which eventually took part in the Pearl Harbor attack. He then took a position in the aviation bureau of Japan's naval affairs ministry. In 1935 Yamamoto was promoted to chief of the bureau, which gave him authority over Japan's entire naval air program, including carrier aircraft, seaplanes, and land-based planes.

In 1936 Yamamoto joined the Japanese government as vice minister of the navy. In this position, he fought to increase the size of the Japanese navy to match that of the United States, Great Britain, and other world powers. Foreseeing that air power represented the future of naval warfare, he also promoted the construction of aircraft carriers rather than battleships.

During this period, the government of Japan grew increasingly militaristic. Many government leaders wanted to conquer new territory in Asia and the Pacific in order to gain access to raw materials and build an empire. Although Yamamoto felt a strong loyalty to his country, he worried that expanding rapidly by force would lead Japan into a war with the United States. Having spent several years in America, he knew that Japan lacked the natural resources, technology, and industrial capacity to win a prolonged war against the United States. For this reason, Yamamoto opposed Japan's invasion of China in 1937. He also argued against entering into an alliance with Germany, which Japan eventually did in 1940. Yamamoto's antiwar stance made him very unpopular with military extremists in the government. In fact, he received several death threats because of his views.

On August 30, 1939, Yamamoto was promoted to the rank of admiral and appointed commander in chief of the Japanese Combined Fleet. Upon taking command of his country's naval forces, Yamamoto famously warned

Prime Minister Konoye Fumimaro about the potential results of going to war with the United States. "If I am told to fight regardless of the consequences, I shall run wild for the first six months or a year, but I have utterly no confidence for the second or third year," he declared. "I hope you will endeavor to avoid a Japanese-American war."[1]

Plans the Attack on Pearl Harbor

When it became clear that the Japanese government was determined to follow through on its expansionist plans, Yamamoto began preparing for war. He knew that the U.S. Navy's Pacific Fleet, which was stationed at Pearl Harbor in Hawaii, was the only force capable of interfering with Japan's conquest of new territory in the region. He decided that Japan's best chance of prevailing was to launch a preemptive strike to cripple the American navy. Yamamoto developed a plan involving a massive air strike on Pearl Harbor by planes from Japanese aircraft carriers. He gathered information and worked out every technical detail of the plan, then threatened to resign if it was not approved. The new Japanese Prime Minister, General Hideki Tojo, gave his formal approval on October 20, 1941.

Following a month of training, Yamamoto's attack force set sail from Japanese waters on November 26. It consisted of 23 warships, including 6 aircraft carriers with nearly 400 planes, under the command of Admiral Chuichi Nagumo. On December 2 Yamamoto sent Nagumo a message that said "Climb Mount Niitaka 1208." Mount Niitaka was the highest peak in the Japanese empire. This signal meant that all diplomatic options had been exhausted and the attack was scheduled for December 8 Tokyo time, which was December 7 in Hawaii.

The Japanese attack was even more successful than its planner had hoped. Yamamoto's forces achieved complete surprise, devastated the U.S. Pacific Fleet in Pearl Harbor, and destroyed hundreds of American planes on the ground at Hawaiian airfields. The Pearl Harbor attack severely crippled U.S. military capacity in the Pacific while costing the Japanese only twenty-nine planes and fifty-five air crew.

As it turned out, though, the attack also left a number of valuable targets unscathed, including the Pacific Fleet's aircraft carriers and Pearl Harbor's fuel-storage tanks, ship-repair facilities, and submarine base. It also united the American people behind the war and created a burning desire for revenge against Japan. As Yamamoto had predicted, the Japanese ran wild for six months, capturing large swaths of territory in Asia and the Pacific. But once the United States recovered from the attack on Pearl Harbor, Japan's early advantage quickly disappeared.

Falls into a Trap at Midway

Yamamoto played an important role in the battle that marked a key turning point in the Pacific War. It centered around Midway, two small islands about 1,200 miles northwest of Pearl Harbor that featured a harbor and an airfield. Yamamoto felt that capturing Midway would give his fleet a valuable base from which to launch submarine and air attacks on Hawaii and even California. He came up with an elaborate plan to lure the U.S. Pacific Fleet into a trap at Midway in hopes of destroying it once and for all. Without a decisive victory, he worried that Japan's defeat would be only a matter of time.

Yamamoto assembled a huge fleet consisting of more than 200 ships and 100,000 men. He sent part of this fleet northward to create a diversion by attacking the Aleutian islands off the coast of Alaska. While the main Japanese force attacked Midway, a third force would lie in wait to ambush the U.S. Fleet when it came to the rescue from Pearl Harbor.

Unfortunately for Yamamoto, his plan was discovered in advance by American military code breakers. Knowing the time and place of the attack, U.S. Admiral Chester W. Nimitz was able to set a trap of his own. When the Japanese launched their attack on Midway on June 4, 1942, American aircraft carriers were ready. U.S. warplanes located and sank four Japanese aircraft carriers, forcing Yamamoto to make a hasty retreat.

The Battle of Midway was a devastating blow that put Japan on the defensive for the remainder of the war. Naval historian Jonathan Parshall blamed Yamamoto, saying that his "needlessly complex operational scheme at the Battle of Midway dispersed his forces in the face of a still-dangerous foe, and directly led to the disaster there."[2]

Dies in the Pacific War

Allied forces went on the offensive in late 1942 and early 1943, capturing Japanese-held territory in Asia and the Pacific. Recognizing the need to increase the morale of his forces, Yamamoto made visits to several islands in

155

the South Pacific during this time. On April 18, 1943, American code break-ers intercepted reports detailing the Japanese admiral's travel plans. U.S. fighter planes from Henderson Field on Guadalcanal ambushed Yamamoto's plane and shot it down over the Solomon Islands.

The death of Japan's most famous military planner had important impli-cations for both sides in the Pacific War. "The American-educated Japanese commander was recognized as the driving intelligence behind Japanese oper-ations and it was considered that the loss of his expertise could take months, even years, off the war in the Pacific," noted one historian. "The Japanese would be seriously crippled by the loss of so important a military figure in morale alone."[3]

On June 5, 1943, after his remains were returned to Japan, Yamamoto was honored in a full state ceremony. He was considered a national hero in Japan for the boldness and cunning of his plan to attack Pearl Harbor, although his legacy was tarnished somewhat by later defeats. "Yamamoto was perhaps the most imaginative and skillful Japanese admiral to go to war against the United States," wrote one biographer. "Yet his campaigns had all the merits and faults of a gambler's strategy."[4]

Sources

Hoyt, Edwin B. *Yamamoto: The Man Who Planned Pearl Harbor.* New York: McGraw-Hill, 1990.

Potter, John Dean. *Yamamoto: The Man Who Menaced America.* New York: Viking, 1965.

Ryan, James C. "History May Have Given Japanese Admiral Isoroku Yamamoto More Credit for Mili-tary Genius than He Deserved." *World War II,* May 1999, p. 66.

Notes

[1] Quoted in Prange, Gordon W. *At Dawn We Slept: The Untold Story of Pearl Harbor.* New York: McGraw-Hill, 1981, p. 10.

[2] Quoted in Chen, C. Peter. "Isoroku Yamamoto." World War II Database. Available online at http://ww2db.com/person_bio.pht?person_id=1.

[3] Welsh, Douglas. *The USA in World War II: The Pacific Theater.* New York: Galahad Books, 1982, p. 36.

[4] "Admiral Isoroku Yamamoto." In "Beyond the Movie: Pearl Harbor," *National Geographic,* 2001. Available online at http://plasma.nationalgeographic.com/pearlharbor/ngbeyond/people.

PRIMARY SOURCES

The Neutrality Act of 1937

In the aftermath of World War I, the American people were determined to avoid getting involved in another European conflict. They felt that the United States should mind its own business and stay out of world affairs. Such isolationist attitudes helped convince the U.S. Congress to pass a series of Neutrality Acts in the 1930s. An excerpt from one of these laws, the Neutrality Act of 1937, appears below. Like its predecessors, the act forbids American government agencies, businesses, or citizens from providing money, weapons, or any other type of aid to a nation at war. It also prohibits Americans from traveling to war zones or sailing on vessels owned by a nation at war.

EXPORT OF ARMS, AMMUNITION, AND IMPLEMENTS OF WAR

Section 1. (a) Whenever the President shall find that there exists a state of war between, or among, two or more foreign states, the President shall proclaim such fact, and it shall thereafter be unlawful to export, or attempt to export, or cause to be exported, arms, ammunition, or implements of war from any place in the United States to any belligerent state named in such proclamation, or to any neutral state for transshipment to, or for the use of, any such belligerent state.

(b) The President shall, from time to time, by proclamation, extend such embargo upon the export of arms, ammunition, or implements of war to other states as and when they may become involved in such war.

(c) Whenever the President shall find that such a state of civil strife exists in a foreign state and that such civil strife is of a magnitude or is being conducted under such conditions that the export of arms, ammunition, or implements of war from the United States to such foreign state would threaten or endanger the peace of the United States, the President shall proclaim such fact, and it shall thereafter be unlawful to export, or attempt to export, or cause to be exported, arms, ammunition, or implements of war from any place in the United States to such foreign state, or to any neutral state for transshipment to, or for use of, such foreign state.

(d) The President shall, from time to time by proclamation, definitely enumerate the arms, ammunition, and implements of war, the export of which is prohibited by this section....

(e) Whoever, in violation of any of the provisions of this Act, shall export, or attempt to export, or cause to be exported, arms, ammunition, or implements of war from the United States shall be fined not more than $10,000, or imprisoned not more than five years, or both....

EXPORT OF OTHER ARTICLES AND MATERIALS

Section 2. (a) Whenever the President shall have issued a proclamation under the authority of section 1 of this Act and he shall thereafter find that the placing of restrictions on the shipment of certain articles or materials in addition to arms, ammunition, and implements of war from the United States to belligerent states, or to a state wherein civil strife exists, is necessary to promote the security or preserve the peace of the United States or to protect the lives of citizens of the United States, he shall so proclaim, and it shall thereafter be unlawful, for any American vessel to carry such articles or materials to any belligerent state, or to any state wherein civil strife exists, named in such proclamation issued under the authority of section 1 of this Act, or to any neutral state for transshipment to, or for the use of, any such belligerent states or any such state wherein civil strife exists. The President shall by proclamation from time to time definitely enumerate the articles and materials which it shall be unlawful for American vessels to so transport....

FINANCIAL TRANSACTIONS

Section 3. (a) Whenever the President shall have issued a proclamation under the authority of section 1 of this Act, it shall thereafter be unlawful for any person within the United States to purchase, sell, or exchange bonds, securities, or other obligations of the government of any belligerent state or of any state wherein civil strife exists, named in such proclamation, or of any political subdivision of any such state, or of any person acting for or on behalf of the government of any such state, or of any faction or asserted government within any such state wherein civil strife exists, or of any person acting for or on behalf of any faction or asserted government within any such state wherein civil strife exists, issued after the date of such proclamation, or to make any loan or extend any credit to any such government, political subdivision, faction, asserted government, or person, or to solicit or receive any contribution for any such government, political subdivision, faction, asserted government, or person.

PROVIDED, That if the President shall find that such action will serve to protect the commercial or other interest of the United States or its citizens, he may, in his discretion, and to such extent and under such regulations as he may prescribe, except from the operation of this section ordinary commercial credits and short-time obligations in aid of legal transactions and of a character customarily used in normal peacetime commercial transactions. Nothing in this subsection shall be construed to prohibit the solicitation or collection of funds to be used for medical aid and assistance, or for food and clothing to relieve human suffering, when such solicitation or collection of funds is made on behalf of and for use by any person or organization which is not acting for or on behalf of any such government, political subdivision, faction, or asserted government, but all such solicitations and collections of funds shall be subject to the approval of the President and shall be made under such rules and regulations as he shall prescribe....

(c) Whoever shall violate the provisions of this section or of any regulations issued hereunder shall, upon conviction thereof, be fined not more than $50,000 or imprisoned for not more than five years, or both. Should the violation be by a corporation, organization, or association, each officer or agent thereof participating in the violation may be liable to the penalty herein prescribed....

EXCEPTIONS—AMERICAN REPUBLICS

Section 4. This Act shall not apply to an American republic or republics engaged in war against a non-American state or states, provide the American republic is not cooperating with a non-American state or states in such a war.

NATIONAL MUNITIONS CONTROL BOARD

Section 5. (a) There is hereby established a National Munitions Control Board (herein after referred to as the 'Board') to carry out the provisions of this Act. The board shall consist of the Secretary of State, who shall be chairman and executive officer of the Board, the Secretary of the Treasury, the Secretary of War, the Secretary of the Navy, and the Secretary of Commerce. Except as otherwise provided in this Act, or by other law, the administration of this Act is vested in the Department of State. The Secretary of State shall promulgate such rules and regulations with regard to the enforcement of this section as he may deem necessary to carry out its provisions. The Board shall be convened by the chairman and shall hold at least one meeting a year.

(b) Every person who engages in the business of manufacturing, exporting, or importing any of the arms, ammunition, or implements of war referred to in this Act, whether as an exporter, importer, manufacturer, or dealer, shall register with the Secretary of State his name, place of business, and places of business in the United States, and a list of the arms, ammunition, and implements of war which he manufactures, imports, or exports....

AMERICAN VESSELS PROHIBITED FROM CARRYING ARMS TO BELLIGERENT STATES

Section 6. (a) Whenever the President shall have issued a proclamation under the authority of section 1 of this Act, it shall thereafter be unlawful, until such proclamation is revoked, for any American vessel to carry any arms, ammunition, or implements of war to any belligerent state, or to any state wherein civil strife exists, named in such proclamation, or to any neutral state for transshipment to, or for the use of, any such belligerent state or any such state wherein civil strife exists.

(b) Whoever, in violation of the provisions of this section, shall take, or attempt to take, or shall authorize, hire, or solicit another to take, any American vessel carrying such cargo out of port or from the jurisdiction of the United States shall be fined not more than $10,000, or imprisoned not more than five years, or both; and in addition, such vessel, and her tackle, apparel, furniture, and equipment, and the arms, ammunition, and implements of war on board, shall be forfeited to the United States.

USE OF AMERICAN PORTS AS BASE OF SUPPLY

Section 7. (a) Whenever, during any war in which the United States is neutral, the President, or any person thereunto authorized by him, shall have cause to believe that any vessel, domestic or foreign, whether requiring clearance or not, is about to carry out of a port of the United States, fuel, men, arms, ammunition, implements of war, or other supplies to any warship, tender, or supply ship of a belligerent state, but the evidence is not deemed sufficient to justify forbidding the departure of the vessel as provided for by section 1, title V, chapter 30, of the Act approved June 15, 1917, and if, in the President's judgment, such action will serve to maintain peace between the United States and foreign states, or to protect the commercial interests of the United States and its citizens, or to promote the security or neutrality of the United States, he shall have the power and it shall be his duty to require the owner, master, or person in command thereof, before departing from a port of the United States, to give a bond to the United States, with sufficient sureties, in such amount as he shall deem proper, conditioned that the vessel will not deliver the men, or any part of the cargo, to any warship, tender, or supply ship of the belligerent state.

(b) If the President, or any person thereunto authorized by him, shall find that a vessel, domestic or foreign, in a port of the United States, has previously cleared from a port of the United States during such war and delivered its cargo or any part thereof to a warship, tender, or supply ship of a belligerent state, he may prohibit the departure of such vessel during the duration of the war.

SUBMARINES AND ARMED MERCHANT VESSELS

Section 8. Whenever, during any war in which the United States is neutral, the President shall find that special restrictions placed on the use of the ports and territorial waters of the United States by the submarines or armed merchant vessels of a foreign state, will serve to maintain peace between the United States and foreign states, or to protect the commercial interests of the United States and its citizens, or to promote the security of the United States, and shall make proclamation thereof, it shall thereafter be unlawful for any such submarine or armed merchant vessel to enter a port or the territorial waters of the United States or to depart thereof, except under such conditions and subject to such limitations as the President may prescribe. Whenever, in his judgment, the conditions which have caused him to issue his proclamation have ceased to exist, he shall revoke his proclamation and the provisions of this section shall thereupon cease to apply.

TRAVEL ON VESSELS OF BELLIGERENT STATES

Section 9. Whenever the President shall have issued a proclamation under the authority of section 1 of this Act it shall thereafter be unlawful for any citizen of the United States to travel on any vessel of the state or states named in such proclamation, except in accordance with such rules and regulations as the President shall prescribe....

ARMING OF AMERICAN MERCHANT VESSELS PROHIBITED

Section 10. Whenever the President shall have issued a proclamation under the authority of section 1, it shall thereafter be unlawful, until such proclamation is revoked, for any American vessel engaged in commerce with any belligerent state, or any state wherein civil strife exists, named in such proclamation, to be armed or to carry any armament, arms, ammunition, or implements of war, except small arms and ammunition therefor which the President may deem necessary and shall publicly designate for the preservation of discipline aboard such vessels....

Source: U.S. Congress. "Neutrality Act of 1937." May 1, 1937. Available online at Teaching American History, Ashbrook Center for Public Affairs, Ashland University, http://www.teachingamericanhistory.org.

The Tripartite Pact of 1940

Japan entered into a formal military alliance with Germany and Italy on September 27, 1940, when leaders of the three nations signed the Tripartite Pact. They agreed to cooperate with each other in "the establishment of a new order" in the world. Each nation recognized the others' spheres of interest and promised not to interfere in activities there. They also agreed to come to each other's defense in case of attack. Japanese leaders hoped that the Tripartite Pact, and the potential for war in both Europe and the Pacific, would help convince the United States to stay on the sidelines.

The governments of Germany, Italy and Japan, considering it as a condition precedent of any lasting peace that all nations of the world be given each its own proper place, have decided to stand by and co-operate with one another in regard to their efforts in greater East Asia and regions of Europe respectively wherein it is their prime purpose to establish and maintain a new order of things calculated to promote the mutual prosperity and welfare of the peoples concerned.

Furthermore, it is the desire of the three governments to extend co-operation to such nations in other spheres of the world as may be inclined to put forth endeavours along lines similar to their own, in order that their ultimate aspirations for world peace may thus be realized.

Accordingly, the governments of Germany, Italy and Japan have agreed as follows:

ARTICLE ONE

Japan recognizes and respects the leadership of Germany and Italy in establishment of a new order in Europe.

ARTICLE TWO

Germany and Italy recognize and respect the leadership of Japan in the establishment of a new order in greater East Asia.

ARTICLE THREE

Germany, Italy and Japan agree to co-operate in their efforts on aforesaid lines. They further undertake to assist one another with all political, economic and military means when one of the three contracting powers is attacked by a power at present not involved in the European war or in the Chinese-Japanese conflict.

ARTICLE FOUR

With the view to implementing the present pact, joint technical commissions, members which are to be appointed by the respective governments of Germany, Italy and Japan will meet without delay.

ARTICLE FIVE

Germany, Italy and Japan affirm that the aforesaid terms do not in any way affect the political status which exists at present as between each of the three contracting powers and Soviet Russia.

ARTICLE SIX

The present pact shall come into effect immediately upon signature and shall remain in force 10 years from the date of its coming into force. At the proper time before expiration of said term, the high contracting parties shall at the request of any of them enter into negotiations for its renewal.

In faith whereof, the undersigned duly authorized by their respective governments have signed this pact and have affixed hereto their signatures.

Done in triplicate at Berlin, the 27th day of September, 1940, in the 19th year of the fascist era, corresponding to the 27th day of the ninth month of the 15th year of Showa (the reign of Emperor Hirohito).

Source: "Tripartite Pact of 1940." Signed at Berlin, September 27, 1940. The Avalon Project, Yale Law School. Available online at http://avalon.law.yale.edu/wwii/triparti.asp.

The Japanese Attack Plan

The Japanese attack on Pearl Harbor on December 7, 1941, proceeded according to a detailed plan that was prepared well in advance. The document below includes two formal orders issued by Admiral Chuichi Nagumo, commander of the Japanese naval task force that executed the attack, to the ships in his fleet. All copies of the original orders were destroyed during the war. During the postwar occupation of Japan, however, the orders were reconstructed by former Japanese naval officers from personal notes and memory.

Carrier Striking Task Force Operations Order No. 1
3 November 1941
To: Carrier Striking Task Force

1. The Carrier Striking Task Force will proceed to the Hawaiian Area with utmost secrecy and, at the outbreak of the war, will launch a resolute surprise attack on and deal a fatal blow to the enemy fleet in the Hawaiian Area. The initial air attack is scheduled at 0330 hours, X Day. Upon completion of the air attacks, the Task Force will immediately withdraw and return to Japan and, after taking on new supplies, take its position for Second Period Operations. In the event that, during this operation, an enemy fleet attempts to intercept our force or a powerful enemy force is encountered and there is danger of attack, the Task Force will launch a counterattack.

2. The disposition of Force [chart omitted].

3. The Operation of Each Force.

   a. General

While exercising strict antiaircraft and antisubmarine measures and making every effort to conceal its position and movements, the entire force (except the Midway Bombardment Unit) in accordance with special orders will depart as a group from Hitokappu Bay at a speed of 12-14 knots. The force refueling en route whenever possible will arrive at the standby point (42 N, 165 W). In the event bad weather prevents refueling en route to the standby point, the screening unit will be ordered to return to the home base. Subsequent to the issuance of the order designating X Day (the day of the outbreak of hostilities), the force will proceed to the approaching point (32 N, 157 W).

Around 0700 hours, X − 1 Day the Task Force will turn southward at high speed (approximately 24 knots) from the vicinity of the approaching point. It will arrive at the take-off point (200 nautical miles north of the enemy fleet anchorage) at 0100 hours X – 1 Day (0530 Honolulu time) and commit the entire air strength to attack the enemy fleet and important airfields on Oahu.

Upon completion of the air attacks, the Task Force will assemble the aircraft, skirt 800 nautical miles north of Midway, return about X + 15 Day to the western part of the Inland Sea via the assembly point (30 N, 165 E) and prepare for Second Period Operations. In the event of a fuel shortage the Task Force will proceed to Truk via the assembly point.

The force may skirt near Midway in the event that consideration of an enemy counter-attack is unnecessary due to successful air attacks or if such action is necessitated by fuel shortage.

In this event, the 5th Carrier Division with the support of the *Kirishima* from the 3rd Battleship Division will leave the Task Force on the night of X Day or the early morning of X + 1 Day and carry out air attacks on Midway in the early morning of X + 2 Day.

If a powerful enemy force intercepts our return route, the Task Force will break through the Hawaiian Islands area southward and proceed to the Marshall Islands.

b. Patrol Unit

The patrol unit will accompany the main force. In the event the screening unit is returned to the home base, the patrol unit will screen the advance of the main force and the launching and the landing of aircraft. After the air attacks, the patrol unit will station itself between the flank of the main force and the enemy. In the event of an enemy fleet sortie, the patrol unit will shadow the enemy and in a favorable situation attack him.

c. The Midway Bombardment Unit

The Midway Bombardment Unit will depart from Tokyo Bay around X – 6 Day and, after refueling, secretly approach Midway. It will arrive on the night of X Day and shell the air base. The unit will then withdraw and, after refueling, return to the western part of the Inland Sea. The oiler *Shiriya* will accompany the bombardment unit on this mission and will be responsible for the refueling operation.

d. Supply Force

The supply force will accompany the main force to the approaching point, carrying out refuelings, separate from the main force, skirt 800 nautical miles north of Midway, return to the assembly point by 0800 hours, X + 6 Day, and stand by.

4. The Task Force may suspend operations en route to the Hawaiian area and return to Hitokappu Bay, Hokkaido or Mutsu Bay, depending upon the situation.

Commander
Carrier Striking Task Force
Nagumo, Chuichi

Carrier Striking Task Force Operations Order No. 3
23 November 1941
To: Carrier Striking Task Force

The Hawaiian operations air attack plan has been decided as follows:

1. The Operation of the Air Attack Forces

The force will be 700 nautical miles due north of point Z (set at the western extremity of the Island of Lanai) at 0600 hours X – 1 Day and advance on a course of 180 degrees from 0700 hours X – 1 Day at an increased speed of 24 knots.

Air attacks will be carried out by launching the first attack units 230 nautical miles due north of Z point at 0130 hours X Day, and the second attack unit at 200 nautical miles due north of Z point at 0245 hours.

After the launching of the second attack units is completed, the task force will withdraw northward at a speed of about 24 knots. The first attack units are scheduled to return between 0530 and 0600 hours and the second attack units are scheduled to return between 0645 and 0715 hours.

Immediately after the return of the first and second attack units, preparations for the next attack will be completed. At this time, carrier attack planes capable of carrying torpedoes will be armed with such as long as the supply lasts.

If the destruction of enemy land-based air strength progresses favorably, repeated attacks will be made immediately and thus decisive results will be achieved.

In the event that a powerful enemy surface fleet appears, it will be attacked.

169

2. Organization of the Air Attack Units [chart omitted].

3. Targets

a. The First Attack Units

The targets for the first group will be limited to about four battleships and four aircraft carriers; the order of targets will be battleships and then aircraft carriers.

The second group will attack the enemy land-based air strength according to the following assignment:

• The 15 Attack Unit: Hangars and aircraft on Ford Island

• The 16 Attack Unit: Hangars and aircraft on Wheeler Field

• The targets of Fighter Combat Units will be enemy aircraft in the air and on the ground.

b. The Second Attack Units

• The first group will attack the enemy air bases according to the following assignment:

• The 5 Attack Unit: Aircraft and hangars on Kaneohe, Ford Island and Barbers Point.

• The 6 Attack Unit: Hangars and aircraft on Hickam Field.

• The targets for the second group will be limited to four or five enemy aircraft carriers. If the number of targets is insufficient, they will select targets in the order of cruisers and battleships.

• The Fighter Combat Units will attack the enemy aircraft in the air and on the ground.

4. Attack Procedure

a. The First Attack Units

(1) With the element of surprise as the principle, attacks will be carried out by the torpedo unit and bomber unit of the First Group, and then the Second Group.

(2) During the initial phase of the attack, the Fighter Combat Units will, in one formation, storm the enemy skies about the same time as the First Group, and contact and destroy chiefly the enemy interceptor planes.

In the event that no enemy aircraft are encountered in the air, the units will immediately shift to the strafing of parked aircraft as follows:

- 1st and 2nd Fighter Combat Units: Ford Island and Hickam Field.

- 3rd and 4th Fighter Combat Units: Wheeler Field and Barbers Point.

- 5th and 6th Fighter Combat Units: Kaneohe

(3) In the event that the advantage of surprise attack cannot be expected due to strict enemy security, the approach and attack will be made in the order of the Fighter Combat Units, Dive Bombing Units, Horizontal Bombing Units and the Torpedo Attacking Units.

b. The Second Attack Units

All units will storm the enemy skies almost simultaneously and launch the attacks.

Although the general outline of the operations of the Fighter Combat Units corresponds to that of the First Attack Units, the strafing will be carried out according to the following in case there are no enemy aircraft in the air.

- 1st and 2nd Fighter Combat Units: Ford Island and Hickam Field

- 3rd and 4th Fighter Combat Units: Wheeler Field and Kaneohe

c. The general outline of attack in the event that enemy aircraft carriers and the main body of the U.S. Fleet are in anchorages outside Pearl Harbor are:

(1) The organization and targets are the same as mentioned above. The First Attack Units of the First Group, however, will increase the number of torpedo bombers as much as possible.

(2) Escorted by the Fighter Combat Units, the Air Attack Units will proceed in a group and attack the designated targets in the order of the enemy fleet anchorages and the Island of Oahu. If attacks on the enemy fleet anchorages progress favorably, however, the Fighter Combat Units and the 2nd Group of the First Air Attack Unit will immediately proceed to the Island of Oahu. Upon completion of the attacks, the anchorage attack unit will return directly to the carriers.

d. Rendezvous for Return to Carriers

(1) The rendezvous point will be 20 nautical miles at 340 degrees from the western extremity (Kaena Point) of the Island of Oahu. The rendezvous altitude will be 1,000 meters. (If this vicinity is covered with clouds, it will be below the cloud ceiling.)

(2) The Attack Units will wait at the rendezvous point for about 30 minutes and return to their carriers, after being joined by the Fighter Combat Units.

(3) While returning to carriers, the Fighter Combat Unit will become the rear guards for the whole unit and intercept any enemy pursuit.

5. Reconnaissance

a. Pre-operation Reconnaissance

Pre-operation reconnaissance will not be carried out unless otherwise ordered.

b. Immediate Pre-attack Reconnaissance

Two reconnaissance seaplanes of the 8th Cruiser Division will take off at 0030 hours, X Day, secretly reconnoiter Pearl Harbor and Lahaina Anchorage and report the presence of the enemy fleet (chiefly carriers and the main body of the fleet).

c. Scouting Patrol

The reconnaissance seaplanes of the 8th Cruiser Division will take off at 0300 hours and will carry out an extensive search of the waters between the enemy and the friendly forces and the waters adjacent to the two channels situated to the east and west of the Island of Oahu. They will observe and report the presence and activities of the enemy sortie force and enemy aircraft on counter-attack missions.

d. Before returning to its carrier, after the attack, an element of fighters designated by the Fighter Combat Unit Commander will fly as low and as fast as circumstances permit and observe and determine the extent of damage inflicted upon the enemy aircraft and ships.

Air Security Disposition No. 1 Method B will be followed from one hour before sunrise until 45 minutes after sunset on the day of the air attack.

Commander
Carrier Striking Task Force
Nagumo, Chuichi

Source: Nagumo, Chuichi. "Carrier Striking Task Force Operations Order Numbers 1 and 3." November 23, 1941. From Japanese Monograph No. 97, "Pearl Harbor Operations: General Outline of Orders and Plans." Prepared by Military History Section Headquarters, Army Forces Far East. Distributed by Office of the Chief of Military History, Department of the Army. Available online at http://www.ibiblio.org/pha/monos/097/index.html.

President Franklin D. Roosevelt Appeals for Peace

On December 6, 1941—the day before Japanese planes attacked Pearl Harbor—President Franklin D. Roosevelt wrote a letter to Japan's sacred ruler, Emperor Hirohito. In this letter, which appears below, Roosevelt describes the growing tensions between the United States and Japan as a "keg of dynamite." He requests the Emperor's help to avoid war in the Pacific.

Almost a century ago the President of the United States addressed to the Emperor of Japan a message extending an offer of friendship of the people of the United States to the people of Japan. That offer was accepted, and in the long period of unbroken peace and friendship which has followed, our respective Nations, through the virtues of their peoples and the wisdom of their rulers, have prospered and have substantially helped humanity.

Only in situations of extraordinary importance to our two countries need I address to Your Majesty messages on matters of state. I feel I should now so address you because of the deep and far-reaching emergency which appears to be in formation.

Developments are occurring in the Pacific area which threaten to deprive each of our Nations and all humanity of the beneficial influence of the long peace between our two countries. Those developments contain tragic possibilities.

The people of the United States, believing in peace and in the right of Nations to live and let live, have eagerly watched the conversations between our two Governments during these past months. We have hoped for a termination of the present conflict between Japan and China. We have hoped that a peace of the Pacific could be consummated in such a way that nationalities of many diverse peoples could exist side by side without fear of invasion; that unbearable burdens of armaments could be lifted for them all; and that all peoples would resume commerce without discrimination against or in favor of any Nation.

I am certain that it will be clear to Your Majesty, as it is to me, that in seeking these great objectives both Japan and the United States should agree to eliminate any form of military threat. This seemed essential to the attainment of the high objectives.

More than a year ago Your Majesty's Government concluded an agreement with the Vichy Government by which five or six thousand Japanese troops were permitted to enter into Northern French Indo-China for the protection of Japanese troops which were operating against China further north. And this spring and summer the Vichy Government permitted further Japanese military forces to enter into Southern French Indo-China for the common defense of French Indo-China. I think I am correct in saying that no attack has been made upon Indo-China, nor that any has been contemplated.

During the past few weeks it has become clear to the world that Japanese military, naval, and air forces have been sent to Southern Indo-China in such large numbers as to create a reasonable doubt on the part of other Nations that this continuing concentration in Indo-China is not defensive in its character.

Because these continuing concentrations in Indo-China have reached such large proportions and because they extend now to the southeast and the southwest corners of that peninsula, it is only reasonable that the people of the Philippines, of the hundreds of islands of the East Indies, of Malaya, and of Thailand itself are asking themselves whether these forces of Japan are preparing or intending to make attack in one or more of these many directions.

I am sure that Your Majesty will understand that the fear of all these peoples is a legitimate fear inasmuch as it involves their peace and their national existence. I am sure that Your Majesty will understand why the people of the United States in such large numbers look askance at the establishment of military, naval, and air bases manned and equipped so greatly as to constitute armed forces capable of measures of offense.

It is clear that a continuance of such a situation is unthinkable.

None of the peoples whom I have spoken of above can sit either indefinitely or permanently on a keg of dynamite.

There is absolutely no thought on the part of the United States of invading Indo-China if every Japanese soldier or sailor were to be withdrawn therefrom.

I think that we can obtain the same assurance from the Governments of the East Indies, the Governments of Malaya, and the Government of Thailand. I would even undertake to ask for the same assurance on the part of the Government of China. Thus a withdrawal of the Japanese forces from Indo-China would result in the assurance of peace throughout the whole of the South Pacific area.

I address myself to Your Majesty at this moment in the fervent hope that Your Majesty may, as I am doing, give thought in this definite emergency to ways of dispelling the dark clouds. I am confident that both of us, for the sake of the peoples not only of our own great countries but for the sake of humanity in neighboring territories, have a sacred duty to restore traditional amity and prevent further death and destruction in the world.

Source: Roosevelt, Franklin D. "Appeal to Emperor Hirohito to Avoid War in the Pacific." December 6, 1941. From Woolley, John T., and Gerhard Peters, eds. *The American Presidency Project*. Santa Barbara, CA: University of California. Available online at http://www.presidency.ucsb.edu/ws/?pid=16052.

Japanese Pilot Mitsuo Fuchida Leads the Attack

The lead pilot in the Japanese attack on Pearl Harbor was Commander Mitsuo Fuchida. His recol-lections of the attack were first published in English in his 1955 book Midway: The Battle that Doomed Japan—The Japanese Navy's Story. *In the excerpt below, Fuchida describes arriving over Hawaii, giving the order to attack, and witnessing the destruction of U.S. ships and air bases.*

One hour and forty minutes after leaving the carriers I knew that we should be nearing our goal. Small openings in the thick cloud cover afforded occasional glimpses of the ocean, as I strained my eyes for the first sight of land. Suddenly a long white line of breaking surf appeared directly beneath my plane. It was the northern shore of Oahu.

Veering right toward the west coast of the island, we could see that the sky over Pearl Harbor was clear. Presently the harbor itself became visible across the central Oahu plain, a film of morning mist hovering over it. I peered intently through my binoculars at the ships riding peacefully at anchor. One by one I counted them. Yes, the battleships were there all right, eight of them! But our last lingering hope of finding any carriers present was now gone. Not one was to be seen.

It was 0749 when I ordered my radioman to send the command, "Attack!" He immediately began tapping out the pre-arranged code signal: "TO, TO, TO..."

Leading the whole group, Lieutenant Commander Murata's torpedo bombers headed downward to launch their torpedoes, while Lieutenant Commander Itayay's fighters raced forward to sweep enemy fighters from the air. Takahashi's dive-bomber group had climbed for altitude and was out of sight. My bombers, meanwhile, made a circuit toward Barbers Point to keep pace with the attack schedule. No enemy fighters were in the air, nor were there any gun flashes from the ground.

The effectiveness of our attack was now certain, and a message, "Surprise attack successful!" was accordingly sent to *Akagi* [flagship of the Japan-ese attack fleet] at 0753. The message was received by the carrier and duly relayed to the homeland....

The attack was opened with the first bomb falling on Wheeler Field, followed shortly by dive-bombing attacks upon Hickam Field and the bases at Ford Island. Fearful that smoke from these attacks might obscure his targets, Lieutenant Commander Murata cut short his group's approach toward the battleships anchored east of Ford Island and released torpedoes. A series of white waterspouts soon rose in the harbor.

Lieutenant Commander Itaya's fighters, meanwhile, had full command of the air over Pearl Harbor. About four enemy fighters which took off were promptly shot down. By 0800 there were no enemy planes in the air, and our fighters began strafing the airfields.

My level-bombing group had entered on its bombing run toward the battleships moored to the east of Ford Island. On reaching an altitude of 3,000 meters, I had the sighting bomber take position in front of my plane.

As we closed in, enemy antiaircraft fire began to concentrate on us. Dark gray puffs burst all around. Most of them came from ships' batteries, but land batteries were also active. Suddenly my plane bounced as if struck by a club. When I looked back to see what had happened, the radioman said: "The fuselage is holed and the rudder wire damaged." We were fortunate that the plane was still under control, for it was imperative to fly a steady course as we approached the target. Now it was nearly time for "Ready to release," and I concentrated my attention on the lead plane to note the instant his bomb was dropped. Suddenly a cloud came between the bombsight and the target, and just as I was thinking that we had already overshot, the lead plane banked slightly and turned right toward Honolulu. We had missed the release point because of the cloud and would have to try again.

While my group circled for another attempt, others made their runs, some trying as many as three before succeeding. We were about to begin our second bombing run when there was a colossal explosion [on the USS *Arizona*] in battleship row. A huge column of dark red smoke rose to 1,000 meters. It must have been the explosion of a ship's powder magazine. The shock wave was felt even in my plane, several miles away from the harbor.

We began our run and met with fierce antiaircraft concentrations. This time the lead bomber was successful, and the other planes of the group followed suit promptly upon seeing the leader's bombs fall. I immediately lay flat on the cockpit floor and slid open a peephole cover in order to observe the fall of the bombs. I watched four bombs plummet toward the earth. The target—

two battleships moored side by side—lay ahead. The bombs became smaller and smaller and finally disappeared. I held my breath until two tiny puffs of smoke flashed suddenly on the ship to the left, and I shouted, "Two hits!"

When an armor-piercing bomb with a time fuse hits the target, the result is almost unnoticeable from a great altitude. On the other hand, those which miss are quite obvious because they leave concentric waves to ripple out from the point of contact, and I saw two of these below. I presumed that it was battleship *Maryland* we had hit.

As the bombers completed their runs they headed north to return to the carriers. Pearl Harbor and the air bases had been pretty well wrecked by the fierce strafings and bombings. The imposing naval array of an hour before was gone. Antiaircraft fire had become greatly intensified, but in my continued observations I saw no enemy fighter planes. Our command of the air was unchallenged.

Source: Fuchida, Mitsuo, and Masatake Okumiya. "Attack At Pearl Harbor, 1941—The Japanese View," Available online at EyeWitness to History, http://www.eyewitnessto history.com/pfpearl2.htm.

A U.S. Navy Crewman Remembers Chaos and Casualties

One of the ships moored in Pearl Harbor on the morning of December 7, 1941, was the USS Utah, *an obsolete battleship that had been dismantled and covered with wooden decking to serve as a target ship in training exercises. The* Utah *was struck by several torpedoes during the first wave of the Japanese attack, as some enemy pilots apparently mistook it for an aircraft carrier. The ship capsized within minutes, taking the lives of 58 sailors. Pharmacist's Mate Second Class Lee Soucy was stationed aboard the* Utah *at the time of the attack. In the oral history excerpted below, Soucy remembers escaping from his sinking ship and swimming to shore, where he uses his first aid training to help injured servicemen.*

I had just had breakfast and was looking out a porthole in sick bay when someone said, "What the hell are all those planes doing up there on a Sunday?" Someone else said, "It must be those crazy Marines. They'd be the only ones out maneuvering on a Sunday." When I looked up in the sky I saw five or six planes starting their descent. Then when the first bombs dropped on the hangars at Ford Island, I thought, "Those guys are missing us by a mile." Inasmuch as practice bombing was a daily occurrence to us, it was not too unusual for planes to drop bombs, but the time and place were quite out of line. We could not imagine bombing practice in port. It occurred to me and to most of the others that someone had really goofed this time and put live bombs on those planes by mistake.

In any event, even after I saw a huge fireball and cloud of black smoke rise from the hangers on Ford Island and heard explosions, it did not occur to me that these were enemy planes. It was too incredible! Simply beyond imagination! "What a SNAFU," I moaned.

As I watched the explosions on Ford Island in amazement and disbelief, I felt the ship lurch. We didn't know it then, but we were being bombed and torpedoed by planes approaching from the opposite (port) side.

The bugler and bosun's mate were on the fantail ready to raise the colors at 8 o'clock. In a matter of seconds, the bugler sounded "General Quarters." I grabbed my first aid bag and headed for my battle station amidship.

A number of the ship's tremors are vaguely imprinted in my mind, but I remember one jolt quite vividly. As I was running down the passageway toward my battle station, another torpedo or bomb hit and shook the ship severely. I was knocked off balance and through the log room door. I got up a little dazed and immediately darted down the ladder below the armored deck. I forgot my first aid kit.

By then the ship was already listing [leaning over on its side]. There were a few men down below who looked dumbfounded and wondered out loud, "What's going on?" I felt around my shoulder in great alarm. No first aid kit! Being out of uniform is one thing, but being at a battle station without proper equipment is more than embarrassing.

After a minute or two below the armored deck, we heard another bugle call, then the bosun's whistle followed by the boatswain's chant, "Abandon ship.... Abandon ship."

We scampered up the ladder. As I raced toward the open side of the deck, an officer stood by a stack of life preservers and tossed the jackets at us as we ran by. When I reached the open deck, the ship was listing precipitously. I thought about the huge amount of ammunition we had on board and that it would surely blow up soon. I wanted to get away from the ship fast, so I discarded my life jacket. I didn't want a Mae West [nickname for an inflatable life preserver vest] slowing me down.

Another thing that jolted my memory was how rough the beach on Ford Island was. The day previous, I had been part of a fire and rescue party dispatched to fight a small fire on Ford Island. The fire was out by the time we got there but I remember distinctly the rugged beach, so I tied double knots in my shoes whereas just about everyone else kicked theirs off.

I was tensely poised for a running dive off the partially exposed hull when the ship lunged again and threw me off balance. I ended up with my bottom sliding across and down the barnacle-encrusted bottom of the ship.

When the ship had jolted, I thought we had been hit by another bomb or torpedo, but later it was determined that the mooring lines snapped which caused the 21,000-ton ship to jerk so violently as she keeled over.

Nevertheless, after I bobbed up to the surface of the water to get my bearings, I spotted a motor launch with a coxswain [sailor in charge of a boat and crew] fishing men out of the water with his boat hook. I started to swim toward the launch. After a few strokes, a hail of bullets hit the water a few feet in front of me in line with the launch. As the strafer banked, I noticed the big red insignias [the rising sun emblem of the Japanese Empire] on his wing tips. Until then, I really had not known who attacked us. At some point, I had heard someone shout, "Where did those Germans come from?" I quickly decided that a boat full of men would be a more likely strafing target than a lone swimmer, so I changed course and hightailed it for Ford Island.

I reached the beach exhausted and as I tried to catch my breath, another pharmacist's mate, Gordon Sumner, from the *Utah*, stumbled out of the water. I remember how elated I was to see him. There is no doubt in my mind that bewilderment, if not misery, loves company. I remember I felt guilty that I had not made any effort to recover my first aid kit. Sumner had his wrapped around his shoulders.

While we both tried to get our wind back, a jeep came speeding by and came to a screeching halt. One of the two officers in the vehicle had spotted our Red Cross brassards [badges worn around the arm] and hailed us aboard. They took us to a two- or three-story concrete BOQ (bachelor officer's quarters) facing Battleship Row to set up an emergency treatment station for several oil-covered casualties [injured men] strewn across the concrete floor. Most of them were from the capsized or flaming battleships. It did not take long to exhaust the supplies in Sumner's bag.

A line officer came by to inquire how we were getting along. We told him that we had run out of everything and were in urgent need of bandages and some kind of solvent or alcohol to cleanse wounds. He ordered someone to strip the beds and make rolls of bandages with the sheets. Then he turned to us and said, "Alcohol? Alcohol?" he repeated. "Will whiskey do?"

Before we could mull it over, he took off and in a few minutes he returned and plunked a case of scotch at our feet. Another person who accompanied him had an armful of bottles of a variety of liquors. I am sure denatured [rubbing or medical] alcohol could not have served our purpose better for washing off the sticky oil, as well as providing some antiseptic effect for a variety of wounds and burns.

Despite the confusion, pain, and suffering, there was some gusty humor amidst the pathos and chaos. At one point, an exhausted swimmer, covered with a gooey film of black oil, saw me walking around with a washcloth in one hand and a bottle of booze in the other. He hollered, "Hey Doc, could I have a shot of that medicine?" I handed him the bottle of whichever medicine I had at the time. He took a hefty swig. He had no sooner swallowed the "medicine" then he spewed it out along with black mucoidal [mucus-like] globs of oil. He lay back a minute after he stopped vomiting, then said, "Doc, I lost that medicine. How about another dose?"

Perhaps my internal as well as external application of booze was not accepted medical practice, but it sure made me popular with the old salts. Actually, it probably was a good medical procedure if it induced vomiting. Retaining contaminated water and oil in one's stomach was not good for one's health.

I remember another incident. A low-flying enemy pilot was strafing toward our concrete haven while I was on my knees trying to determine what to do for a prostrate casualty. Although the sailor, or marine, was in bad shape, he raised his head feebly when he saw the plane approach and shouted, "Open the doors and let the sonofabitch in."

Events which occurred in seconds take minutes to recount. During the lull, regular medical personnel from Ford Island Dispensary arrived with proper supplies and equipment and released Sumner and me so we could rejoin other *Utah* survivors for reassignment.

When the supplies ran out at our first aid station, I suggested to Sumner that he volunteer to go to the Naval Dispensary for some more. When he returned, he mentioned that he had a close call. A bomb landed in the patio while he was at the dispensary. He didn't mention any injury so I shrugged it off. After all, under the circumstances, what was one bomb more or less. That afternoon, while we were both walking along a lanai (screened porch) at the dispensary, he pointed to a crater in the patio. "That's where the bomb hit I told you about." "Where were you?" I asked. He pointed to a spot not far away. I said, "Come on, if you had been that close, you'd have been killed." To which he replied, "Oh, it didn't go off. I fled the area in a hurry."

Sometime after dark, a squadron of scout planes from the carrier *Enterprise* (two hundred or so miles out at sea), their fuel nearly depleted, came in for a landing on Ford Island. All hell broke loose and the sky lit up from tracer bullets from numerous antiaircraft guns. As the *Enterprise* planes approached some understandably trigger-happy gunners opened fire; then all gunners followed suit and shot down all but one of our planes. At least, that's what I was told. Earlier that evening, many of the *Utah* survivors had been taken to the USS *Argonne* (AP-4), a transport. Gunners manning .50 caliber machine guns on the partially submerged USS *California* directly across from the *Argonne* hit the ship while shooting at the planes. A stray, armor-piercing bullet penetrated *Argonne*'s thin bulkhead, went through a *Utah* survivor's arm, and spent itself in another sailor's heart. He died instantly.

The name Price has been stored in my memory bank for a long time as this fatality but, at a recent reunion of *Utah* survivors, another ex-shipmate, Gilbert Meyer, insisted that Price was not the one killed. I didn't argue too long because I recalled meeting two men at the Pearl Harbor Naval Hospital several weeks after the raid who walked around with their own obituaries in their wallets—clippings from hometown newspapers.

Source: Soucy, Lee. "Oral History of the Pearl Harbor Attack, 7 December 1941: Pharma-cist's Mate Second Class Lee Soucy." Washington, D.C.: U.S. Department of the Navy, Naval Historical Center, 1999. Available online at http://www.history.navy.mil/faqs/faq66-3a.htm.

A High School Student Describes How the Attack Changed Her Life

The document below is an excerpt from the diary of a 17-year-old high school senior who was living at Hickam Field—a U.S. Army Air Force Base located near the entrance to Pearl Harbor in Hawaii—with her family in 1941. When the Japanese attacked Pearl Harbor on December 7, 182 people were killed at Hickam, 57 American planes were destroyed, and the base's runways, hangars, armory, barracks, and mess hall were severely damaged.

In her diary, E.B. (Betty) Leonard records the dramatic changes that took place in her life as a result of the Pearl Harbor attack. The entries prior to the surprise Japanese raid are full of the typical concerns of a teenage girl, such as writing out Christmas cards, doing her homework, and seeing movies with friends. The entries for December 7 describe the harrowing experience from the perspective of a civilian caught in a war zone. In the entries following the attack, Leonard writes about scenes of destruction, nightly blackouts, and the possibility of being evacuated to the mainland. When preparing the diary for publication, Leonard chose to delete the last names of people mentioned; otherwise, the content is the same as when it was written.

Saturday, December 6, 1941

Washed my hair finally. It's warm again, so it dried real fast. Read the paper and then it was time to eat lunch. Listened to the Shriner's football game over the radio. The University beat Willamette 20-6. I spent all afternoon reading funny books and trying to get our transportation figured out for tonight. Finally fixed it so Hester took us and Dad brought us home. We (Kay and I) were ushering at Punahou for the play "Mr. and Mrs. North." It was pretty good. We got home about ten of twelve and I'm very sleepy. Lani invited us to dinner Tuesday.

Sunday, December 7, 1941

BOMBED! 8:00 in the morning. Unknown attacker so far! Pearl Harbor in flames! Also Hickam hangar line. So far no houses bombed here.

5 of 11:00. We've left the Post. It got too hot. The PX [Post Exchange, a general store on the base] is in flames, also the barracks. We made a dash dur-

---

ing a lull. Left everything we own there. Found out the attackers are Japs. Rats!!! A couple of non-com's [non-commissioned officers] houses demolished. Hope Kay is O.K. We're at M's. It's all so sudden and surprising I can't believe it's really happening. It's awful. School is discontinued until further notice.... There goes my graduation.

Shortwave: Direct hit on barracks, 350 killed. Wonder if I knew any of them. Been quiet all afternoon. Left Bill on duty at the U. Blackout all night of course!

[The following was typed on a separate piece of paper attached to the diary page.]

I was awakened at eight o'clock on the morning of December 7th by an explosion from Pearl Harbor. I got up thinking something exciting was probably going on over there. Little did I know! When I reached the kitchen the whole family, excluding Pop, was looking over at the Navy Yard. It was being consumed by black smoke and more terrific explosions. We didn't know what was going on, but I didn't like it because the first explosion looked as if it was right on top of Marie's house. I went and told Pop that (he in the meantime had gotten dressed and was leaving) and he said, "Who cares about Marie when you and Mom might be killed!" Then I became extremely worried, as did we all. Mom and I went out on the front porch to get a better look and three planes went zooming over our heads so close we could have touched them. They had red circles on their wings. Then we caught on! About that time bombs started dropping all over Hickam. We stayed at the windows, not knowing what else to do, and watched the fireworks. It was just like the news reels of Europe, only worse. We saw a bunch of soldiers come running full tilt towards us from the barracks and just then a whole line of bombs fell behind them knocking them all to the ground. We were deluged in a cloud of dust and had to run around closing all the windows. I got back to the front door just in time to see Pop calmly walking back to the house through it all. He said we could leave if a lull came. Also that a Mrs. B was coming down to our house and to wait for her. Then he left again. In the meantime a bunch of soldiers had come into our garage to hide. They were entirely taken by surprise and most of them didn't even have a gun or anything. One of them asked for a drink of water saying he was sick. He had just been so close to where a bomb fell that he had been showered with debris. He said he was scared, and I was too, so I couldn't say that I blamed him. I saw an officer out in the front yard, so Mom said to ask him if he thought it would be wise for us to try to leave. He said, "I would hate to say because we don't know whether they are bombing in town or not, and besides this is your home." I no sooner got back into the house than a terrible barrage came down just over by the Post Exchange. That's just a block kitty corner from us, so the noise and concussion was terrific. Mom and I were still standing in the doorway and we saw the PX get hit. I was getting more worried by the minute about this time as they seemed to be closing in the circle they had been making around us. (The Japs were flying around in a circle bombing us, Pearl Harbor, and machine-gunning Fort Kam.) A second terrific bunch of explosions followed the first by a few minutes only. I found out later these had landed in the baseball diamond just a second after Dad had walked across it. He ran back to see if the men in a radio truck there had been hit. All but one had and they were carted off in an ambulance. I went dashing into my room to look and saw that the barracks was on fire, also the big depot hangar. I hated to go into my room because the planes kept machine-gunning the street just outside my window and I kept expecting to see a string of bullets come through my roof any minute. We had all gotten dressed in the meantime and had packed a suitcase and were ready to leave any time. Finally, after two and a half hours, the planes went away and we left. I gave the soldiers in the garage two and a half packages of my chewing gum before I left and they nearly died of joy at sight of it. Poor guys!!

As we left the Post, we looked around to see what damage had been done to the place. The barracks was all on fire, the big depot was on fire, the theater was burned to the ground already, the PX was wrecked, the whole hangar line was blown up on the far side of Operations, a couple of the noncoms' houses were very badly blown out, there was debris all over everywhere, and Pearl Harbor was just a solid wall of smoke which we found out later was burning oil from the boats that had been hit. Reports are that nothing was hit there except boats.

As we drove into town we found the highway blocked solid in all three lanes coming out to the Post as the radio had been calling for all personnel of the Army or Navy to return to their posts at once. We were forced to drive out in the gutter, and every now and then we had to move aside from there to let an ambulance go by. The people in town were standing along the street watching it all with very dazed looks. Of course, they didn't know what was going on as the radio hadn't said a thing about it. (We turned it on at home before we left and there amidst all the concussion and noise all we could get was church music.) We ran into Bill on the way into town and made him come back with us. (He had been at the University practicing shooting and had missed it all.) He was mad because he wanted to go and see the fireworks. Ha! Lowyd was with us so we dumped him at the U. where he had a room. Left Jack with him, and Mom and I went up to the M's in Moana Valley. Decided to stay there until further notice so we went back and got Jack. Bill stayed at the U. on duty in the ROTC [Reserve Officers' Training Corps].

Monday, 8 December 1941

War was declared by Congress!!!

Dad called last night. He's OK. Said the barracks was completely destroyed. Soldiers are being quartered in houses. Hope they enjoy my room. Mom, Gaye, and I went down town. Bought me a toothbrush. Sent wires to the folks back in the States. Went to the U. to see Bill and Lowyd. Saw Lowyd, but not Bill. He was at the Armory. He's signed up in the Home Guard for three years or until the war is over. The Dope! Now if we have to leave, he'll have to stay here. Dad came up to see us. He's tired!! Poor guy looked as if he were about to fall over. Julia and Pat M. came to visit us, too. Still wonder where Kay, Jane, Pat F., and Marie are. Dad says there aren't any women or kids on the Post.

Tuesday, 9 December 1941

Slept for a few hours last night. We all sang songs in the dark so we didn't have to go to bed so early.

Mom, Jack, and I went out to the Post to get some clothes and pack a suitcase or two in case we get sent back to the States real sudden like. Mrs. B. went with us. She stayed there, however, and Dad made us leave. The Post is a wreck. The PX is all smashed and so is the depot and the barracks. Every single wing of the barracks! I can't see how it could be so thoroughly gone!

Stopped in town to see the D's. Mrs. D. is of course very worried. Came back to M's for dinner. Brought my accordion back and tried to play during blackout, but I couldn't.

Wednesday, 10 December 1941

Got up and took a shower (my first since the war began). Mom and I went to town. All is running as usual there, but they evidently weren't working yesterday or the day before. The dime store was crowded, but the counters were terribly bare. Except the Xmas gifts counters. Christmas shopping seems to have dropped off for more vital shopping.

Found out Kay is staying at Cerana's. Tried to call, but she wasn't home. Dad says they're building bombproof shelters around the houses on the Post so the families can move back. Hope they hurry! (Think I should go down for a music lesson today. Ha!) All the windows downtown are taped to prevent breaking. Some are very artistically done. Some very sloppy.

Thursday, 11 December, 1941

War declared against us by Germany and Italy.

Went out to the Post at nine. Dad is feeling much better. In fact, he seems quite cheerful. We picked up Elaine and took her out with us. She worked like a fiend cleaning up the house. Mom and I fixed up Jack's room with tarpaper so the men could read or something after blackout. Dad said it was a relief to have a clean house for a change.

Went on a tour of the Post. Boy, is it a mess. The hangars on the Kam. side of the Post were all smashed. I've never seen anything quite so wrecked. A lot of cars parked over that way were burned and smashed too.

Got all packed in suitcases and the wardrobe trunk in case we are evacuated. Hope we aren't! I feel safer on dry land!

Source: Leonard, E.B. "Ginger's Diary." December 6-11, 1941. Available online at http://www.gingersdiary.com/diary.html.

Roosevelt Requests a Declaration of War with Japan

The day after the Pearl Harbor attack, President Franklin D. Roosevelt made the following address before a joint session of the U.S. Congress. In this historic speech, he describes December 7, 1941, as "a date which will live in infamy." Roosevelt condemns the Japanese government for starting a war while peace negotiations were still underway, and he requests a formal declaration of war against Japan. The president also expresses great confidence that the United States will prevail.

Mr. Vice President, and Mr. Speaker, and Members of the Senate and House of Representatives:

Yesterday, December 7, 1941—a date which will live in infamy—the United States of America was suddenly and deliberately attacked by naval and air forces of the Empire of Japan.

The United States was at peace with that Nation and, at the solicitation of Japan, was still in conversation with its Government and its Emperor looking toward the maintenance of peace in the Pacific. Indeed, one hour after Japanese air squadrons had commenced bombing in the American Island of Oahu, the Japanese Ambassador to the United States and his colleague delivered to our Secretary of State a formal reply to a recent American message. And while this reply stated that it seemed useless to continue the existing diplomatic negotiations, it contained no threat or hint of war or of armed attack.

It will be recorded that the distance of Hawaii from Japan makes it obvious that the attack was deliberately planned many days or even weeks ago. During the intervening time the Japanese Government has deliberately sought to deceive the United States by false statements and expressions of hope for continued peace.

The attack yesterday on the Hawaiian Islands has caused severe damage to American naval and military forces. I regret to tell you that very many American lives have been lost. In addition American ships have been reported torpedoed on the high seas between San Francisco and Honolulu.

Yesterday the Japanese Government also launched an attack against Malaya.

Last night Japanese forces attacked Hong Kong.

Last night Japanese forces attacked Guam.

Last night Japanese forces attacked the Philippine Islands.

Last night the Japanese attacked Wake Island. And this morning the Japanese attacked Midway Island.

Japan has, therefore, undertaken a surprise offensive extending throughout the Pacific area. The facts of yesterday and today speak for themselves. The people of the United States have already formed their opinions and well understand the implications to the very life and safety of our Nation.

As Commander in Chief of the Army and Navy I have directed that all measures be taken for our defense.

But always will our whole Nation remember the character of the onslaught against us.

No matter how long it may take us to overcome this premeditated invasion, the American people in their righteous might will win through to absolute victory. I believe that I interpret the will of the Congress and of the people when I assert that we will not only defend ourselves to the uttermost but will make it very certain that this form of treachery shall never again endanger us.

Hostilities exist. There is no blinking at the fact that our people, our territory, and our interests are in grave danger.

With confidence in our armed forces—with the unbounding determination of our people—we will gain the inevitable triumph—so help us God.

I ask that the Congress declare that since the unprovoked and dastardly attack by Japan on Sunday, December 7, 1941, a state of war has existed between the United States and the Japanese Empire.

Source: Roosevelt, Franklin D. "Address to Congress Requesting a Declaration of War with Japan." December 8, 1941. From Woolley, John T., and Gerhard Peters, eds. *The American Presidency Project.* Santa Barbara, CA: University of California. Available online at http://www.presidency.ucsb.edu/ws/?pid=16053.

The U.S. Congress Declares War

On December 8, 1941, President Franklin D. Roosevelt asked the U.S. Congress to respond to the Pearl Harbor attack by declaring war against Japan. Congress granted his request that same day by a vote of 82-0 in the Senate and 388-1 in the House of Representatives. The full text of the joint resolution appears below.

Joint Resolution Declaring That a State of War Exists Between The Imperial Government of Japan and the Government And the People of the United States and Making Provisions To Prosecute the Same, 8 December 1941

Whereas the Imperial Government of Japan has committed unprovoked acts of war against the Government and the people of the United States of America:

Therefore be it

Resolved by the Senate and House of Representatives of the United States of America in Congress assembled, That the state of war between the United States and the Imperial Government of Japan which has thus been thrust upon the United States is hereby formally declared; and the President is hereby authorized and directed to employ the entire naval and military forces of the United States and the resources of the Government to carry on war against the imperial Government of Japan; and, to bring the conflict to a successful termination, all of the resources of the country are hereby pledged by the Congress of the United States.

Approved, December 8, 1941, 4:10 p.m., E. S. T.

Source: U.S. Congress. "Joint Resolution Declaring That a State of War Exists Between The Imperial Government of Japan and the Government And the People of the United States and Making Provisions To Prosecute the Same, 8 December 1941." Available online at Mount Holyoke College International Relations Program, http://www.mt holyoke.edu/acad/intrel/WorldWar2/declare.htm

Roosevelt Calls the American People to Action

On December 9, 1941—the day after the United States declared war against Japan—President Franklin D. Roosevelt outlined the historic challenge facing the nation in a radio address to the American people. This speech, which was part of a series of weekly radio addresses known as Fireside Chats, is reprinted below. The president acknowledges the danger that Axis aggression poses to the security of the United States and the world, but he expresses confidence that America will rise to the challenge and defeat its enemies. He also calls upon every U.S. citizen to do their patriotic duty to aid the war effort.

The sudden criminal attacks perpetrated by the Japanese in the Pacific provide the climax of a decade of international immorality.

Powerful and resourceful gangsters have banded together to make war upon the whole human race. Their challenge has now been flung at the United States of America. The Japanese have treacherously violated the long-standing peace between us. Many American soldiers and sailors have been killed by enemy action. American ships have been sunk; American airplanes have been destroyed.

The Congress and the people of the United States have accepted that challenge.

Together with other free peoples, we are now fighting to maintain our right to live among our world neighbors in freedom and in common decency, without fear of assault.

I have prepared the full record of our past relations with Japan, and it will be submitted to the Congress. It begins with the visit of Commodore Perry to Japan eighty-eight years ago. It ends with the visit of two Japanese emissaries to the Secretary of State last Sunday, an hour after Japanese forces had loosed their bombs and machine guns against our flag, our forces, and our citizens.

I can say with utmost confidence that no Americans, today or a thousand years hence, need feel anything but pride in our patience and in our efforts through all the years toward achieving a peace in the Pacific which would be fair and honorable to every Nation, large or small. And no honest person, today or a thousand years hence, will be able to suppress a sense of indignation and horror at the treachery committed by the military dictators of Japan, under the very shadow of the flag of peace borne by their special envoys in our midst.

The course that Japan has followed for the past ten years in Asia has paralleled the course of Hitler and Mussolini in Europe and in Africa. Today, it has become far more than a parallel. It is actual collaboration so well calculated that all the continents of the world, and all the oceans, are now considered by the Axis strategists as one gigantic battlefield.

In 1931, ten years ago, Japan invaded Manchukuo—without warning.

In 1935, Italy invaded Ethiopia—without warning.

In 1938, Hitler occupied Austria—without warning.

In 1939, Hitler invaded Czechoslovakia—without warning.

Later in 1939, Hitler invaded Poland—without warning.

In 1940, Hitler invaded Norway, Denmark, the Netherlands, Belgium, and Luxembourg—without warning.

In 1940, Italy attacked France and later Greece—without warning.

And this year, in 1941, the Axis powers attacked Yugoslavia and Greece and they dominated the Balkans—without warning. In 1941, also, Hitler invaded Russia—without warning.

And now Japan has attacked Malaya and Thailand—and the United States—without warning.

It is all of one pattern.

We are now in this war. We are all in it—all the way. Every single man, woman, and child is a partner in the most tremendous undertaking of our American history. We must share together the bad news and the good news, the defeats and the victories—the changing fortunes of war.

So far, the news has been all bad. We have suffered a serious set-back in Hawaii. Our forces in the Philippines, which include the brave people of that Commonwealth, are taking punishment, but are defending themselves vigorously. The reports from Guam and Wake and Midway islands are still confused, but we must be prepared for the announcement that all these three outposts have been seized.

The casualty lists of these first few days will undoubtedly be large. I deeply feel the anxiety of all of the families of the men in our armed forces and the relatives of people in cities which have been bombed. I can only give them my solemn promise that they will get news just as quickly as possible.

This Government will put its trust in the stamina of the American people, and will give the facts to the public just as soon as two conditions have been fulfilled: first, that the information has been definitely and officially confirmed; and, second, that the release of the information at the time it is received will not prove valuable to the enemy directly or indirectly.

Most earnestly I urge my countrymen to reject all rumors. These ugly little hints of complete disaster fly thick and fast in wartime. They have to be examined and appraised.

As an example, I can tell you frankly that until further surveys are made, I have not sufficient information to state the exact damage which has been done to our naval vessels at Pearl Harbor. Admittedly the damage is serious. But no one can say how serious, until we know how much of this damage can be repaired and how quickly the necessary repairs can be made.

I cite as another example a statement made on Sunday night that a Japanese carrier had been located and sunk off the Canal Zone. And when you hear statements that are attributed to what they call "an authoritative source," you can be reasonably sure from now on that under these war circumstances the "authoritative source" is not any person in authority.

Many rumors and reports which we now hear originate with enemy sources. For instance, today the Japanese are claiming that as a result of their one action against Hawaii they have gained naval supremacy in the Pacific. This is an old trick of propaganda which has been used innumerable times by the Nazis. The purposes of such fantastic claims are, of course, to spread fear and confusion among us, and to goad us into revealing military information which our enemies are desperately anxious to obtain.

Our Government will not be caught in this obvious trap—and neither will the people of the United States.

It must be remembered by each and every one of us that our free and rapid communication these days must be greatly restricted in wartime. It is not possible to receive full, speedy, accurate reports from distant areas of combat. This is particularly true where naval operations are concerned. For in these days of the marvels of radio it is often impossible for the commanders of various units to report their activities by radio at all, for the very simple reason that this information would become available to the enemy, and would disclose their position and their plan of defense or attack.

Of necessity there will be delays in officially confirming or denying reports of operations but we will not hide facts from the country if we know the facts and if the enemy will not be aided by their disclosure.

To all newspapers and radio stations—all those who reach the eyes and ears of the American people—I say this: You have a most grave responsibility to the Nation now and for the duration of this war.

If you feel that your Government is not disclosing enough of the truth, you have every right to say so. But—in the absence of all the facts, as revealed by official sources—you have no right in the ethics of patriotism to deal out unconfirmed reports in such a way as to make people believe that they are gospel truth.

Every citizen, in every walk of life, shares this same responsibility. The lives of our soldiers and sailors—the whole future of this Nation—depend upon the manner in which each and every one of us fulfills his obligation to our country.

Now a word about the recent past—and the future. A year and a half has elapsed since the fall of France, when the whole world first realized the mechanized might which the Axis Nations had been building for so many years. America has used that year and a half to great advantage. Knowing that the attack might reach us in all too short a time, we immediately began greatly to increase our industrial strength and our capacity to meet the demands of modern warfare.

Precious months were gained by sending vast quantities of our war material to the Nations of the world still able to resist Axis aggression. Our policy rested on the fundamental truth that the defense of any country resisting Hitler or Japan was in the long run the defense of our own country. That policy has been justified. It has given us time, invaluable time, to build our American assembly lines of production.

Assembly lines are now in operation. Others are being rushed to completion. A steady stream of tanks and planes, of guns and ships, and shells and equipment—that is what these eighteen months have given us.

But it is all only a beginning of what still has to be done. We must be set to face a long war against crafty and powerful bandits. The attack at Pearl Harbor can be repeated at any one of many points, points in both oceans and along both our coast lines and against all the rest of the hemisphere.

It will not only be a long war, it will be a hard war. That is the basis on which we now lay all our plans. That is the yardstick by which we measure what we shall need and demand; money, materials, doubled and quadrupled production—ever-increasing. The production must be not only for our own Army and Navy and Air Forces. It must reinforce the other armies and navies and air forces fighting the Nazis and the war lords of Japan throughout the Americas and throughout the world.

I have been working today on the subject of production. Your Government has decided on two broad policies.

The first is to speed up all existing production by working on a seven-day-week basis in every war industry, including the production of essential raw materials.

The second policy, now being put into form, is to rush additions to the capacity of production by building more new plants, by adding to old plants, and by using the many smaller plants for war needs.

Over the hard road of the past months, we have at times met obstacles and difficulties, divisions and disputes, indifference and callousness. That is now all past—and, I am sure, forgotten.

The fact is that the country now has an organization in Washington built around men and women who are recognized experts in their own fields. I think the country knows that the people who are actually responsible in each and every one of these many fields are pulling together with a teamwork that has never before been excelled.

On the road ahead there lies hard work—grueling work day and night, every hour and every minute.

I was about to add that ahead there lies sacrifice for all of us.

But it is not correct to use that word. The United States does not consider it a sacrifice to do all one can, to give one's best to our Nation, when the Nation is fighting for its existence and its future life.

It is not a sacrifice for any man, old or young, to be in the Army or the Navy of the United States. Rather is it a privilege.

It is not a sacrifice for the industrialist or the wage earner, the farmer or the shopkeeper, the trainman or the doctor, to pay more taxes, to buy more bonds, to forego extra profits, to work longer or harder at the task for which he is best fitted. Rather is it a privilege.

It is not a sacrifice to do without many things to which we are accustomed if the national defense calls for doing without.

A review this morning leads me to the conclusion that at present we shall not have to curtail the normal use of articles of food. There is enough food today for all of us and enough left over to send to those who are fighting on the same side with us.

But there will be a clear and definite shortage of metals of many kinds for civilian use, for the very good reason that in our increased program we shall need for war purposes more than half of that portion of the principal metals which during the past year have gone into articles for civilian use. Yes, we shall have to give up many things entirely.

And I am sure that the people in every part of the Nation are prepared in their individual living to win this war. I am sure that they will cheerfully help to pay a large part of its financial cost while it goes on. I am sure they will cheerfully give up those material things that they are asked to give up.

And I am sure that they will retain all those great spiritual things without which we cannot win through.

I repeat that the United States can accept no result save victory, final and complete. Not only must the shame of Japanese treachery be wiped out, but the sources of international brutality, wherever they exist, must be absolutely and finally broken.

In my message to the Congress yesterday I said that we "will make it very certain that this form of treachery shall never again endanger us." In order to achieve that certainty, we must begin the great task that is before us by abandoning once and for all the illusion that we can ever again isolate ourselves from the rest of humanity.

In these past few years—and, most violently, in the past three days—we have learned a terrible lesson.

It is our obligation to our dead—it is our sacred obligation to their children and to our children—that we must never forget what we have learned.

And what we all have learned is this:

There is no such thing as security for any Nation—or any individual—in a world ruled by the principles of gangsterism.

There is no such thing as impregnable defense against powerful aggressors who sneak up in the dark and strike without warning.

We have learned that our ocean-girt hemisphere is not immune from severe attack—that we cannot measure our safety in terms of miles on any map any more.

We may acknowledge that our enemies have performed a brilliant feat of deception, perfectly timed and executed with great skill. It was a thoroughly dishonorable deed, but we must face the fact that modern warfare as conducted in the Nazi manner is a dirty business. We don't like it—we didn't want to get in it—but we are in it and we're going to fight it with everything we've got.

I do not think any American has any doubt of our ability to administer proper punishment to the perpetrators of these crimes.

Your Government knows that for weeks Germany has been telling Japan that if Japan did not attack the United States, Japan would not share in dividing the spoils with Germany when peace came. She was promised by Germany that if she came in she would receive the complete and perpetual control of the whole of the Pacific area—and that means not only the Far East, but also all of the islands in the Pacific, and also a stranglehold on the west coast of North, Central, and South America.

We know also that Germany and Japan are conducting their military and naval operations in accordance with a joint plan. That plan considers all peoples and Nations which are not helping the Axis powers as common enemies of each and every one of the Axis powers.

That is their simple and obvious grand strategy. And that is why the American people must realize that it can be matched only with similar grand strategy. We must realize for example that Japanese successes against the United States in the Pacific are helpful to German operations in Libya; that any German success against the Caucasus is inevitably an assistance to Japan in her operations against the Dutch East Indies; that a German attack against Algiers or Morocco opens the way to a German attack against South America, and the Canal.

On the other side of the picture, we must learn also to know that guerrilla warfare against the Germans in, let us say, Serbia or Norway helps us; that a successful Russian offensive against the Germans helps us; and that British successes on land or sea in any part of the world strengthen our hands.

Remember always that Germany and Italy, regardless of any formal declaration of war, consider themselves at war with the United States at this moment just as much as they consider themselves at war with Britain or Russia. And Germany puts all the other Republics of the Americas into the same category of enemies. The people of our sister Republics of this hemisphere can be honored by that fact.

The true goal we seek is far above and beyond the ugly field of battle. When we resort to force, as now we must, we are determined that this force shall be directed toward ultimate good as well as against immediate evil. We Americans are not destroyers—we are builders.

We are now in the midst of a war, not for conquest, not for vengeance, but for a world in which this Nation, and all that this Nation represents, will be safe for our children. We expect to eliminate the danger from Japan, but it would serve us ill if we accomplished that and found that the rest of the world was dominated by Hitler and Mussolini.

We are going to win the war and we are going to win the peace that follows.

And in the difficult hours of this day—through dark days that may be yet to come—we will know that the vast majority of the members of the human race are on our side. Many of them are fighting with us. All of them are praying for us. For in representing our cause, we represent theirs as well—our hope and their hope for liberty under God.

Source: Roosevelt, Franklin D. "Fireside Chat." December 9, 1941. From Woolley, John T., and Gerhard Peters, eds. *The American Presidency Project*. Santa Barbara, CA: University of California. Available online at http://www.presidency.ucsb.edu/ws/?pid=16056.

Japan Surrenders

World War II officially ended on September 2, 1945, when representatives of the Japanese government signed the instrument of surrender in a special ceremony held on board the battleship USS Missouri *in Tokyo Bay. General Douglas MacArthur, as the Supreme Commander of the Allied Powers, presided over the simple, half-hour ceremony. The text of the formal surrender document appears below.*

We, acting by command of and in behalf of the Emperor of Japan, the Japanese Government and the Japanese Imperial General Headquarters, hereby accept the provisions set forth in the declaration issued by the heads of the Governments of the United States, China, and Great Britain on 26 July 1945 at Potsdam, and subsequently adhered to by the Union of Soviet Socialist Republics, which four powers are hereafter referred to as the Allied Powers.

We hereby proclaim the unconditional surrender to the Allied Powers of the Japanese Imperial General Headquarters and of all Japanese armed forces and all armed forces under the Japanese control wherever situated.

We hereby command all Japanese forces wherever situated and the Japanese people to cease hostilities forthwith, to preserve and save from damage all ships, aircraft, and military and civil property and to comply with all requirements which may be imposed by the Supreme Commander for the Allied Powers or by agencies of the Japanese Government at his direction.

We hereby command the Japanese Imperial Headquarters to issue at once orders to the Commanders of all Japanese forces and all forces under Japanese control wherever situated to surrender unconditionally themselves and all forces under their control.

We hereby command all civil, military and naval officials to obey and enforce all proclamations, and orders and directives deemed by the Supreme Commander for the Allied Powers to be proper to effectuate this surrender and issued by him or under his authority and we direct all such officials to remain at their posts and to continue to perform their non-combatant duties unless specifically relieved by him or under his authority.

We hereby undertake for the Emperor, the Japanese Government and their successors to carry out the provisions of the Potsdam Declaration in good faith, and to issue whatever orders and take whatever actions may be required by the Supreme Commander for the Allied Powers or by any other designated representative of the Allied Powers for the purpose of giving effect to that Declaration.

We hereby command the Japanese Imperial Government and the Japanese Imperial General Headquarters at once to liberate all allied prisoners of war and civilian internees now under Japanese control and to provide for their protection, care, maintenance and immediate transportation to places as directed.

The authority of the Emperor and the Japanese Government to rule the state shall be subject to the Supreme Commander for the Allied Powers who will take such steps as he deems proper to effectuate these terms of surrender.

Signed at TOKYO BAY, JAPAN at 0904 on the SECOND day of SEPTEMBER, 1945

MAMORU SHIGEMITSU
By Command and in behalf of the Emperor
of Japan and the Japanese Government

YOSHIJIRO UMEZU
By Command and in behalf of the Japanese
Imperial General Headquarters

Accepted at TOKYO BAY, JAPAN at 0903 on the SECOND day of SEPTEMBER, 1945, for the United States, Republic of China, United Kingdom and the Union of Soviet Socialist Republics, and in the interests of the other United Nations at war with Japan.

DOUGLAS MAC ARTHUR
Supreme Commander for the Allied Powers

C.W. NIMITZ
United States Representative

HSU YUNG-CH'ANG
Republic of China Representative

BRUCE FRASER
United Kingdom Representative

KUZMA DEREVYANKO
Union of Soviet Socialist Republics Representative

THOMAS BLAMEY
Commonwealth of Australia
Representative

L. MOORE COSGRAVE
Dominion of Canada Representative

JACQUES LE CLERC
Provisional Government of the French
Republic Representative

C.E.L. HELFRICH
Kingdom of the Netherlands
Representative

LEONARD M. ISITT
Dominion of New Zealand Representative

Source: "Instrument of Surrender." Signed September 2, 1945. Washington, D.C.: U.S. National Archives and Records Administration. Available online at http://www. archives.gov/exhibits/featured_documents/japanese_surrender_document/.

President Harry S. Truman Announces the End of the War

As representatives of Japan formally surrendered to end the war, President Harry S. Truman recognized the momentous occasion in a radio address to the nation. The text of this speech—delivered on the evening of September 1, 1945, Washington time—is reprinted below. Describing the successful Allied war effort as "a victory of liberty over tyranny," Truman praises the contributions and sacrifices of the American people. He also expresses hope that the victory will result in "a world of peace rounded on justice, fair dealing, and tolerance."

My fellow Americans, and the Supreme Allied Commander, General MacArthur, in Tokyo Bay:

The thoughts and hopes of all America—indeed of all the civilized world—are centered tonight on the battleship *Missouri*. There on that small piece of American soil anchored in Tokyo Harbor the Japanese have just officially laid down their arms. They have signed terms of unconditional surrender.

Four years ago, the thoughts and fears of the whole civilized world were centered on another piece of American soil—Pearl Harbor. The mighty threat to civilization which began there is now laid at rest. It was a long road to Tokyo—and a bloody one.

We shall not forget Pearl Harbor.

The Japanese militarists will not forget the U.S.S. *Missouri*.

The evil done by the Japanese war lords can never be repaired or forgotten. But their power to destroy and kill has been taken from them. Their armies and what is left of their Navy are now impotent.

To all of us there comes first a sense of gratitude to Almighty God who sustained us and our Allies in the dark days of grave danger, who made us to grow from weakness into the strongest fighting force in history, and who has now seen us overcome the forces of tyranny that sought to destroy His civilization.

God grant that in our pride of the hour, we may not forget the hard tasks that are still before us; that we may approach these with the same courage, zeal, and patience with which we faced the trials and problems of the past four years.

Our first thoughts, of course—thoughts of gratefulness and deep obligation—go out to those of our loved ones who have been killed or maimed in this terrible war. On land and sea and in the air, American men and women have given their lives so that this day of ultimate victory might come and assure the survival of a civilized world. No victory can make good their loss.

We think of those whom death in this war has hurt, taking from them fathers, husbands, sons, brothers, and sisters whom they loved. No victory can bring back the faces they longed to see.

Only the knowledge that the victory, which these sacrifices have made possible, will be wisely used, can give them any comfort. It is our responsibility—ours, the living—to see to it that this victory shall be a monument worthy of the dead who died to win it.

We think of all the millions of men and women in our armed forces and merchant marine all over the world who, after years of sacrifice and hardship and peril, have been spared by Providence from harm.

We think of all the men and women and children who during these years have carried on at home, in lonesomeness and anxiety and fear.

Our thoughts go out to the millions of American workers and businessmen, to our farmers and miners—to all those who have built up this country's fighting strength, and who have shipped to our Allies the means to resist and overcome the enemy.

Our thoughts go out to our civil servants and to the thousands of Americans who, at personal sacrifice, have come to serve in our Government during these trying years; to the members of the Selective Service boards and ration boards; to the civilian defense and Red Cross workers; to the men and women in the USO and in the entertainment world—to all those who have helped in this cooperative struggle to preserve liberty and decency in the world.

We think of our departed gallant leader, Franklin D. Roosevelt, defender of democracy, architect of world peace and cooperation.

And our thoughts go out to our gallant Allies in this war: to those who resisted the invaders; to those who were not strong enough to hold out, but who, nevertheless, kept the fires of resistance alive within the souls of their people; to those who stood up against great odds and held the line, until the United Nations together were able to supply the arms and the men with which to overcome the forces of evil.

This is a victory of more than arms alone. This is a victory of liberty over tyranny.

From our war plants rolled the tanks and planes which blasted their way to the heart of our enemies; from our shipyards sprang the ships which bridged all the oceans of the world for our weapons and supplies; from our farms came the food and fiber for our armies and navies and for our Allies in all the corners of the earth; from our mines and factories came the raw materials and the finished products which gave us the equipment to overcome our enemies.

But back of it all were the will and spirit and determination of a free people—who know what freedom is, and who know that it is worth whatever price they had to pay to preserve it.

It was the spirit of liberty which gave us our armed strength and which made our men invincible in battle. We now know that that spirit of liberty, the freedom of the individual, and the personal dignity of man, are the strongest and toughest and most enduring forces in all the world.

And so on V-J Day we take renewed faith and pride in our own way of life. We have had our day of rejoicing over this victory. We have had our day of prayer and devotion. Now let us set aside V-J Day as one of renewed consecration to the principles which have made us the strongest nation on earth and which, in this war, we have striven so mightily to preserve.

Those principles provide the faith, the hope, and the opportunity which help men to improve themselves and their lot. Liberty does not make all men perfect nor all society secure. But it has provided more solid progress and happiness and decency for more people than any other philosophy of government in history. And this day has shown again that it provides the greatest strength and the greatest power which man has ever reached.

We know that under it we can meet the hard problems of peace which have come upon us. A free people with free Allies, who can develop an atomic bomb, can use the same skill and energy and determination to overcome all the difficulties ahead.

Victory always has its burdens and its responsibilities as well as its rejoicing.

But we face the future and all its dangers with great confidence and great hope. America can build for itself a future of employment and security. Together with the United Nations, it can build a world of peace rounded on justice, fair dealing, and tolerance.

As President of the United States, I proclaim Sunday, September the second, 1945, to be V-J Day—the day of formal surrender by Japan. It is not yet the day for the formal proclamation of the end of the war nor of the cessation of hostilities. But it is a day which we Americans shall always remember as a day of retribution—as we remember that other day, the day of infamy.

From this day we move forward. We move toward a new era of security at home. With the other United Nations we move toward a new and better world of cooperation, of peace and international good will and cooperation.

God's help has brought us to this day of victory. With His help we will attain that peace and prosperity for ourselves and all the world in the years ahead.

Source: Truman, Harry S. "Radio Address to the American People after the Signing of the Terms of Unconditional Surrender by Japan." September 1, 1945. From Woolley, John T., and Gerhard Peters, eds. The American Presidency Project. Santa Barbara, CA: University of California. Available online at http://www.presidency.ucsb.edu/ws/?pid= 12366.

IMPORTANT PEOPLE, PLACES, AND TERMS

Allied Powers

The alliance between France, England, Russia, the United States, and other countries during World War II.

Amphibious

A type of military operation using a combination of air, land, and sea forces.

Atomic bomb

A powerful explosive device created in 1945 through a top-secret project and used by the United States to destroy the cities of Hiroshima and Nagasaki in Japan.

Axis Powers

The alliance between Nazi Germany, Fascist Italy, and Imperialist Japan during World War II.

Bataan Death March

An atrocity committed in May 1942 when Japanese soldiers forced captured American and Filipino troops to march 65 miles across the Bataan peninsula in the Philippines in extreme heat with no access to food, water, or medicine, causing the death of an estimated 20,000 prisoners.

Battleship Row

An area in the center of Pearl Harbor, along the southeastern shore of Ford Island, where the battleships of the U.S. Pacific Fleet were anchored on the day of the attack.

Cold War

A period of intense political and military rivalry between the United States and Soviet Union that began in the aftermath of World War II and lasted until the breakup of the Soviet Union in 1991.

Communism
A political system in which the state controls all economic activity. In practice, Communist governments typically establish single-party rule and place significant limits on citizens' rights and freedoms.

Congressional Medal of Honor
The highest honor bestowed by the U.S. government on military personnel for valor in service to the country.

Coral Sea, Battle of the
A May 1942 engagement in which Allied forces turned back a Japanese advance on Port Moresby, New Zealand.

Churchill, Winston (1874-1965)
Prime Minister of Great Britain during World War II.

Doolittle Raid
An air strike on Tokyo, Japan, conducted by a squadron of American long-range bombers led by James H. Doolittle in April 1942.

Embargo
A diplomatic measure that limits foreign trade with a particular nation as a way to punish its policies or actions.

Escort carrier
A small aircraft carrier used to support amphibious landings and accompany supply shipments and troop transports during the Pacific War.

Fascism
A political and social system in which a strong central government controls most aspects of citizens' lives.

Fleet carrier
A large aircraft carrier, capable of holding 80 to 100 planes, used to locate and destroy Japanese vessels during the Pacific War.

Fuchida, Mitsuo (1902-1976)
Japanese Navy pilot who led the Pearl Harbor strike force.

Great Depression
A period of severe economic crisis that began with a crash in the value of the American stock market in October 1929. Marked by bank failures, business collapses, unemployment, and poverty, the downturn affected countries around the world until the early 1940s.

Guadalcanal, Battle of

The first successful Allied offensive in the Pacific War, it centered around an island in the Solomon chain north of Australia and lasted from August 1942 to February 1943.

Halsey, William "Bull" (1882-1959)

U.S. Navy admiral who commanded Allied naval operations in the southern Pacific during World War II.

Hirohito, Emperor (1901-1989)

Sacred ruler of Japan who surrendered to Allied leaders on August 15, 1945.

Hiroshima, Japan

City that was destroyed by an atomic bomb dropped by U.S. warplanes on August 6, 1945.

Hitler, Adolf (1889-1945)

Nazi leader who rose to power in Germany in 1933, conquered most of Europe by 1939, and was defeated by the Allies in 1945.

Hull, Cordell (1871-1955)

U.S. Secretary of State who led diplomatic negotiations with Japan in the months leading up to the Pearl Harbor attack.

Internment

A U.S. government policy adopted following the Pearl Harbor attack that involved rounding up Japanese Americans and holding them in detention facilities for the duration of the war.

Island hopping

An offensive strategy used by Allied forces in the Pacific during World War II that involved making amphibious assaults on selected Japanese-held islands with strategic value, then using those islands as bases for further assaults.

Isolationism

The view that the best way for a nation to maintain its power and security is to remain isolated from the rest of the world and not intervene in conflicts outside its borders.

Iwo Jima, Battle of
A bloody fight between U.S. Marines and entrenched Japanese troops for control of a small volcanic island about 700 miles from Japan which resulted in an important Allied victory in March 1944.

Japanese home islands
The four main islands comprising the nation of Japan before and after the Pacific War: Honshu, Hokkaido, Kyushu, and Shikoku.

Kamikazes
A force of novice Japanese pilots who carried out suicide missions by crashing their bomb-filled planes into Allied ships.

Kimmel, Husband E. (1882-1968)
U.S. Navy admiral in charge of the U.S. Pacific Fleet at the time of the Pearl Harbor attack.

League of Nations
An international body, similar to the modern United Nations, created following World War I to help member nations resolve their differences in a peaceful manner.

Leyte Gulf, Battle of
A lopsided 1944 naval battle in the Philippines in which Allied planes destroyed four Japanese aircraft carriers.

MacArthur, Douglas (1880-1964)
U.S. Army general who led Allied operations in the southern Pacific during World War II and oversaw the postwar occupation and reconstruction of Japan.

Marianas
A chain in the central Pacific consisting of three main islands—Saipan, Tinian, and Guam—that were captured as part of the Allied island-hopping campaign in 1944.

Marshall, George C. (1880-1959)
U.S. Army Chief of Staff in Washington, D.C., at the time of the Pearl Harbor attack.

Midway, Battle of
A June 1942 engagement in the Pacific War in which the United States turned back a major Japanese offensive and destroyed four valuable enemy aircraft carriers.

Miller, Doris (1919-1943)
First African-American sailor to receive the Navy Cross, for his heroism on board the U.S.S. *West Virginia* during the Pearl Harbor attack.

Mitscher, Marc (1887-1947)
U.S. Navy admiral who commanded a carrier task force in the central Pacific during the island-hopping campaign.

Mount Suribachi
Rocky volcanic peak on the Pacific island of Iwo Jima that was the site of a famous flag-raising by U.S. Marines in February 1944.

Mussolini, Benito (1883-1945)
Fascist dictator who rose to power in Italy in 1922 and joined forces with Nazi Germany and Imperialist Japan to form the Axis Powers during World War II.

Nagasaki, Japan
Port city that was destroyed by an atomic bomb dropped by a U.S. warplane on August 9, 1945.

Nagumo, Chuichi (1887-1944)
Japanese Navy admiral who commanded the Pearl Harbor attack force and died in the Japanese defeat at Saipan in the Marianas.

Nazi Party
The National Socialist German Workers' Party, which rose to power in Germany under the leadership of Adolf Hitler in 1933.

Neutrality Acts
A series of U.S. laws passed in the 1930s that prohibited government agencies, businesses, or citizens from providing money, weapons, or any other type of aid to a nation at war.

Nimitz, Chester W. (1885-1966)
U.S. Navy admiral who took command of the Pacific Fleet following the Pearl Harbor attack and led the Allies to victory in the Pacific.

Nomura, Kichisaburo (1877-1964)
Japanese ambassador to the United States who led diplomatic negotiations between the two countries in the months leading up to the Pearl Harbor attack.

Occupation
A situation where the winner of a war stations a military force within the borders of a conquered nation, such as when U.S. troops under General Douglas MacArthur occupied Japan following World War II.

Okinawa, Battle of
A bloody fight between Allied ground forces and entrenched Japanese troops on an island 370 miles south of Japan which raged from April 1 to June 22, 1945.

Pacific War
The engagements of World War II that took place in and around the Pacific Ocean between Allied and Japanese forces.

Pearl Harbor
Site of a major U.S. Navy base on the island of Oahu in Hawaii that was attacked by Japan on December 7, 1941.

Philippines
A group of Pacific islands south of Japan that were captured by Japanese forces in 1942 and liberated by Allied forces in 1945.

Potsdam Declaration
A document issued by Allied leaders on July 26, 1945, outlining the terms of unconditional surrender that Japan must accept in order to end the Pacific War.

Revisionists
Critics who claim that U.S. and British government leaders knew in advance of the Japanese plan to attack Pearl Harbor, but allowed the attack to happen in order to increase public support for the United States to enter World War II.

Rochefort, Joseph J. (1898-1976)
Leader of a group of U.S. Navy code breakers who intercepted secret Japanese messages that provided information vital to the Allied victory at Midway in 1942.

Roosevelt, Franklin D. (1882-1945)
President of the United States during the Great Depression and World War II.

SCAP
Supreme Commander of the Allied Powers, a title held by U.S. General Douglas MacArthur during the postwar occupation and reconstruction of Japan.

Short, Walter C. (1880-1949)
U.S. Army general in charge of the defense of Hawaii during the Pearl Harbor attack.

Spruance, Raymond (1886-1969)
U.S. Navy admiral who commanded the Allied task force that defeated the Japanese fleet in the Battle of Midway.

Stalin, Joseph (1879-1953)
Communist dictator who led the Soviet Union during World War II.

Stark, Harold R. (1880-1972)
U.S. Chief of Naval Operations in Washington, D.C., during the Pearl Harbor attack.

Third World
A collective term for small, developing nations.

Tojo, Hideki (1885-1948)
General who took charge of Japan's military government in October 1941, approved the Pearl Harbor attack, and was executed for war crimes during the U.S. occupation of Japan.

Tripartite Pact
A document formalizing the military and political alliance entered into on September 27, 1940, by Nazi Germany, Fascist Italy, and Imperialist Japan.

Treaty of Versailles
Peace agreement signed in 1918 that officially ended World War I.

Truman, Harry S. (1884-1972)
President of the United States who ended World War II by authorizing the use of atomic weapons against Japan.

USS

A designation for a naval vessel meaning "United States Ship."

USS *Arizona* Memorial

A structure built above the sunken battleship in Pearl Harbor that serves as a shrine for the U.S. servicemen killed in the 1941 attack.

Wilson, Woodrow (1856-1924)

U.S. President who led the United States during World War I and was instrumental in founding the League of Nations.

World War I

A conflict that lasted from August 1914 until November 1918 and pitted the Central Powers (Germany, Austria-Hungary, and the Ottoman Empire) against the Allied Powers (France, England, Russia, and the United States).

World War II

A conflict that lasted from September 1939 until August 1945 and pitted the Axis Powers (Germany, Italy, and Japan) against the Allied Powers (France, England, Canada, Australia, the Soviet Union, the United States, and others).

Yamamoto, Isoroku (1884-1943)

Commander in chief of the Imperial Japanese Combined Fleet and main military strategist behind the Pearl Harbor attack.

CHRONOLOGY

1880

Douglas MacArthur is born in Little Rock, Arkansas, on January 26.

Walter C. Short, commanding officer of U.S. Army ground and air defenses at Pearl Harbor, is born on March 30 in Fillmore, Illinois.

1882

Husband E. Kimmel, commander in chief of the U.S. Pacific Fleet during the Pearl Harbor attack, is born in Henderson, Kentucky, on February 26.

1884

Isoroku Yamamoto, mastermind behind the Pearl Harbor attack, is born on April 4 in Nagaoka, Honshu Province, Japan.

1885

Chester W. Nimitz is born on February 24 in Fredericksburg, Texas.

1898

Hawaii is annexed by the United States.

1902

Mitsuo Fuchida, lead pilot in the Pearl Harbor attack, is born in Nara Prefecture, Japan, on December 2.

1908

The Pearl Harbor Naval Shipyard opens on the Hawaiian island of Oahu.

1914

World War I begins in Europe.

1917

The United States enters World War I.

1918

The Allied Powers (France, England, Russia, and the United States) defeat the Central Powers (Germany, Austria-Hungary, and the Ottoman Empire) to end World War I.

1922

Fascist dictator Benito Mussolini rises to power in Italy.

1929

A crash in the value of the American stock market in October marks the beginning of the severe economic crisis known as the Great Depression.

1931

Japan takes over Manchuria, a resource-rich region of northeastern China.

1933

Adolf Hitler and the Nazi Party rise to power in Germany.

1936

Hitler sends German troops into the Rhineland, a neutral territory on the border of France that had been taken away from Germany following World War I.

1937

On July 7, following an incident in which Chinese forces supposedly fired upon Japanese troops, Japan launches a full-scale invasion of China.

1938

Nazi Germany takes over the neighboring country of Austria and a region of Czecho-slovakia called Sudetenland.

1939

After signing a non-aggression pact with Soviet dictator Joseph Stalin, Hitler invades Poland.

France and England respond by declaring war on Nazi Germany on September 3.

1940

In February, the U.S. Pacific Fleet adopts Pearl Harbor, Hawaii, as its new home port.

On June 22, France surrenders to Germany, leaving England as the only nation standing between Hitler and the conquest of western Europe.

Taking advantage of Germany's victory, Japan invades the French colonies in Southeast Asia known as French Indochina.

Admiral Isoroku Yamamoto becomes commander in chief of the Imperial Japanese Combined Fleet on August 30.

On September 27, Nazi Germany, Fascist Italy, and Imperialist Japan forge a formal alliance by signing the Tripartite Pact. The three nations become known collectively as the Axis Powers.

Franklin D. Roosevelt is elected to a third term as president of the United States.

On November 11, the British Royal Navy uses planes launched from an aircraft carrier to cripple Mussolini's main fleet in Taranto, Italy.

On December 29, Roosevelt makes his famous "Arsenal of Democracy" speech with the goal of rallying the American people in support of the Allies in Europe.

1941

In January, Yamamoto develops a plan to attack the U.S. Navy base at Pearl Harbor and threatens to resign if Japanese leaders do not adopt it.

On February 1, Admiral Husband E. Kimmel becomes commander in chief of the U.S. Pacific Fleet at Pearl Harbor.

In March, the U.S. Congress passes the Lend-Lease Act to provide the Allies with warships without officially entering World War II.

In July, Roosevelt responds to Japanese aggression by placing an embargo prohibiting the sale of all raw materials and manufactured goods to Japan.

On October 9, Roosevelt approves a top-secret project to create an atomic bomb.

General Hideki Tojo becomes prime minister of Japan's military government on October 16.

On October 20, Tojo formally approves the plan to attack Pearl Harbor.

Japanese diplomats present their "last word" proposal to the U.S. government on November 20.

On November 26, U.S. Secretary of State Cordell Hull responds with a counterproposal.

The next day, when Japan rejects Hull's proposal, U.S. military leaders in Washington, D.C., issue a "war warning" to commanding officers in the Pacific, including those at Pearl Harbor.

On December 2, Yamamoto issues the final attack order to the Japanese attack force; U.S. military tracking systems lose contact with six aircraft carriers in the Japanese fleet; U.S. military code breakers intercept a message from Tokyo telling all Japanese consulates in the United States to destroy their code machines and sensitive documents.

On December 7, Japan attacks the U.S. military base at Pearl Harbor in Hawaii.

The following day, Roosevelt addresses a joint session of Congress and requests a declaration of war against Japan.

Japan invades Thailand, Hong Kong, and Malaya, and attacks U.S. military bases on the Pacific islands of Wake and Guam.

Japan's fellow Axis Powers, Germany and Italy, declare war on the United States on December 11.

On December 18, Roosevelt orders the first of many official inquiries into the Pearl Harbor attack.

On December 22, Japanese troops land in the Philippines.

1942

The committee investigating the Pearl Harbor attack, led by Supreme Court Justice Owen J. Roberts, releases a report in January finding Admiral Kimmel and General Short guilty of dereliction of duty; they retire on March 1.

U.S. Army General Douglas MacArthur is ordered to Australia, but he vows to return to liberate the Philippines.

On February 15, the British fortress at Singapore surrenders to Japanese forces.

In March, a team of U.S. military cryptanalysts at Pearl Harbor under the command of Joseph J. Rochefort succeed in breaking the Japanese naval communications code JN-25.

Japan continues to conquer new territory in Asia and the Pacific, including Burma, Indonesia, and the Dutch East Indies.

Throughout the spring, the U.S. government rounds up Japanese Americans and places them in internment camps for the duration of the war.

On April 18, a squadron of American long-range bombers led by James H. Doolittle conducts an air strike on Tokyo, Japan, increasing U.S. morale and raising concerns among Japanese leaders.

In May, Allied troops surrender in the Philippines and an estimated 20,000 die during the Bataan Death March.

That same month, Allied forces turn back a Japanese advance on Port Moresby, New Zealand, in the Battle of the Coral Sea.

On May 27, Cook Third Class Doris Miller becomes the first African-American sailor to receive the Navy Cross for his heroism on board the USS *West Virginia* during the Pearl Harbor attack.

Using information from intercepted Japanese messages, the U.S. Navy turns back a major Japanese offensive in June at the Battle of Midway.

On August 7, the Allies launch their first offensive operation in the Pacific War at Guadalcanal in the Solomon Islands.

1943

In February, amphibious Allied forces succeed in capturing Guadalcanal.

Scientists work to develop an atomic bomb as part of the top-secret Manhattan Project.

The Allies formally launch the island-hopping campaign, formally known as Operation Cartwheel, against Japan in the Pacific.

On April 18, U.S. fighters intercept a plane carrying Admiral Yamamoto, commander in chief of the Imperial Japanese Combined Fleet, and shoot it down over the Solomon Islands.

After a bloody battle, U.S. Marines capture the Japanese stronghold on Tarawa atoll in the Gilbert Islands in November.

1944

On June 6, Allied forces in Europe storm the beaches of Normandy, France, in a successful invasion that eventually ends the German occupation of France.

218

Allied troops under the command of General Douglas MacArthur land in the Philippines on October 20.

1945

On February 19, 30,000 U.S. Marines land on Iwo Jima, a small volcanic island about 700 miles from Japan.

On February 23, MacArthur makes a triumphant return to the capital city of Manila in the Philippines.

That same day, an exhausted but triumphant group of servicemen plants an American flag on top of Mount Suribachi, the highest peak on Iwo Jima.

Allied planes from captured island air bases conduct air raids on Japanese cities, including an incendiary attack that destroys 95 percent of Tokyo on March 9.

On March 14, U.S. Navy forces begin bombing Japanese defenses on the Pacific island of Okinawa, 370 miles south of Japan.

After six weeks of bloody fighting that took the lives of 6,800 Americans, Iwo Jima is declared secure on March 26.

On April 1, U.S. Marines land on Okinawa.

President Franklin D. Roosevelt dies of a brain hemorrhage on April 12, and Vice President Harry S. Truman takes office.

Truman learns of the existence of the atomic bomb on April 25.

On May 8, known as Victory in Europe or V-E Day, Nazi Germany surrenders to the Allies.

Okinawa is captured on June 22, at a cost of 12,000 American lives.

A team of American and British scientists detonate the world's first atomic weapon at a test site in Alamogordo, New Mexico, on July 16.

On July 26, Allied leaders issue the Potsdam Declaration, which outlines the terms of unconditional surrender Japan must accept in order to end the war; Japanese leaders reject it.

On August 6, a U.S. warplane drops an atomic bomb on the Japanese city of Hiroshima, reducing 80 percent of the buildings to rubble and killing an estimated 70,000 people instantly.

Soviet dictator Joseph Stalin declares war on Japan on August 8; the following day, Russian troops invade Manchuria, a disputed region of China under Japanese control.

On August 9, the United States drops a second atomic bomb, on the Japanese city of Nagasaki.

On August 14, known as Victory over Japan or V-J Day, Japanese leaders surrender to end World War II.

In a formal ceremony aboard the battleship USS Missouri in Tokyo Bay, Allied and Japanese leaders sign the official instrument of surrender on September 2.

The last major Japanese Army units in the Pacific are disarmed on October 24.

The Congressional Pearl Harbor Joint Committee convenes on November 15 to conduct the most extensive of several official investigations into the Japanese attack.

By the end of the year, MacArthur has 350,000 U.S. troops stationed in Japan to take part in postwar occupation and reconstruction activities.

1946

The Congressional committee investigating the Pearl Harbor attack issues a 500-page report on July 20 that places primary blame on the officers in charge of defending the base.

1947

A new Japanese constitution takes effect on May 3 that renounces war, establishes civil rights, and creates a democratically elected government.

1948

The Cold War begins with the Soviet blockade of Berlin, Germany; the United States responds by arranging an airlift of supplies to residents of democratic West Berlin.

1949

Short dies of heart failure on March 9.

1950

The Korean War begins and MacArthur is chosen to lead United Nations forces.

1951

After the famous general publicly contradicts administration policy, Truman relieves MacArthur of command in April.

Japanese leaders sign the San Francisco Peace Treaty on September 8.

1952

The San Francisco Peace Treaty takes effect on April 28, ending seven years of foreign occupation and making Japan an independent nation again.

1962

The USS *Arizona* Memorial is dedicated at the site of the sunken battleship in Pearl Harbor on May 30.

1964

After struggling with poor health for several years, MacArthur dies on April 5.

1966

Nimitz dies on February 20.

1968

Kimmel dies on May 14, having tried unsuccessfully to clear his name for many years after the Pearl Harbor attack.

1976

Japanese pilot Mitsuo Fuchida dies on May 30 in Kashiwara, Japan.

1980

The USS *Arizona* Memorial, which receives 1.5 million visitors per year, becomes a national park.

1991

The Cold War ends with the breakup of the Soviet Union.

2001

On September 11, a terrorist attack destroys the World Trade Center towers in New York City and damages the Pentagon building in Washington, D.C.; many people compare the surprise attack and its impact on America to the 1941 attack on Pearl Harbor.

SOURCES FOR
FURTHER STUDY

Friedrich, Otto, et al. *Time* (cover story), December 2, 1991. Available online at http://www.time.com/time/covers/0,16641,1101911202,00.html. Prepared in honor of the 50th anniversary of the Pearl Harbor attack, this special edition of *Time* magazine features a three-part series on the Japanese attack and the Pacific War, survivor recollections, and an essay about U.S.-Japanese relations in the modern era.

Harris, Nathaniel. *A Day That Made History: Pearl Harbor.* North Pomfret, VT: David and Charles, 1986. A detailed juvenile history of the reasons behind the Pearl Harbor attack, the creation of the Japanese attack plan, and the events of December 7, 1941, plus an assessment of why the Americans were taken by surprise.

Klam, Julie. *World War II Chronicles: The Rise of Japan and Pearl Harbor.* North Mankato, MN: Byron Preiss, 2003. A readable juvenile history of the origins of U.S.-Japanese political tensions, the attack on Pearl Harbor, and the war in the Pacific up to the Battle of Midway.

McGowan, Tom. *Cornerstones of Freedom: The Attack on Pearl Harbor.* New York: Children's Press, 2002. This juvenile history includes lots of good pictures of the Pearl Harbor attack and a by-the-minute chronology of December 7, 1941.

Naval Historical Center, U.S. Department of the Navy. "The Pearl Harbor Attack, 7 December 1941." Available online at http://www.history.navy.mil/faqs/faq66-1.htm. This extensive U.S. Navy site features oral histories, survivor accounts, action reports, photographs, and a wealth of other material related to the Pearl Harbor attack.

Pearl Harbor.org. Available online at http://www.pearlharbor.org. This comprehensive site provides a historical overview of the attack, plus links to survivor recollections, documents and speeches, photographs, casualty lists, medal of honor recipients, and other materials.

Prange, Gordon W. *At Dawn We Slept: The Untold Story of Pearl Harbor.* New York: McGraw-Hill, 1981. Exhaustively researched and dramatically written, this best-seller is considered one of the most authoritative records of the events that took place before, during, and after the attack.

U.S. Marine Corps History and Museums Division, "Marines in World War II Commemorative Series." Available online at National Park Service, http://www.nps.gov/archive/

wapa/indepth/extContent. This site includes an extensive series of authoritative articles about Pearl Harbor and various battles in the Pacific during World War II.

Van der Vat, Dan. *Pearl Harbor: The Day of Infamy—An Illustrated History.* Toronto: Madison Press, 2001. Heavily illustrated with historic photographs and dramatic paintings, this book provides an extensive account of the Pearl Harbor attack and includes recollections from survivors.

BIBLIOGRAPHY

Books

Harris, Nathaniel. *A Day That Made History: Pearl Harbor.* North Pomfret, VT: David and Charles, 1986.

Klam, Julie. *World War II Chronicles: The Rise of Japan and Pearl Harbor.* North Mankato, MN: Byron Preiss, 2003.

McGowan, Tom. *Cornerstones of Freedom: The Attack on Pearl Harbor.* New York: Children's Press, 2002.

Prange, Gordon W. *At Dawn We Slept: The Untold Story of Pearl Harbor.* New York: McGraw-Hill, 1981.

Prange, Gordon W. *Pearl Harbor: The Verdict of History.* New York: McGraw-Hill, 1986.

Van der Vat, Dan. *Pearl Harbor: The Day of Infamy—An Illustrated History.* Toronto: Madison Press, 2001.

Welsh, Douglas. *The USA in World War II: The Pacific Theater.* New York: Galahad Books, 1982.

Periodicals

Friedrich, Otto. "Day of Infamy." *Time,* December 2, 1991, p. 30.

Friedrich, Otto. "Down but Not Out." *Time,* December 2, 1991.

Henderson, Phillip G. "Intelligence Gathering and September 11: What the Lessons of History Show." *World and I,* December 2002.

O'Connell, Kim A. "The Ship That Bleeds." *National Parks,* November-December 2001, p. 18.

Posner, Richard A. "Surprise Attack: The Lessons of History." *Commentary,* April 2005, p. 50.

Price, Sean. "Parallels to Pearl Harbor: In 1941, as in 2001, a Surprise Attack on America United the Nation for a Major War." *New York Times Upfront,* November 12, 2001, p. 28.

"25 Years After Pearl Harbor—An Attack That Remade the World," *U.S. News and World Report,* December 12, 1966, p. 47.

Van der Vat, Dan. "Pearl Harbor Revisited." *History Today,* June 2001, p. 2.

Warren, Spencer. "Why America Slept." *National Review,* December 16, 1991, p. 34.

Online

Alexander, Joseph H. "Closing In: Marines in the Seizure of Iwo Jima." From *Marines in World War II Commemorative Series,* National Park Service, War in the Pacific National Historical Park, Guam. Available online at http://www.nps.gov/archive/wapa/indepth/extContent/usmc/pcn-190-003131-00/index.htm.

Anderson, Charles R. "Guadalcanal." Brochure prepared for the U.S. Army Center of Military History, 2003. Available online at http://www.history.army.mil/brochures/72-8/72-8.htm.

Budiansky, Stephen. *Battle of Wits: The Complete Story of Codebreaking in World War II.* Converted for the Web as "Midway: Ambush the Ambushers." Available online at http://worldwar2history.info/Midway/ambush.html.

Burr, William, ed. "The Atomic Bomb and the End of World War II: A Collection of Primary Sources." National Security Archive, August 5, 2005. Available online at http://www.gwu.edu/~nsarchiv/NSAEBB/NSAEBB162/index.htm.

Conn, Stetson, Rose C. Engelman, and Byron Fairchild. *Guarding the United States and Its Outposts.* Washington, D.C.: U.S. Army Center of Military History, 2000, p. 176. Available online at http://www.history.army.mil/books/wwii/guard-us/ch7.htm.

Friedrich, Otto, et al. *Time* (cover story on 50th anniversary of Pearl Harbor attack), December 2, 1991. Available online at http://www.time.com/time/covers/0,16641,1101911202,00.html.

"Japan in the Twentieth Century, 1920-1996." *DISCovering World History.* Gale, 2003. Reproduced in *History Resource Center Online.* Farmington Hills, MI: Gale, http://galenet.galegroup.com/servlet/HistRC/.

"Japan's Iwo Jima Strategy." Available online at http://www.iwojima.com/battle/battlea.htm.

National Park Service, "A Guide to the War in the Pacific." Available online at http://www.nps.gov/archive/wapa/indepth/extContent/wapa/guides.

National Park Service, USS *Arizona* Memorial. Available online at http://www.nps.gov/archive/usar/extendweb1.html.

"Oral Histories of the Pearl Harbor Attack, 7 December 1941." U.S. Department of the Navy, Naval Historical Center, June 8, 2001. Available online at http://www.history.navy.mil/faqs/.

Wallin, Homer N. *Pearl Harbor: Why, How, Fleet Salvage and Final Appraisal.* Washington, D.C.: Government Printing Office, 1968, pp. 297-327. Available online at "Reports by Survivors of Pearl Harbor Attack," U.S. Department of the Navy, Navy Historical Center, http://www.history.navy.mil/docs/wwii/pearl/survivors2.htm.

"Wars and Battles: Island Hopping, 1942-45—Pacific Theater, World War II." Available online at http://www.u-s-history.com/pages/h1671.html.

"World War II." *Encyclopedia of the American Military.* Detroit: Gale Research, 1997. Reproduced in *History Resource Center.* Farmington Hills, MI: Gale, http://galenet.gale group.com/servlet/HistRC/.

"World War II: Background to Involvement, 1939-45." *Discovering U.S. History.* Detroit: Gale Research, 1997. Reproduced in *History Resource Center.* Farmington Hills, MI: Gale, http://galenet.galegroup.com/servlet/HistRC/.

PHOTO AND ILLUSTRATION CREDITS

Cover and Title Page: FSA-OWI Photograph Collection, Library of Congress Prints and Photographs Division, LC-USW33-018433-C.

Chapter One: Courtesy of the Franklin D. Roosevelt Digital Archives (p. 7); Photo by Heinrich Hoffmann, Library of Congress Prints and Photographs Division, LC-USZ62-97567 (p. 9); New York World-Telegram & Sun Newspaper Photograph Collection, Library of Congress Prints and Photographs Division, LC-USZ62-111644 (p. 11).

Chapter Two: Official U.S. Navy Photograph, from the collections of the Naval Historical Center (p. 17); Library of Congress Prints and Photographs Division, LC-USZ62-52710 (p. 23); U.S. Naval Historical Center Photograph (pp. 26, 30); FSA-OWI Photograph Collection, Library of Congress Prints and Photographs Division, LC-USW3-004283-D (p. 28).

Chapter Three: Official U.S. Navy Photograph, now in the collections of the National Archives (pp. 35, 46); New York World-Telegram & the Sun Newspaper Photograph Collection, Library of Congress Prints and Photographs Division, LC-USZ62-129810 (p. 37); U.S. Naval Historical Center Photograph (p. 39); Courtesy of the Franklin D. Roosevelt Digital Archives (pp. 42, 44).

Chapter Four: FSA-OWI Photograph Collection, Library of Congress Prints and Photographs Division, LC-USE6-D-007400 (p. 52); FSA-OWI Photograph Collection, Library of Congress Prints and Photographs Division, LC-USW33-018433-C (p. 55); Official U.S. Navy Photograph, now in the collections of the National Archives (pp. 56, 58, 61); Photo attributed to Clem Albers, FSA-OWI Photograph Collection, Library of Congress Prints and Photographs Division, LC-USZ62-44093 (p. 63).

Chapter Five: FSA-OWI Photograph Collection, Library of Congress Prints and Photographs Division, LC-USZ62-15185 (p. 71); Poster from Hilts Publishing Co., Library of Congress Prints and Photographs Division, LC-USZ62-114394 (p. 72); National Archives photo no. 208-AA-288BB(2) (p. 76); Official U.S. Navy Photograph, now in the collections of the National Archives (pp. 78, 84); Courtesy of the Franklin D. Roosevelt Digital Archives (p. 80).

Chapter Six: Defense Department Photo (Marine Corps), Library of Congress Prints and Photographs Division, LC-USZ62-99263 (p. 89); Library of Congress Prints and Photographs Division, LC-USZ62-99394 (p. 92); Official U.S. Navy Photograph, now in the collections of the National Archives (p. 94); Official U.S. Marine Corps Photograph, from the collections of the Naval Historical Center. Original photo taken by Staff Sergeant Louis R. Lowery, USMC, staff photographer for "Leatherneck" magazine. (p. 97); U.S. Air Force Photo (p. 103); Photograph from the Army Signal Corps Collection in the U. S. National Archives (p. 105).

Chapter Seven: U.S. Navy photo by Mass Communication Specialist 1st Class Tiffini M. Jones (p. 110); U.S. Navy photo by Mass Communication Specialist 1st Class Shane Tuck (p. 114); U.S. Navy photo by Photographer's Mate 2nd Class Carol Warden (p. 119).

Biographies: Keystone/Getty Images (p. 123); U.S. Naval Historical Center Photograph (p. 127); Photo by U.S Army, Library of Congress Prints and Photographs Division, LC-USZ62-21027 (p. 131); Official U.S. Navy Photograph, now in the collections of the National Archives (p. 136); U.S. Naval Historical Center Photograph, Collection of Fleet Admiral Chester W. Nimitz, USN (p. 139); Courtesy of the Franklin D. Roosevelt Digital Archives (p. 144); Popperfoto/Getty Images (p. 148); U.S. Naval Historical Center Photograph, official portrait by Shugaku Homma, 1943 (p. 152).

INDEX